USING A LAW LIBRARY

98 A

A Student's Guide to Legal Research Skills

USING A LAW LIBRARY

A Student's Guide to Legal Research Skills

Peter Clinch, BA (Hons), MA, MPhil, PhD, MIInfSc

Law Librarian, Lancashire Polytechnic

BLACKSTONE PRESS LIMITED

First published in Great Britain 1992 by Blackstone Press Limited,
9-15 Aldine Street, London W12 8AW. Telephone 081-740 1173

ISBN: 1 85431 191 3

British Library Cataloguing in Publication Data
A CIP catalogue record for this book is available from the British Library.

Typeset by Style Photosetting Ltd, Mayfield, East Sussex
Printed by BPCC Wheatons Ltd, Exeter

Contents

1.1   Where is your nearest law library?   1.2   Using the law library   1.2.1
What is the general arrangement of the stock?   1.2.2   How is each type of
material arranged on the shelves?   1.2.3   Is all the stock of the library
available for you to borrow?   1.2.4   How do you discover whether the
library has the book you require?   1.2.5   Which parts of the catalogue
should you use to answer particular information needs?   1.2.6   How do you
discover if the library has the periodical you require?   1.2.7   Special points
you should remember when searching the catalogue for law books   1.2.8
What if the library appears not to have the book or periodical you require?

3.1   The structure of the literature   3.2   Primary legislation   3.2.1   Bills
of Parliament   Tracing information on Bills of the current session of
Parliament   Tracing information on Bills of a past session of Parliament
3.2.2   Acts of Parliament   Is this Public General Act in force?   Has any
section or schedule of the Act been amended or repealed by subsequent

legislation? Tracing Acts currently in force by subject Tracing historical, i.e., repealed, legislation by subject Are there any cases on this Act or section of an Act? Have any statutory instruments been made under this Act? Have any case notes or articles been written about this Act? 3.3 Secondary legislation 3.3.1 Statutory instruments You know the title of an SI but not the year or running number. How do you trace a copy of it? Is this SI, the title, year and number of which you know, in force? Has this SI been amended? Which SIs have been made under this Act? Is this SI still in force? Has this SI been considered by the courts? Have any notes or articles been written in periodicals about this SI? 3.3.2 Statutory Codes of Practice 3.3.3 By-laws 3.4 Case law Tracing a report of a case where only the names of the parties are known Has this case been considered by the courts on a subsequent occasion? Tracing cases on a subject Have there been any case notes or articles on this case? 3.5 Extra-legal sources 3.6 Textbooks 3.7 Encyclopaedias 3.8 Periodicals 3.9 Research literature 3.10 Reference works 3.11 Official publications How to find details of official publications on a subject How to find details on Law Commission publications How to trace details of an official publication when all you know is the name of the chairman How to trace if statistics are published on a topic

4.1 Introduction 4.2 Primary sources 4.2.1 Community treaties 4.2.2 Secondary legislation Tracing the text of EC legislation on a subject Tracing draft legislation Has this EC Directive become law? Is this piece of EC legislation still in force? Has this EC legislation been considered in any cases before the European Court of Justice? 4.2.3 Case law Tracing a report of an EC case by name or by case reference number Tracing EC cases by subject Has this ECJ case been referred to subsequently? Tracing recent judgments 4.3 Secondary sources

6.1 Recording research progress 6.2 Footnoting and compiling bibliographies

Contents

Acknowledgements

This book is the product of over 25 years contact with the subject of law, first as an undergraduate, then as a local authority planner attempting to research and apply the law, and finally, over the past 13 or more years, as a librarian teaching students how to research it for themselves. The format and content of this book have been influenced by these experiences and I am indebted to all the people with whom I have come into contact, but particularly law staff, students and my library colleagues at Lancashire Polytechnic. Knowingly, and sometimes unwittingly, they have contributed to this work, by means of their interest, comment and 'off the cuff' remarks on the law and the difficulties of researching it. I must also pay tribute to those authors who have preceded me and whose work has influenced mine: John Pemberton, Adrian Blunt, Derek Way, Robert Logan, Jean Dane and Philip Thomas, and John Jeffries and Christine Miskin.

I am grateful to the following for reading and commenting on various parts of the text: Frank Hallett, Parliamentary Liaison Officer (HMSO) for the section on Bills of Parliament and generously providing figure 3.3; Barbara Denyer, Training Manager (LEXIS), and the Lawtel editors, under the direction of Dr Lawrence Impey, for all the sections on the two on-line information retrieval services.

Acknowledgements and thanks are due to a number of people and organisations for permission to reproduce pages from their publications:

Butterworth Law Publishers Ltd (*All England Law Reports*);
H.W. Wilson Co. (*Index to Legal Periodicals*);
Legal Information Resources Ltd (*A Legal Thesaurus* and *Legal Journals Index*);
Sweet & Maxwell (*Current Law Yearbook, Current Law Case Citator 1988* and *Current Law Legislation Citator 1988*).

Crown copyright in the extracts from an Act and statutory instrument is acknowledged.

Notwithstanding this assistance freely given, any omissions or errors are entirely my responsibility.

Special thanks are due to Corina Rogerson for her patient application in converting my jigsaw manuscript into an accurate typescript.

Finally, I am indebted to my wife, Verity, for enduring my preoccupation over such a long time, and to young Graham for his patience when I was 'not to be disturbed'. To them this book is dedicated.

Peter Clinch
April 1992

Table of Figures

Introduction

'Knowledge is of two kinds, we know a subject ourselves, or we know where we can find information upon it' (Samuel Johnson).

ABOUT THIS BOOK AND HOW TO USE IT

The study of law is changing. It is becoming less about learning mechanically the facts contained in books noted on lecturers' reading lists, and more about the ability to analyse a legal problem, identify and employ the written and computerised sources appropriate to its solution, and present the results of that analysis and research as a coherently organised, written or verbal presentation. This book is about the skill of legal research. The skills of analysis and communication are dealt with in two other Blackstone Press publications: *Learning Legal Rules* (Holland and Webb 1991) and *Learning Legal Skills* (Lee and Fox 1991).

The aim of this book, then, is to provide students studying English and European Communities law with a basic knowledge of the research sources and techniques relevant to the literature of law. Throughout this book the phrase 'English law' should be taken to include the law of England and Wales, unless otherwise stated. Traditionally legal research has been about how to use a law library, but in today's study of law, a student must be able not only to find particular books on the shelves but also correctly identify and confidently use, from the wide range of information now available in both print and electronic formats, those publications and databases appropriate to the solution of legal problems. The heart of this book is about acquiring these skills and techniques.

Experience shows that many students have great difficulty in developing adequate research skills for three reasons: first, they are confused by the distinction between publications containing the full and authoritative text of the law and publications which contain either unofficial versions or commentary; secondly, they are bewildered by the wide range of publications and databases containing legal information and have difficulty in matching the most appropriate source to the problem in hand; thirdly, some of the techniques required to correctly exploit these publications and databases appear complex and are a discouragement to further learning.

This book adopts two entirely novel approaches in an attempt to overcome these difficulties. First, it is clearly structured not only as far as the sequence of chapters is concerned, but in the way information is presented under standard headings for each source of legal information discussed. Secondly, wherever possible, use is made of diagrams and charts to outline the content and use of publications and provide step-by-step instruction in undertaking particular research problems.

The heart of the book lies in Part 2, 'Research Sources Described', which comprises three chapters, on the source materials of English law, European Communities law, and on keeping up to date, an aspect of legal research frequently neglected. Wrapped around this core are Part 1, dealing with some initial steps in legal research, finding and using a law library, and the effective use of catalogues and indexes; and Part 3, covering how to record and present research results, including the discussion of methods to be used in extended research (such as for projects or final-year dissertations) to record progress and findings, and the purpose and techniques for the construction of footnotes and bibliographies (lists of references detailing the material you cite). Much of the information presented in Part 3 is often neglected by books and lectures on legal research, but knowledge and understanding of these techniques will improve your confidence in managing and presenting research.

The discussion of each source of legal information in Part 2 is presented under a series of standard headings. Each heading is further subdivided. This structure is applied quite rigidly, though where, in a very few instances, only a little information is to be conveyed, subdivision is not used. The guiding aim has been to ensure information is clearly presented and readily accessible. The standard headings and subheadings for each legal source discussed in chapters 3 and 4 are as follows:

A **Description**   subdivided into a discussion of the **definition** and purpose of a particular original source material, a description of its **origin** and **structure**, information on its **publication and general availability** in libraries and details of the recommended form of **citation** (the way of referring to the source when writing about it).

B **Exploitation**   subdivided into paragraphs, each describing a different publication which will help you find and use the source material, with step by step instructions, often in diagrammatic form, on how to use key publications.

C **Electronic sources**   subdivided into paragraphs, each briefly describing a computer database containing either the text of the original sources described in section A or publications used to exploit them, described in section B.

D Research strategies   an account, using diagrams and charts where possible, to illustrate step by step how to use the publications and databases described in sections A, B and C to answer your most frequent research needs.

This rigid structure and the use of copious diagrams and charts makes the book appear more like a workshop manual than a conventional student text – and that is as it should be, for skills are not learnt by reading books from cover to cover, but through the application of small amounts of book knowledge to resolve particular, practical difficulties or problems. As far as possible, each section of the book is self-contained, and through the system of subdivision it should be easy to find the particular information required to solve a research problem. Some publications and databases include information on more than one legal source so some duplication of text is inevitable, but every effort has been made to keep repetition to a minimum.

The use of diagrams and charts is a considerable innovation. Very few law books contain illustrations of any kind but experience of teaching legal research over a number of years indicates that a diagram or chart is of more value to a student than pages of text or a lengthy verbal explanation. In the section on research strategies (section D), cross-references are provided in the charts and diagrams to the discussion of particular publications in section B, so linking the research steps to be followed in solving a particular information need to the detailed use of particular publications.

One feature of this book which may come as a surprise is the lack of 'worked examples'. There are two reasons for this: first, the law changes with such rapidity and the details of a volume, page and/or paragraph number provided in indexes to publications alter so much, that it is difficult to follow the worked example even a short time after the exercise was compiled. Secondly, there is a temptation to select examples to illustrate as many research difficulties as possible, regardless of whether the difficulty is met frequently or rarely. Again, experience indicates that students find it easier to follow a step-by-step presentation of research *principles* rather than become faced with the *detail* of a particular legal problem.

A final remark. This book is intended for use by students; it is not intended as a work of reference for law librarians and information officers. It therefore makes no claim to being a comprehensive treatment but merely aims to highlight basic information sources and provide an introduction to legal research techniques. If you have difficulty with a legal research problem this book cannot answer, then do make use of the skill and experience of the staff of your local law library or information service – they are there to help!

PART 1

INITIAL STEPS IN LEGAL RESEARCH

Chapter 1

Finding and using a law library

1.1 WHERE IS YOUR NEAREST LAW LIBRARY?

As a law student you will have automatic access to the library in the university, polytechnic or college at which you are studying. But, if you are studying law following a distance learning or correspondence course at home, or wish to study during the vacations away from your term-time base, or are preparing a final year project or dissertation on a topic for which your usual law library has little material, you will want to discover the nearest law library which can provide the type and size of collection which will satisfy your research needs.

In its 1988 edition (a new edition is in preparation), the *Directory of Law Libraries in the British Isles*, compiled by Christine Miskin for the British and Irish Association of Law Librarians, lists over 300 libraries, including academic libraries (the collective term for those in universities, polytechnics and colleges), public libraries, libraries of government departments, Inns of Court, national and local law societies, law firms and law courts themselves. Libraries are listed under each of the constituent countries of the British Isles, and then alphabetically by town, so it's easy to trace a library local to your base. Each entry gives details of the size of the collection, but most importantly a named contact. Before you set off to visit a law library other than one with which you are familiar, it is essential to contact the librarian beforehand, as many libraries outside the academic and public library service are private and normally available only to members. You may need to obtain permission to use them. Whilst you can walk straight into a public library you will discover that most will have only a very basic law collection. Normally you can use academic libraries for reference purposes only (that is, you can browse but you won't be able to borrow) unless you are a member of that educational institution, or you belong to another academic library which has made special reciprocal arrangements with the library you intend to use. Such a reciprocal scheme operates amongst polytechnic libraries in the London area, for example; it is called the London Plus Scheme and is available to part-time students registered at any one of the polytechnics belonging to the scheme.

Check beforehand whether the library you wish to visit does, in fact, stock the publications you wish to use – the *Directory* provides only a very general idea of each library's stock. Opening hours are noted in the *Directory* but in view of expenditure cuts faced by all libraries, they may have been reduced, so that is another point to check.

In school or public libraries, the whole library service is usually centralised – all the books available to library users are kept in a single building. However, academic libraries frequently organise their collections quite differently, to take into account the needs of different groups of library users and the extent to which the university, polytechnic or college buildings are scattered over a geographical area. Some academic libraries have a single building housing the bookstock of all subjects; the law collection may be part of the main sequence of books, or it is sometimes set apart because the types of publication and the needs of law library users are rather different from those of other subjects. Other academic libraries may have a central library, with branches, frequently referred to as site, campus or departmental libraries, scattered over several buildings. Often these branch libraries are located close to the teaching departments they serve.

So, make a point of studying any leaflet guides or floor plans displayed in the library. If in doubt about where the law collection is shelved, ask library staff for assistance.

1.2   USING THE LAW LIBRARY

There is a strong chance that when you enter a law library for the first time you will experience bewilderment and apprehension, possibly leading to panic. Bewilderment at the hundreds of shelves and numerous rows of books, apprehension at the thought of trying to find your way round the stock, and panic that you will never be able to find the information you want in the time available.

Relax! Libraries are laid out in a logical way; there are catalogues to help you identify whether the library has the book you need and, finally, but most important of all, there will usually be an enquiry desk or information point where library staff will be available to assist you. Never be afraid to ask for help; it is an important part of the job of library and information staff to ensure, to the best of their ability, that customers' information needs are satisfied, so that they are encouraged to use the collections again in the future.

1.2.1   What is the general arrangement of the stock?

If you are attending a course of study at a university, polytechnic or college it is likely that during the early days of the first term you will be given a tour of the library. What follows in this chapter is meant to provide background information and a skeleton framework within which to set the detail of the particular library you are to use. There is a checklist in appendix 1 which you can use to find out how well you know how to use any law library.

Libraries usually contain two broad categories of material: books and periodicals (also called journals or, more popularly, magazines). They are usually shelved separately from one another. One reason for this is that periodicals comprise titles which are added to, more or less regularly, by the publication of new issues. So, space has to be left on the shelves between one title and the next to accommodate future issues. Some periodicals have new issues published as frequently as weekly and a few even daily.

Therefore, in law libraries you will find documents which are published in the same way as periodicals, such as Acts of Parliament, law reports as well as law periodicals, shelved separately from books.

1.2.2   How is each type of material arranged on the shelves?

Books are usually grouped according to their subject. This is achieved by means of a subject classification scheme. Several different schemes are in use; each employs numbers or a combination of numbers and letters to indicate the subject of a book. The classification number or mark – often abbreviated to class number or class mark – is placed near the bottom of the spine of each book. If you are familiar with school or public libraries you may have noticed they mostly use a scheme of numbers, the third and fourth separated by a decimal point. This is the Dewey decimal classification scheme. It is also used in some universities, polytechnics and colleges. Another scheme you will find in academic libraries is the Library of Congress classification scheme which uses a combination of letters and numbers. Whichever scheme your library employs the purposes of the classification are the same: to bring together on the shelves books on the same subject, and to indicate where in the library a particular book is to be found.

Periodicals may be arranged in one of several different ways: either by subject and then alphabetically by title within each subject, or just alphabetically by title. In some of the larger law libraries you may find periodicals arranged according to the jurisdiction (the geographical area over which the laws of a particular legislature or decisions of the courts extend) to which they usually refer. So, for example, English law periodicals will be shelved separately from European Communities or French or United States periodicals.

Libraries often have separate sequences for a number of specialised groups of publications: reference books, such as dictionaries, general encyclopaedias, directories etc.; and bibliographic works – a large group of publications ranging from lists of the total publishing output of a particular country to lists of books and/or individual articles contained in periodicals on a particular subject, such as law. Government publications or the publications of international organisations such as the European Communities, sometimes form a separate collection depending, in part, on how much of this huge publishing output is collected by the particular library.

You may also find another distinction made in the stock of the library: very large books (called 'folios', or 'quartos' in some libraries, or 'oversize' in others) may be shelved separately from ordinary size books. At the other end of the scale, some libraries, especially universities, keep very thin books (pamphlets) in a separate sequence. Recent changes in photocopying law mean that some libraries will stock photocopies made under licence of parts of books or articles from periodicals – these may be kept apart from the rest of the stock, perhaps in an area to which you will not have direct access so that you will need to ask staff to obtain the item you require.

1.2.3 Is all the stock of the library available for you to borrow?

Not all the stock of the library will be available for loan, and in law libraries in particular, where there is a very strong dependence on periodicals rather than books, a large part of the stock will be for use only in the library. However, libraries usually provide photocopying services, either self-service or undertaken by staff, where small sections of books or periodicals may be copied subject to the provisions of copyright law. Notices in the photocopy service areas will explain what is permitted under the law.

Usually you will be able to borrow copies of most books, though some of the more expensive or loose-leaf publications (which require regular updating by library staff) may be for use only in the library. Sometimes you will find several copies of the same basic text are available for loan, and each copy may be for a different loan period (the length of time you can borrow a book). The loan period is usually determined by the book's popularity – the level of demand for the title. Some libraries keep copies of the most frequently borrowed titles in a separate collection; you may have to ask library staff to obtain the book you require from this collection as it is sometimes placed behind a service desk or issue counter. The loan period for this stock may be very brief, perhaps just a few hours. The intention is that you may be required to read only one chapter of a book each week or fortnight, and you can borrow the book for a few hours, long enough to read the text required, return it to the library, and one of your colleagues on the course can then borrow the book. Often this collection contains copies of 'set' or 'recommended' texts for your course – copies which you should **buy** for your own personal use. Do not let the fact that the library has copies of recommended books prevent you from buying your own, because the number of students wishing to read a particular recommended book before an essay or seminar deadline, will usually far exceed the library's capacity to meet this peak in demand.

1.2.4 How do you discover whether the library has the book you require?

The key is the library catalogue. Many libraries now use computers on which to hold and display details of the stock, but in some libraries parts of the stock, frequently books purchased before the computer system was installed, will be recorded on microform or card catalogues. Microform catalogues comprise rolls or sheets of plastic film containing photo-reduced images of the details of books. The rolls or sheets of plastic are read using a piece of equipment called a microform reader. Card catalogues are contained in large banks of wooden drawers – the traditional image, along with leather-bound books, of a scholarly library!

No matter the medium by which the stock of the library is recorded and displayed, you will usually find at least three separate parts to the catalogue or ways of finding details about the stock:

(a)   *The author section* arranges details of the stock alphabetically by the authors' surnames. If no author's name is given in the book (perhaps it has been issued by a large organisation such as a government department) then an entry will be given under the name of the issuing body. Sometimes libraries also include for all books additional entries filed alphabetically by the title of the book, and this combined author and title catalogue may be referred to as a *name* catalogue.

(b)   *The subject section* is arranged alphabetically by subject and provides class marks where books on each topic are shelved.

(c)   *The classified section* arranges class marks in numerical or alphabetical order according to the classification scheme used, with details of the authors and titles of books allocated to each subject. This section of the catalogue is usually consulted only after you have found the appropriate class mark in the subject section, for the topic in which you are interested.

1.2.5   Which parts of the catalogue should you use to answer particular information needs?

If you know who wrote the book you are looking for, use the author section and remember to search by the first letter of the author's *surname*. If the library has books by more than one author of the same surname, search entries for the forename or initials of the author in whom you are interested.

Although an alphabetical arrangement of authors' names or book titles may sound straightforward enough to use, there are, unfortunately, two ways of organising the entries in alphabetical order. One uses a 'letter-by-letter' arrangement, the other 'word-by-word'. In 'letter-by-letter', any spaces between words are ignored and the whole name or title is treated as one long word. In 'word-by-word', the first word determines the overall order of entries and where two entries have the same first word, the second word determines the detailed order. Here are examples to illustrate the difference.

Letter-by-letter	*Word-by-word*
Law Centres Federation	Law Centres Federation
Law Commission	Law Commission
Lawler, S.D.	Law Reform Committee
Lawless, Clive	Law Society
Law Reform Committee	Lawler, S.D
Law Society	Lawless, Clive

If you know the title of the book but not the author's name and the library
has a name or title catalogue, use it to find out if the book is in stock. *Ignore*
an indefinite or definite article ('a', 'an', 'the' in English) at the beginning of
the title.

If you wish to browse for books on a subject and you have no authors or titles
in mind, use the subject section to find the appropriate class marks then either
go to the shelves or use the classified section of the catalogue.

If you know the class mark for a subject you can go straight to the shelves
and browse, but books in your chosen section may be on loan, and some may
be shelved in other parts of the library because they are large size, or
pamphlets or reference books. You will not have any idea, therefore, of what
the full stock of the library may be. To obtain a full picture, it is better to use
the classified section of the catalogue to identify particular authors and titles
before you go to the shelves.

If the library has a computerised catalogue you will need to use a computer
terminal with a screen and keyboard. Most systems provide users with a list
of options, otherwise known as a 'menu', from which to choose the search
path you wish to follow. Computerised systems often offer more ways of
searching the database than the three outlined above and will also tell you the
current position, whether, for example, the book you want is on loan, when
it is due to be returned, or if it is on the shelves now. Some systems allow you
to reserve or recall books you require which are presently on loan, by typing
instructions at the computer terminal. Instruction leaflets are usually
available to help you obtain the best results from using the library catalogue.

1.2.6   How do you discover if the library has the periodical you require?

Libraries with microform or card catalogues usually have a separate section
of the catalogue devoted to a list, usually in alphabetical order by title, of the
periodicals they keep in stock. This periodicals catalogue or 'holdings list' as
it is sometimes termed, will give details of the particular issues and their dates
of publication which the library keeps, and an indication of where on the
shelves they are located.

If a library has a computerised catalogue then its periodicals catalogue may
be within the title section of the book catalogue.

The way information is given about the issues of a particular title held by
the library can sometimes cause a little confusion. Here is an example with an
explanation.

New Law Journal v118 (1968) – v120 (1970), v124 (1974) -

This means the library stocks *New Law Journal* from volume 118 of 1968 to
volume 120 of 1970, then there are some volumes not in stock, before the
holdings of the title recommence at volume 124 of 1974 and continue *complete
to the present*. Where some individual issues are missing from a set, too many
to list individually on the public catalogue, the word 'incomplete' or 'incomp'
may be given at the end of the entry.

1.2.7 Special points you should remember when searching the catalogue for law books

New editions of law books appear frequently because law is one of the most dynamic subjects in all knowledge. Libraries frequently retain old, out-of-date editions because they can have a value to those studying the development of law – legal historians. Entries for these books will, of course, appear in the library catalogue, so you should take particular care when using the catalogue *and* when searching the library shelves to obtain the particular edition of the work you may have been directed to either by a lecturer or in your reading. If no guidance has been given on the edition to use then a good rule of thumb is to consult the most up-to-date you can trace. You can check which edition is the latest available by using either publishers' catalogues or general lists of books such as *Whitaker's Books in Print* (see 3.6B2.1) which virtually every library will possess. Publishers' catalogues may not be on public display in the library but ask library staff if you can consult copies kept to assist the library in purchasing its stock. The rule of thumb should also be borne in mind if you are tempted to purchase law books second-hand; make sure the edition on offer *is* the latest available, otherwise you may be parting with good money for a publication of little practical use.

Law books written by famous authors frequently continue to be known by the name of the original author even though that person died long ago. An example is Joseph Chitty, *Contracts*, first published in 1826 and now in its 26th edition. Joseph Chitty died in 1838. Subsequent editions have been prepared by other authors such as Anthony G. Guest, and when using the library catalogue you should be able to trace entries under these names as well. In addition, since the book is popularly known as *Chitty on Contracts*, you may find an additional entry in the title catalogue in this form.

Quite a large number of well-known law books are written by *joint authors*, that is, two or more authors are responsible for the text, for example: Hepple and Matthews, *Tort: Cases and Materials*. Usually the library author catalogue will have two entries, one under Hepple, B.A., and the other under Matthews, M.H., so you can successfully search under either name. This is particularly helpful where one of the authors has a very commonly occurring surname, such as Smith, as in Smith and Hogan, *Criminal Law*. Save time and effort and search under Hogan!

Lawyers can be rather lax about giving *the surname and forenames or initials of authors* to whom they are referring; frequently only the surname is given. Tracing Smith, *Casebook on Contract* in a library catalogue will be a very time-consuming task. If, however, the catalogue has a title section, search that instead! Also, why not consider encouraging others to follow a more helpful policy and when *you* write about an author, give the surname *with* initials or forenames.

Some famous law authors have *double barrelled names* such as O. Hood-Phillips. Libraries adopt different practices and it is worth checking the catalogue under Phillips and, if unsuccessful, Hood-Phillips, before declaring the library does not stock his books.

A substantial number of legal publications are prepared by *organisations* rather than individuals, for example: the Law Commission, the Home Office, the Law Society. To find an entry in the library catalogue use the author section and search under the name of the organisation, ignoring 'the' at the beginning of the name.

HMSO, which stands for Her Majesty's Stationery Office, is a *publisher* of a very wide range of materials lawyers use (see 3.11). HMSO is not the author of law books. You should avoid the common trap of trying to search the library author catalogue under HMSO for entries on the particular official publication you require. Instead, either search the author catalogue by the name of the organisation which prepared the document (e.g., Home Office, Law Commission), or the title, or name, catalogue by the title of the publication.

1.2.8   What if the library appears not to have the book or periodical you require?

First, make sure you have used the correct section of the catalogue for your search. For example, here are three fairly common errors in catalogue use:

(a)   Picking a word from the title of a book and searching the subject section of the catalogue, then the classified in the hope of finding an entry.

(b)   Searching the author section of the book catalogue for an entry for the author of a periodical article you are trying to trace – no library catalogue indexes the contents of periodicals except where an article has been photocopied and added to stock, and this is not a common occurrence.

(c)   Searching the title section of the catalogue for the title of a periodical. This can be achieved successfully on some computerised catalogues, but if only microform or card catalogues are available, information about the periodicals stocked by the library is kept in a separate periodicals catalogue.

Secondly, make sure you are using the correct spelling of the author's name or the title of the book or periodical. Try some alternatives. If that fails ask library staff for advice.

Thirdly, when you have exhausted the two foregoing possibilities, then the chances are the library probably does not stock what you require. But do not give up! All academic and public libraries in the UK are members of a national inter-library loan service, which enables them to trace and obtain from other libraries copies of books and periodicals which they, themselves, do not possess. The service is also part of an international network. If the information you have about a particular book or periodical article is *full and accurate* – and these are vital requirements – you can make an application through your local library for the item to be obtained for you. If you are preparing a final-year project or dissertation you will probably need to use the inter-library loan service quite often; more details are given in appendix 2.

Chapter 2

Effective use of catalogues and indexes

This short chapter describes some techniques for making the most effective use of library catalogues and indexes in all types of legal publication. Law is a subject so dependent on written words and their meaning that having the skill to extract all the required information from a catalogue or index is one of the basic abilities a lawyer should possess.

When you have analysed a legal topic or problem with which you have to deal, you may have formed a list of words or phrases in your mind which sum the matter up. The challenge before you is to accurately match *your* list with the words provided in library catalogues and publication indexes so that you can quickly and accurately find the information about the topic or problem you require.

The language of law is particularly rich and you will discover that in many instances no two indexes to publications are likely to use exactly the same words to describe a particular legal concept. There are several reasons for this: first, the authors may be considering the concept from different viewpoints and in different contexts. Secondly, the index compiler, who is normally a different person from the author, will not only echo the author's approach but develop the structure and content of the index in a way which will be most helpful for the intended readership. So a student textbook on industrial relations law, for example, may use different subject headings from a three-volume practitioners' encyclopaedia on the same subject. Further, a good index will use a single word or phrase to describe a fact or concept which, in the text of the book, may have been referred to by several different words and in several different ways – the index will bring all references to the same matter together at the same point.

To ensure that when you use an index you refer to all the possible words which might be used to describe the concept in which you are interested, you should master the use of a word association technique, such as cartwheeling.

An example of this technique is given in figure 2.1.

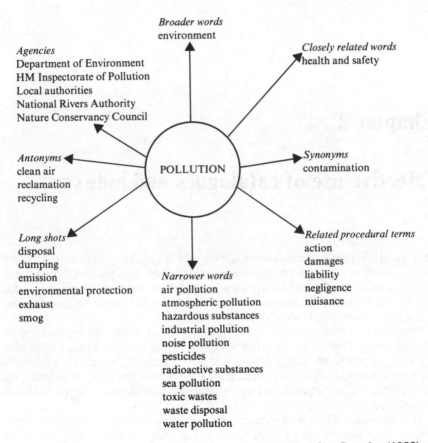

Broader words
environment

Agencies
Department of Environment
HM Inspectorate of Pollution
Local authorities
National Rivers Authority
Nature Conservancy Council

Closely related words
health and safety

Antonyms
clean air
reclamation
recycling

POLLUTION

Synonyms
contamination

Long shots
disposal
dumping
emission
environmental protection
exhaust
smog

Narrower words
air pollution
atmospheric pollution
hazardous substances
industrial pollution
noise pollution
pesticides
radioactive substances
sea pollution
toxic wastes
waste disposal
water pollution

Related procedural terms
action
damages
liability
negligence
nuisance

Figure 2.1   Cartwheel for the word 'pollution'. After Statsky (1982).

Place the concept in which you are intrested at the centre of the page, then cluster in groups around it words which have a broader meaning, closely related terms, synonyms (words with the same meaning), related terms, narrower words and so on.

To help you compile these groups of words use ordinary English dictionaries, such as the *Oxford English Dictionary*, or law dictionaries, or a specialised publication – a legal thesaurus. An example of one published for English law is *A Legal Thesaurus*, 2nd edition, edited by Christine Miskin and Alison Napier, published by Legal Information Resources Ltd. It is an alphabetical listing of legal terms against each of which are noted broader terms, narrower terms and related terms. So, in the example shown in figure 2.2, for the word 'negligence', 12 narrower terms are given ranging in alphabetical order from accidents to wrongful birth; three broader terms and one related term (contributory negligence) complete the list.

NEGLIGENCE   (G)
    NT: ACCIDENTS
    NT: DUTY OF CARE
    NT: ECONOMIC LOSS
    NT: FORSEEABILITY
    NT: LATENT DAMAGE
    NT: NERVOUS SHOCK
    NT: PERSONAL INJURIES
    NT: PRODUCT LIABILITY
    NT: PROFESSIONAL NEGLIGENCE
    NT: RES IPSA LOQUITOR
    NT: STANDARD OF CARE
    NT: WRONGFUL BIRTH
    BT: MENS REA
    BT: TORTIOUS LIABILITY
    BT: TORTS
    RT: CONTRIBUTORY NEGLIGENCE

NEGOTIABLE INSTRUMENTS   (G)
    NT: BANKERS DRAFTS
    NT: BILLS OF EXCHANGE
    NT: COMMERCIAL CREDITS
    NT: SHARE WARRANTS
    NT: STERLING COMMERCIAL PAPER
    NT: SWAP AGREEMENTS
    BT: BANKING
    BT: CHOSES IN ACTION

NEGOTIATION   (G)
    BT: DISPUTE RESOLUTION
    BT: GRIEVANCE PROCEDURES

NEIGHBOUR NOTIFICATION   (G)

NEIGHBOURHOOD ADVICE CENTRES   (G)
    BT: LEGAL ADVICE CENTRES

Figure 2.2   Extract from *A Legal Thesaurus* (1988).

Having compiled your cartwheel you can run the list of terms you have discovered against the index entries in the book or encyclopaedia you are using, and so be more certain of extracting all the information relevant to your problem. Constructing a cartwheel takes time but in the early stages of your law course you will be trying to understand the relationships between legal concepts and the words used to describe them, so learning the discipline of using a word association technique will be worthwhile.

A final word about the different types of index you are likely to come across in your legal research. Publishers usually group indexes at the back of a book or in the last volume of a multi-volume encyclopaedia, or even as a separate index volume if the main text of the publication is so extensive. Alphabetical lists of the subjects covered by the publication are commonplace. However, you will find in law publications some specialised indexes, and these are frequently placed at the *front*: they include alphabetical lists of the titles of Acts and court cases referred to in the text, or even chronological lists of Acts and other statutory materials referred to, the oldest placed first in the list.

The main points to ask yourself when using indexes are:

(a)   What information is being searched for: a subject, a title, the name of an organisation?

(b)   Which types of index are available in the publication? Check the contents page at the front.

(c)   Where are the indexes placed: at the front, at the back, in a separate volume?

This checklist may seem like 'teaching Grandma to suck eggs' but few students stop to think about these points and so fail to fully benefit from the thoughtful and careful work of the indexer.

PART 2

RESEARCH SOURCES DESCRIBED

Chapter 3

Researching the law of England and Wales

3.1 THE STRUCTURE OF THE LITERATURE

'*Where* do I start to look for the answer to this legal problem?' This thought commonly crosses the minds of students, and some practitioners, who, having already expended considerable mental effort to identify to their satisfaction the nature of the problem to be solved, now stand in the library wondering which publications are likely to contain the solution. Two of the most basic research skills are to understand that there is a structure to the literature of law,and to know how the component parts relate to one another so that relevant sources can be matched and applied to information needs.

The literature of English law may be divided into two broad categories: the primary sources and the secondary sources, as shown in figure 3.1.

The basis of this distinction is that the primary sources are the law itself whilst the secondary are commentaries on it.

The primary sources comprise original and authoritative statements of the law, sub-divided into three: legislation – law made by Parliament; case law – the decisions of the courts; and a minor, frequently overlooked yet valuable, group of sources, which might be collectively referred to as 'extra-legal'.

Legislation is itself divided into primary (original) and secondary (delegated or subordinate), the distinction being that primary legislation, in general, becomes law only after detailed debate and scrutiny within Parliament culminating in approval by the Sovereign, whilst secondary legislation is, generally speaking, prepared by an authority outside Parliament (usually a Minister of the Crown), under powers given by Parliament through primary legislation. Secondary legislation contains detailed rules and regulations, which it would be impractical to include within primary legislation, in an

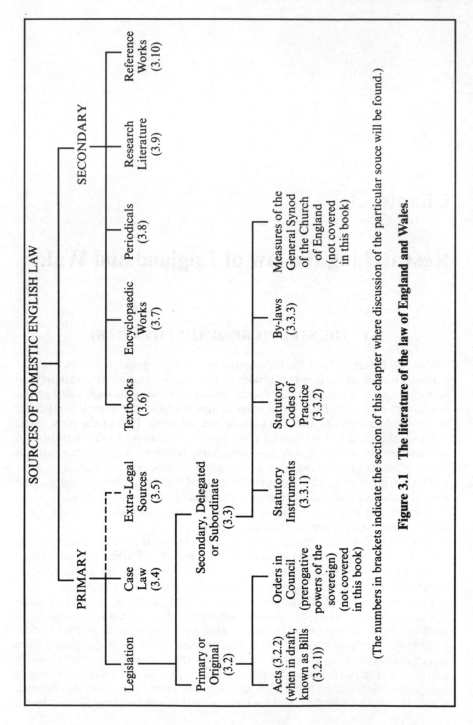

Figure 3.1   The literature of the law of England and Wales.

(The numbers in brackets indicate the section of this chapter where discussion of the particular souce will be found.)

attempt to cover every contingency the legislation might involve. The usual practice is for primary legislation to contain the broad outlines of a particular scheme and secondary legislation to contain the detail.

Primary or original legislation can take the form of an Act of Parliament or an Order in Council, but since the latter are only infrequently issued and their main application is in relation to the armed forces, the civil service or emergency powers, further discussion of Orders in Council as primary legislation is omitted. However, law students must be aware of how to trace and use draft versions of Acts of Parliament, better known as Bills of Parliament. Bills of Parliament contain proposals which, if enacted, would either introduce new provisions or amend, repeal or consolidate the existing law – a knowledge of such current proposals and their likely effect will impress examiners. Bills of both the current and past sessions of Parliament are valuable to students undertaking final-year projects or higher-degree research. Bills are often heavily amended and revised as they pass through Parliament, and tracing these changes provides insights into the development of the law and the lobby work of pressure groups. The ability to trace Bills which failed to receive Parliamentary support and have never become law is also useful – in recent years, more Public Bills have failed to become Acts than the number which have successfully completed the legislative process. Many will have been contentious, some may have failed through lack of Parliamentary time, but all contain pertinent views on how the law should develop to either cause or reflect change in society. The different types of Bills and Acts are discussed in 3.2.1 and 3.2.2 respectively.

Secondary legislation may be split into four categories: statutory instruments, codes of practice, by-laws and Measures of the General Synod of the Church of England. Only the first three will be covered in this book as rarely, if ever, even in legal practice, will a lawyer need access to Church of England Measures. The differences between statutory instruments, statutory codes of practice and by-laws, and how to trace these publications are explained in 3.3.1, 3.3.2 and 3.3.3 respectively.

The second subdivision of the primary sources of law comprises case or judge-made law – the decisions of the courts. Built up from over seven centuries of work of the courts, the sheer volume of decisions and number of different source publications available means, that of all the categories of primary legal sources, case law frequently causes students the most research difficulty. However, as with other legal sources, the key to mastering legal research skills lies in recognising and understanding patterns and structures, and for case law they are (a) the historical development of law report publishing and (b) the characteristics and use of a range of case-locating publications such as indexes, digests and *Citators*, available to assist research; see 3.4.

The third subdivision of the primary sources of law, the extra-legal, comprises what are generally referred to as non-statutory codes of practice. The individual documents may be called either codes of practice, codes of conduct, guidance or standards, but they have two things in common: they are issued without the authority of Parliament by a variety of public and private organisations, and secondly, they are not legally enforceable in their own right. They are not found in all areas of legal study but most frequently in business, commercial and consumer law. They can be difficult to track down in legal research, but 3.5 provides assistance.

Standing distinct from the primary sources of the literature of English law are five secondary, an even more extensive and varied group, comprising commentaries, explanations, reviews or guides to the primary sources. They are: textbooks (3.6) comprising books of authority, modern textbooks, casebooks, practice books and precedent books; encyclopaedic works (3.7); periodicals (3.8), also referred to as journals; research literature (3.9), such as postgraduate theses and other research publications; and reference works (3.10), including dictionaries and directories.

So far the outline of the structure of legal literature has been based on the type of information or form of publication. However, no guide to legal research skills would be complete without a section devoted to the output of probably the most prolific and diverse publisher in the UK – the government. The government publishes legal information in virtually every one of the forms so far described. Ways of tracking down government publications will be explained in the final section of this chapter (3.11).

3.2 PRIMARY LEGISLATION

3.2.1 Bills of Parliament

3.2.1A DESCRIPTION

3.2.1A1 Definition

A Bill is a draft version of a proposed Act of Parliament, a document containing the text of a piece of legislation. A Bill may be introduced in Parliament in either the House of Lords or the House of Commons but must successfully pass through several stages in both Houses before it can be submitted to the Sovereign for Royal Assent. Once the Sovereign has signified assent the Bill becomes an Act of Parliament.

There are three classes of Bill: Public, Private and Hybrid (see figure 3.2).

Public Bills (which, if successful, will become Public General Acts) relate to matters of *public policy* and are introduced directly by members of Parliament. If a Public Bill is introduced by a member of the government (for example, a Minister) the Bill will be referred to as a Government Bill; if it is introduced by a private member of Parliament (in the Commons an individual Member of Parliament (MP) or in the Lords an individual peer) it is formally referred to as an 'unofficial Member's Bill', or more familiarly as a Private Member's Bill. A Private Member's Bill should not be confused with the second class of Bills, Private Bills. A Private Bill (which, if successful, will become a Private Act, or more correctly a Local or Personal Act) is a Bill which relates to an individual or small group of people, a public company or corporation or a local authority – its application is restricted in scope to particular people, organisations or a geographical location. As a further

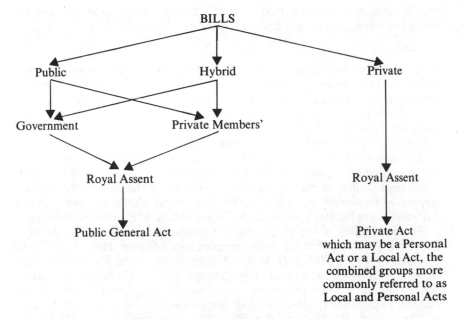

Figure 3.2   Types of Bill of Parliament

distinction, a Private Bill is presented to Parliament in the form of a petition, by the parties whom the legislation is intended to benefit, acting through a specialist firm of Parliamentary Agents, and not a member of Parliament. A Private Bill also follows a quite different Parliamentary procedure from a Public Bill. The Greater Manchester (Light Rapid Transit System) Bill, which received the Royal Assent in 1990, is an example. It provides for the construction and operation of a 'tram' system on the public road and rail networks.

The third category of Bill is known as a Hybrid Bill which, as the name suggests, is a Public Bill which may in certain respects affect Private rights, and is dealt with by a special procedure. The Channel Tunnel Bill, which received the Royal Assent in 1987, not only provides for the construction and operation of the railway tunnel, but also the compulsory purchase of land around Folkestone for roads and other works.

One type of Bill you will frequently come across is a consolidation Bill, normally found amongst Public Bills. It does not introduce any new law but seeks to tidy up existing legislation by bringing together scattered elements in one Bill. A recent example has become the Companies Act 1985, which comprises 747 sections and 25 schedules consolidating legislation from 1948 to 1983.

As a law student you are likely only to use Public Bills, but once in legal practice, especially with a local authority or a statutory undertaker (for example, an electricity, gas or water authority), skill in researching private legislation may be required. In the rest of 3.2.1, therefore, the accent is on the skills and techniques required when researching Public Bills.

3.2.1A2   Origin

Bills themselves have draft versions. They are prepared by specialist lawyers known as Parliamentary counsel. The draft versions are not normally published but reports of the Law Commission (see 3.11) frequently include a draft Public Bill in its entirety or selected clauses, to show how recommendations for the reform of a legal topic should be given effect.

It is important to understand the broad outline of the procedure followed by Parliament when considering Bills because they are reprinted, incorporating amendments, at several stages in the Parliamentary process. It is crucial, when researching, to match the correct version of the Bill to the relevant *Reports of Parliamentary Debates (Hansard)*, in which the arguments put by MPs and peers for and against the Bill's provisions, are reported verbatim.

The procedures of the House of Commons and House of Lords when considering a Public Bill are quite complex and different. Figure 3.3, kindly supplied by Frank Hallett (HMSO), highlights the crucial points for legal research purposes, relating each stage through which a Bill may pass to (a) the times when the Bill may be printed or reprinted (marked 'Bill' in the columns headed 'Reported in (publication)', (b) the places where reports of the debates will be printed (*Hansard* and *Reports of Standing Committees of the House*), (c) when amendments will be printed, and (d) where details of the progress of business on the Bill will be found (*Minute, Journal*).

A Bill may be first presented in either the House of Commons or the House of Lords. In the first House it would require support at all stages through to transfer stage when it would go to the other House to follow a similar path again. If amendments have been made in the other House, an exchange of messages occurs between the Houses until the differences are resolved, and finally the Bill is sent for Royal Assent by the Sovereign. A Bill may be printed up to six times during the Parliamentary process, each printing may include agreed amendments to the original document. The timing of these key events is noted in figure 3.3 by the word 'Bill' appearing in the columns headed 'Reported in (publication)'. They are after first reading (both Houses), after committee stage if amended in committee (both Houses), and following report stage, if amended (both Houses, though this does not usually occur in the Commons).

There are a few more points to bear in mind. First, there are several ways in which a Member of Parliament in the House of Commons can introduce a Bill. One is under the so-called 'ten-minute rule', when the Member gives a brief explanatory statement on the objects of the proposed Bill. This statement will be reported verbatim in *Hansard*. If, as a result of the statement, the Commons do *not* give leave to introduce the Bill, then the Bill will not be published, and the only public statement about it will be the MP's speech. Secondly, a Bill can be defeated at several other stages in the Parliamentary process, notably at the second reading and third reading stages in either House. The second reading normally commences with a speech by

HOUSE OF COMMONS		HOUSE OF LORDS	
STAGE	REPORTED IN (PUBLICATION)	STAGE	REPORTED IN (PUBLICATION)
Presentation (First Reading)	Bill, Order Paper, Votes and Proceedings, Hansard, Journal	Presentation (First Reading)	Bill, Minute, Hansard, Journal
Second Reading (General Debate) (approval to continue)	Order Paper, Hansard, Votes and Proceedings, Journal	Second Reading (General Debate) (approval to continue)	Minute, Hansard, Journal
Amendments (can now be tabled)	Notices of Amendments	Amendments (can now be tabled)	Peers Amendments, Marshalled Lists
Committee Stage (amends Bill) (usually Standing Committee, can be a whole House Committee)	Amendments, Standing Committee Debate (or Hansard if whole House Committee), Votes and Proceedings, Journal, Minutes of Proceedings, Notices of Amendments, Committee Business, Bill (if amended)	Committee Stage (normally whole House, can be a Public Bill Committee)	Amendments, Marshalled Lists, Hansard, Minute, (or Public Bill Committee Official Report), Journal and Bill (if amended)
Report Stage (Can further amend Bill)	Order Paper, Amendments possible, Hansard, Votes and Proceedings, Journal, Notices of Amendments, Bill (not normally printed)	Report Stage (can further amend Bill)	Amendments, Marshalled Lists, Hansard, Minute, Journal and Bill (if amended)
Third Reading (Can further amend Bill)	Amendments possible, Order Paper, Hansard, Votes and Proceedings, Journal, Notices of Amendments	Third Reading (can further amend Bill)	Amendments possible, Hansard, Minute, Journal
Transfer or Consideration Stage Messages	Lords Reasons and Amendments, Commons Amendments, Votes and Proceedings, Notices of Amendments, Hansard, Journal	Transfer or Consideration Stage Messages	Commons Reasons and Amendments, Lords Amendments, Marshalled Lists, Hansard, Minute, Journal
Royal Assent	Votes and Proceedings, Hansard, Journal	Royal Assent (Notice to Commons)	Hansard, Minute, Journal

Figure 3.3 Legislation procedures and related publications for Parliamentary Bills. Source Hallett (1992).

the Bill's proposer followed by a debate on the general principles of the proposed legislation. If the Bill successfully receives a second reading it will go to the committee stage where detailed consideration, line by line, word by word, is given to the Bill's proposals. There is no vote at the end of the committee stage, but at the report stage amendments made in committee and, in the House of Commons only, any new amendments, are considered. Again, there is no vote at the conclusion of this stage but there is following the brief proceedings of the third reading. For legal researchers the committee stage, especially in the House of Commons, has the most interest, for the Bill is here considered by a Standing Committee of, on average, about 20 MPs. The discussions are reported verbatim, not in *Hansard*, but in a separate series: *Reports of Standing Committees of the House*. On a few occasions the Commons sits as a committee of the whole House, and in that case the debate on the Bill is printed in *Hansard* itself.

For further information on Public, Private and Hybrid Bill procedure consult the authoritative source used in Parliament itself: Erskine May's *Treatise on the Law, Privileges, Proceedings and Usage of Parliament* (often referred to as Erskine May's *Parliamentary Practice*), published by Butterworths and frequently revised through new editions.

In general, for a Public Bill to become law it must complete its passage through both Houses within a session of Parliament, which is usually a period of about a year between one Queen's Speech and the next. One exception, recently topical, is where a Bill passes successfully through the House of Commons but is defeated in the House of Lords in two successive Parliamentary sessions. Even without the support of the House of Lords, providing certain procedural details have been followed, the Bill can be sent for Royal Assent. This procedure, laid down in the Parliament Act 1911, as amended by the Parliament Act 1949, has been used on only four occasions, and most recently in 1991 when the House of Lords blocked the War Crimes Bill for the second time. The length of each Parliamentary session is determined by the government of the day, but the normal pattern is for the State Opening of Parliament, when the Queen's Speech is delivered, to take place in early November, so marking the beginning of a fresh session of Parliament, with no Bills yet introduced. The Queen's Speech itself will set out in general terms the legislation which the government intends to introduce into Parliament during the session. Nearly a year later, just before the next Queen's Speech, the session is brought to an end by prorogation, and any Bills which have yet to complete their passage are lost. This frequently happens with Private Members' Bills, most getting no further than the first reading stage, a few to second reading and an even fewer number beyond. All will fail to become law because the session was brought to a close before all Parliamentary stages were completed. Commonly only around 10 per cent of all Private Members' Bills satisfactorily complete the Parliamentary process and become law (see Drewry 1989). Government Bills, however, fare much better, and once introduced into Parliament are highly likely to complete all stages by the end of the session and become law. When a General Election is called Parliament is dissolved and all Public Bills will be lost. The only exception to this general position is that some Private Bills and Hybrid Bills can be carried over from one session of Parliament to the next, provided specific resolutions to that effect are agreed by the House or Houses which have already given them consideration.

3.2.1A3   Structure

A Public Bill comprises nine different parts, not all of which are essential.

(a)   Short title – this is the title under which the eventual Act will be generally known. It is given in three places: at the head of the Bill, in a clause of the Bill (usually the last) and on the outside of the back cover.

(b)   Arrangement of clauses – a table at the front of most printings of all but the briefest of Bills sets out in order the parts, chapters and clauses into which the text is divided, with their respective titles (see appendix 3 for further details of the terminology for the divisions of a Bill).

(c)   Long title – this sets out in general terms the purposes of the Bill. It appears twice in a Bill, once above the enacting formula, and also on the outside of the back cover.

(d)   Preamble – its purpose is to state the reasons for and the expected effects of the proposed legislation. A preamble is rarely incorporated in Public Bills nowadays but still appears in Bills of great constitutional importance or in a Bill giving effect to international conventions.

(e)   Enacting formula – this short paragraph summarises the legislative authority of Parliament and precedes the first clause of the Bill.

(f)   Clauses – the Bill is divided into a series of numbered clauses, each with a descriptive title, known as a 'side note' or 'marginal note' printed in the margin. The word clause is often abbreviated in writing to 'cl'.

Clauses may be divided into subsections, subsections into paragraphs, and paragraphs into subparagraphs – see appendix 3. Towards the end of the Bill, or if appropriate, at the end of one of its parts, formal clauses are placed which contain very important information for the legal researcher:

(i)   Definition clauses, indicated by the marginal note 'interpretation', give the meaning of certain key words used in the text of the Bill.

(ii)   Saving clauses, indicated by the marginal note 'savings' or similar, have the function of saving or preserving rather than altering an existing right or powers; it has been said that they are often included by way of reassurance, for avoidance of doubt or from abundance of caution. They often begin with a phrase: 'Nothing in this section shall be construed as . . .'.

(iii)   The short title clause, indicated by the marginal note 'short title', sets out the title under which the Act will be cited amongst the statutes. This title is also given at the head of the Bill and on the outside of the back cover.

(iv)   Commencement clauses, indicated by the marginal note 'commencement', detail when the Act is to come into force. Since the beginning of the 1982/83 session of Parliament, commencement clauses ought usually to be grouped at the end of a Bill (see Anon (1983)).

(v)   Extent clauses, indicated by the marginal note 'extent', detail the geographical area to which the Bill applies (England and Wales, Scotland, Northern Ireland individually or in any combination, or the United Kingdom as a whole).

When a Bill receives Royal Assent and becomes an Act, the clauses of the Bill become sections of the Act.

(g)   Schedules – at the end of many Bills will be found one or more schedules (abbreviated to 'Sch.') containing detailed provisions dependent on one or more of the preceding clauses, rather like appendices at the back of a book.

(h)   Explanatory memorandum – though not technically part of the Bill, an explanatory memorandum is often attached to the first printing of the Bill in each House. If appropriate a financial memorandum is also included, on the Bill's likely effect on public expenditure. The explanatory memorandum sets out the contents and objects of the Bill and briefly describes, clause by clause in non-technical language, the provisions of the Bill. For the legal researcher this provides a very helpful summary. All Government Bills requiring expenditure must include a financial memorandum, setting out the financial effects with estimates, where possible, of the amount of money involved, and also forecasts of any effects on manpower in the public service, expected as a result of the passing of the Bill.

(i)   Back cover information – printed sideways across the back cover of the Bill, and known as an endorsement, similar to those found on other legal documents, such as court briefs, conveyances, wills, leases etc., are the short and long titles and then several groups of information valuable to the researcher : the name of the MP or peer presenting and the names of up to 11 supporters of the Bill, and details of the stage in the Parliamentary process the particular version of the Bill relates to, the date of the order for the Bill to be printed and the sessional running number for the Bill. The names will indicate whether the Bill is a Government Bill (which will have a high chance of becoming law) or a Private Member's Bill (which will have a greatly reduced chance of becoming law). The stage, printing date and sessional running number assist identification of the version of the Bill to hand.

3.2.1A4   Publication and general availability

Public Bills are published by Her Majesty's Stationery Office (HMSO) and are one of a larger group of publications known as Parliamentary Papers (see 3.11). They can be purchased through HMSO Bookshops or private bookshops acting as agents for HMSO. Bills are normally printed in small quantities and should be available until three months after the end of the session in which they were presented. If out of print, HMSO can arrange for a photocopy of the Bill to be supplied. The Bills themselves are printed on azure (pale green) tinted paper, whilst lists of amendments for consideration by Parliament are printed on white paper. Bills and related papers can be ordered from HMSO on a short-term standing order. This will supply the specific Bill requested, all reprints, related debates and amendments. After the end of each session of Parliament HMSO publishes bound volumes of Sessional Papers, the first two or three volumes of which contain all Public Bills in alphabetical order by title, all the amendments and different versions of a Bill brought together at one point. Sessional indexes are also published to assist searching. However, only major, academic law libraries or libraries having comprehensive collections of British official publications are likely to collect all Public Bills.

Private Bills, on the other hand, are printed at the expense of the promoters themselves and are available from their Parliamentary Agent (the *Weekly Information Bulletin of the House of Commons* – see 3.2.1B1 – provides details of names and addresses of agents for Private Bills being considered in the current session of Parliament). Few libraries collect Private Bills – to obtain copies of old Bills contact the local authority, corporation or individuals concerned.

3.2.1A5 Citation

For Public Bills a serial number appears at the bottom left-hand side of the first page of each Bill. When a Bill is reprinted at any subsequent stage it is given a new number. Traditionally, the number on a Bill originating in the House of Commons appeared in square brackets and those originating in the Lords appeared within curved brackets, but since the mid 1980s, with the change from Royal Octavo to A4 paper size, although Commons Bills continue to be signified in the traditional manner, Lords Bills are now designated 'HL Bill' followed by a number without brackets. Since a new numerical sequence begins with each new session of Parliament, the correct method of citing a Bill should not only include the running number, but also the session, e.g:

HC Bill (1989–90) [51].
HL Bill (1989–90) 57.

3.2.1B EXPLOITATION

3.2.1B1 Weekly Information Bulletin of the House of Commons

Weekly Information Bulletin is compiled by the Public Information Office of the House of Commons Library and published each week Parliament is sitting. Amongst the vast amount of information provided in each issue are two lists, one of Public (including Hybrid) Bills, the other of Private Bills, before Parliament this session. The Bills are listed in alphabetical order by title. The Bill number and the dates when each stage of Parliamentary scrutiny has been reached are given. The dates are specially useful for they assist (a) in identifying the most up-to-date printing of a Bill and (b) in tracing in *Hansard* the reports of debates on the Bill. It is important to note that debates in House of Commons Standing Committees are *not* printed in the same series of *Hansard* as reports of debates on the floor of the House of Commons, but in a separate series. Standing Committee debates are frequently of greatest interest to legal researchers because it is in committee, comprising on average only 20 MPs selected for their interest in and knowledge of the subject area, that the most detailed scrutiny of a Bill occurs (see 3.2.1B4).

3.2.1B2   Current Law Monthly Digest

Although this popular publication carries a table listing the progress of Bills, the content is neither as full nor as up to date as the lists in *Weekly Information Bulletin*.

3.2.1B3   Daily List of Government Publications

In the late afternoon of every working day a list is published of all HMSO and some non-HMSO official publications issued that day. The first part of the list gives details of Parliamentary publications, which includes Bills. HMSO also publishes a *Monthly Catalogue* and an *Annual Catalogue* which also list Bills published. However, all the listings produced by HMSO are primarily intended to help booksellers correctly identify a publication, not assist legal researchers. They do not give much detail of the stages and no detail of the dates of progress of Bills. They merely tell you that different printings of a Bill were made!

3.2.1B4   Hansard

The series titled *Parliamentary Debates (Official Reports)* is popularly known as *Hansard* after the printer of one of the earliest (but not *the* earliest) reports of Parliamentary debates. It is, to all intents and purposes, a verbatim report of what is said in the House of Commons and the House of Lords; it is published in two series, one covering each House. *Hansard* is available the day following the debates reported, with, in addition, a weekly edition, *Weekly Hansard*, merely gathering together the daily parts. Finally, bound volumes are published, a new volume commencing at the start of each session of Parliament. Indexes are available to the weekly and sessional volumes.

There are a number of points to watch when using *Hansard* and its indexes:

(a)   *Hansard* is laid out with two columns of print to a page. References in the indexes refer not to page numbers but column numbers.

(b)   In House of Commons *Hansard* written answers to Parliamentary questions are gathered in a separate section at the end of each volume with column numbering in italics. Take care when looking for the debate on a Bill, that you are not looking in the Parliamentary questions section.

(c)   The indexes are so constructed that references to a debate on a topic are given *after* entries for Parliamentary questions, comments, brief statements etc. on the same topic. Although the debate may occupy the greatest area of text in *Hansard*, the index places the reference to it last in order of priority.

Since 1909 a quite distinct series covering the debates of Standing Committees has also appeared. Parliament may appoint as many Standing Committees as necessary; normally under 10 are appointed each session, designated by the letters 'A', 'B', 'C' etc. Their debates are published only as daily parts and as sessional volumes. Unfortunately, there is no equivalent weekly index to this series and although each individual bound volume has an index, there is no general index to a sessional set. Reference should therefore be made to the *Annual Catalogue of Government Publications* (see note within 3.2.1B3), which lists alphabetically the Bills considered in Standing Committee, identifying the Committee and the dates of sittings.

3.2.1B5   Current Law Statutes Annotated

This publication, covered in more detail in section 3.2.2B2.2.2, reprints the Public General Acts of each session, many with additional editorial notes and commentary. Just below the list of contents at the beginning of each Act, the editors include references to the volume and column numbers in *Hansard*, where reports of the debates in the House of Commons (HC) and House of Lords (HL) are printed, but no references are given for Standing Committee debates. *Current Law Statutes Annotated*, of course, prints only successful Bills which have become law, and is of no use for tracing failed legislation.

3.2.1C   ELECTRONIC SOURCES

See appendix 4 for background information on the use of electronic databases.

3.2.1C1   POLIS

Parliamentary Online Information System (POLIS) is an index to (*not* the text of) proceedings in the UK Parliament. The information is stored on a computer in the south of England and can be accessed by any organisation having appropriate equipment and registered with the database provider, Meridian Systems Management (MSM). The database is not simple to use. MSM offers new subscribers a one-day training course and a set of manuals – at a charge. There are also charges for using the database. Not many libraries have sufficient enquiries on Parliamentary matters to warrant subscribing to the database but those that do find two advantages:

(a)   Very recent information is held on the index – the database is rarely more than a few working days behind the events described – it is therefore far more current than printed indexes.

(b)   The index holds references to all House of Commons Bills laid before Parliament since May 1979, House of Lords Bills since November 1981 and all debates on legislation since November 1982 (as well as information about all other aspects of Parliamentary business), and is far quicker to use than ploughing through many sessional indexes to *Hansard* or Parliamentary Bills and Papers.

However, since the database was originally created and is still updated by the House of Commons Library, to meet its own needs in providing Members of Parliament with answers to their research and information queries, and was not intended for 'external users', it is necessary to have a firm grasp of the technical language of Parliamentary procedure to use the database effectively. Nevertheless, law students studying the progress of a particular Bill through Parliament, or searching for all Bills over the last 10 years on a particular subject may find a POLIS search very useful. So, why not ask staff of your law library if they subscribe to POLIS, and if they do, whether they will undertake a search for you.

3.2.1C2   Lawtel

Information on the progress of Public and Private Bills through Parliament is included in the Legislation section of the database. Summaries of the content of all Government Bills are included on Lawtel as soon as the text is available from HMSO. Private Bills and Private Member's Bills are not included. To obtain this information select 'legislation' from the Lawtel main index and choose the appropriate topic. A general description of Lawtel is given in appendix 5.

3.2.1C3   Hansard on CD-ROM

The full text of the House of Commons Official Report (*Hansard*), from 1988/89 onwards, is available on CD-ROM. One disc is available for each Parliamentary session, and as each session progresses, discs are issued in April, September and January, cumulating the file to the Easter and Summer recesses, and the end of session, respectively. This means the CD-ROM version makes the content of *Hansard* more easily and quickly accessible than printed indexes.

3.2.1D   RESEARCH STRATEGIES

3.2.1D1   Tracing information on Bills of the current session of Parliament

The most up-to-date information will be provided by either of the two electronic sources: POLIS (3.2.1C1) or Lawtel (3.2.1C2). However, whilst POLIS will provide only dates of the stages reached by the Bill, Lawtel will also provide a brief summary of the content of many Bills. Neither provides details of the debates on the Bill. Assuming it is a Public Bill you are researching, you will need to match the 'date' and 'stage' information against part of figure 3.4, to clarify what ought to be available in *Hansard* or elsewhere in Parliamentary publications. For a Public Bill, start at the diamond-shaped 'decision box' with a double border in figure 3.4.

If access to the electronic databases is not available, use the paper source, *Weekly Information Bulletin of the House of Commons* (3.2.1B1) and follow figure 3.4 from the top.

3.2.1D2   Tracing information on Bills of a past session of Parliament

The electronic source POLIS (3.2.1C1) is a good starting-point because the file for House of Commons Bills goes back to May 1979. You can also search by subject, as well as title. Using paper sources is difficult but the following routes could be followed:

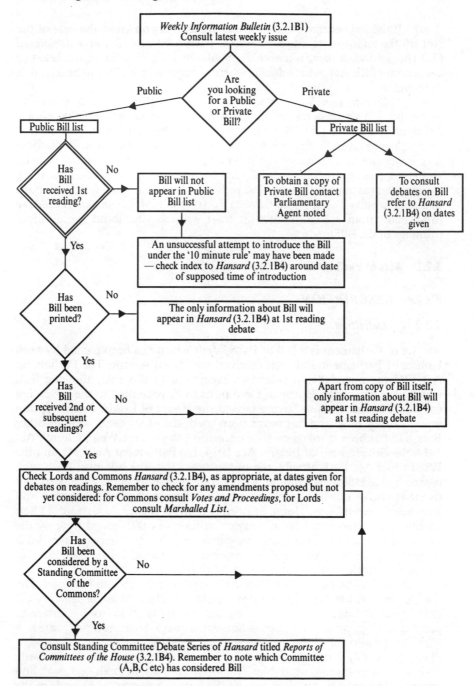

Figure 3.4   Tracing information on Bills of the current session of Parliament.

(a)   If the Bill became a Public General Act and you know the year of the Act try the appropriate annual volume of *Current Law Statutes Annotated* (3.2.1B5) and see if there is a note, immediately following the contents list to the reprint of the Act, which details where debates on the Bill will be found in *Hansard*.

(b)   If *Current Law Statutes Annotated* does not provide this information or the Bill did not become an Act, *either*, use the final issue of the *Weekly Information Bulletin* (3.2.1B1) for the relevant Parliamentary session and follow the procedure in figure 3.4 *or* consult the sessional index to Parliamentary Papers under the title of the Bill to find copies in the Sessional Papers, and check indexes to *Hansard* (3.2.1B4) for Lords, Commons and Standing Committees (as appropriate) to find reports of debates; if the sessional index to Parliamentary Papers is not available try the HMSO *Annual Catalogue* (discussed within 3.2.1B3) which at least will tell you about the different printings of the Bill made.

3.2.2   Acts of Parliament

3.2.2A   DESCRIPTION

3.2.2A1   Definition

An Act of Parliament is a Bill of Parliament which has been passed by both Houses of Parliament and then received the Royal Assent. The Parliament Act 1911 (as amended) provides two exceptions to this rule, allowing Bills which have passed the House of Commons to be presented to the Sovereign for Royal Assent without having passed the House of Lords. One exception is for 'Money Bills' and has never been used; the other deals with all other Bills, and has been invoked on four occasions, to pass the Welsh Church Act 1914, the Government of Ireland Act 1914, the Parliament Act 1949 and the War Crimes Act 1991. Briefly, the procedure is that the Bill must have been passed by the House of Commons in two successive sessions, have been sent to the House of Lords at least one month before the end of the session and have been rejected by the House of Lords in each of those two sessions. Other, specific, time-limits must be met also. On rejection the second time by the House of Lords, unless the House of Commons directs otherwise, the Bill is presented to the Sovereign and, on receiving the Royal Assent, becomes an Act of Parliament.

There are two classes of Act: Public General, and Local and Personal. The distinction is that Public General Acts relate to matters of *public policy* while Local and Personal Acts are restricted in application to a particular geographical location or organisation (such as a local authority area, a harbour or a port) or a group of individuals. As a law student you will be most likely to use only Public General Acts, but once in legal practice, especially with a local authority or public corporation, skill in finding Local and Personal Acts may be required as well. In future, however, as a result of the Transport and Works Act 1992, the authorisation of railway, tramway, canal and other schemes of works will no longer be by means of Local and Personal Acts but by a system of Ministerial orders – statutory instruments (see 3.3.1).

3.2.2A2   Origin

See 3.2.1.

3.2.2A3   Structure

Figure 3.5 reproduces the whole of one Act of Parliament – it is unusual for an Act to be so brief; normally they cover many pages.

An Act of Parliament comprises nine parts, not all of which are essential. As might be expected nearly all correspond to the parts of a Bill discussed in 3.2.1, but there are some important differences.

(a)   Short title – this is the title under which the Act is generally known. It is given in two places: at the head of the Act and in a section of the Act, usually the last. Sometimes in the second or subsequent Act of a series on the same subject, provision is made in the section dealing with the short title for both or all the Acts to be cited together by a short title, for example: the Merchant Shipping Acts 1894 to 1986. Prior to 1845 Acts did not carry clearly defined short titles but the Short Titles Act 1896 and the Statute Law Reform Act 1948 assigned short titles to many of the earlier Acts. This is worth remembering, for if you are searching for an Act of the first half of the 19th century, or earlier, in the indexes to volumes of Acts published at that time, you will have to scan long, rather than short, titles. There is also another difficulty connected with titles of Acts, which is when an Act gains a popular, rather than its correct, title – fortunately, it only rarely occurs with Acts of the 20th century, but can be a problem when studying legal history. Popular titles for Acts most commonly occur when the Act is identified with a personal sponsor or champion of Parliamentary legislation. One of the most notable recent examples is the Butler Act of 1944 (properly, the Education Act 1944), but the period of Georgian and Victorian social reform is littered with popular personal attributions. Another circumstance when popular names occur is when they are used to describe the activity for which the statute legislates: the Ten Hours Act (properly, the Factories Act 1847). More insights into this fascinating problem area are given in an article by Alex Noel-Tod (1989), who has compiled an index (not published) listing close to 1,000 different popular titles. Of published indexes, Noel-Tod identifies three which yield about 250 to 300 popular titles:

(i)   University of London, Institute of Advanced Legal Studies, *Manual of Legal Citations*, part 1, The British Isles (London: The University, 1959), pp. 3 and 4.

(ii)   *Chitty's Statutes of Practical Utility* . . . 6th ed. (London: Sweet & Maxwell, 1913) vol. 16, table of short and popular titles, etc.

(iii)   Craies, W.F., *Craies on Statute Law*, 7th ed. (London: Sweet & Maxwell, 1971), pp. 593–97: appendix A, some popular titles of statutes.

① # Explosives (Age of Purchase &c.) Act 1976

② ## 1976 CHAPTER 26

③ An Act to restrict further the sale to young persons of explosive substances, including fireworks, and to increase the penalties provided by sections 31 and 80 of the Explosives Act 1875.   ④ [22nd July, 1976]

⑤ **B**E IT ENACTED by the Queen's most Excellent Majesty, by and with the advice and consent of the Lord Spiritual and Temporal, and Commons, in this present Parliament assembled, and by the authority of the same, as follows:—

⑦

⑥ 1.—(1) In section 31 of the Explosives Act 1875 (which, as extended by section 39 of that Act, prohibits the sale to children of explosives, including fireworks, and provides that a person who makes a sale in contravention of the said section 31 shall be liable to a penalty not exceeding £20) for the words "any child apparently under the age of thirteen" there shall be substituted the words "any person apparently under the age of sixteen" and for the word "£20" there shall be substituted the word "£200".

Increase of age for purchase of fireworks etc and of certain penalties relating to fireworks etc.

1875 c. 17.

(2) In section 80 of that Act (which provides that a person who lets fireworks off in a highway or public place shall be liable to a penalty not exceeding £20) for the word "£20" there shall be substituted the word "£200".

⑧ 2.—(1) This Act may be cited as the Explosives (Age of Purchase &c.) Act 1976, and this Act and the Explosives Acts 1875 and 1923 may be cited together as the Explosives Acts 1875 to 1976.

Citation, extent and commence- ment.

⑨ (2) This Act shall not extend to Northern Ireland.
⑩ (3) This Act shall come into force at the expiration of one month beginning with the date of its passing.

---

① Short title   (a)
② Official Citation   (b)
③ Long Title   (d)
④ Date of Royal Assent   (e)
⑤ Enacting Formula   (g)

⑥ Section and Subsection   (h)
⑦ Marginal note   (h)
⑧ Citation   (h)(iii)
⑨ Extent   (h)(v)
⑩ Commencement   (h)(iv)

(The letters in parentheses refer to paragraphs in the text where discussion on the element of an Act occur.)

Figure 3.5   A Public and General Act of Parliament.

(b)   Official citation – this is a shorthand way of referring to the Act, comprising a date and running number. Currently, Acts are numbered sequentially, beginning with 1, throughout the calendar year, in the order in which they receive the Royal Assent. Public General Acts are numbered in arabic numerals, Local and Personal Acts are numbered with lower-case roman numerals. So, the example illustrated earlier, the Explosives (Age of Purchase etc.) Act, was the 26th Act to receive the Royal Assent in 1976. In general use the citation may be further abbreviated to 1976, c. 26. ('chapter' may be abbreviated to 'c.', 'ch.' or 'cap.'). The use of the word chapter derives from the medieval period when a single statute emerged from the brief Parliamentary sessions, dealing with many different topics, each constituting a separate chapter of the one statute.

The present system of citation based on the calendar year and a running number was introduced in 1963. Prior to that the official citation was constructed in a far more complex and confusing way, as is explained in 3.2.2A5.

(c)   Arrangement of sections – a table at the front of all but the shorter Acts, sets out in order the parts, chapters and sections into which the text is divided, with their respective titles (see appendix 3 for further details of the terminology for the divisions of an Act).

(d)   Long title – this sets out in general terms the purpose of the Act and, in contrast to its appearance in a Bill, is found only above the enacting formula.

(e)   Date of Royal Assent.

(f)   Preamble – its purpose is to state the reasons for and the expected effects of the proposed legislation. It is rarely incorporated in Public General Acts but is a required feature of Local and Personal Acts.

(g)   Enacting formula – this short paragraph summarises the legislative authority of Parliament and precedes the first section of the Act.

(h)   Sections – an Act is divided into a series of numbered sections, each with a descriptive title, known as a 'side note' or 'marginal note' printed in the margin. The word section is frequently abbreviated in writing to 's.' or, in the plural, 'ss.'. Sections may be divided into subsections (abbreviated to 'subs.'), subsections into paragraphs (abbreviated to 'para.') and paragraphs into subparagraphs (abbreviated to 'subpara.') – see appendix 3 for further details of terminology. Towards the end of the Act or, if appropriate, at the end of one of its parts, formal sections are placed which contain very important information for the legal researcher:

(i)   Definition sections, indicated by the marginal note 'interpretation', give the meaning of certain key words in the text of the Act.

(ii)   Saving sections, indicated by the marginal note 'savings' or similar, have the function of saving or preserving rather than altering an existing right or powers; it has been said that they are often included by way of reassurance, for avoidance of doubt or from abundance of caution. They often begin with a phrase: 'Nothing in this section shall be construed as . . .'

(iii)   The short title section, indicated by the marginal note 'short title', or sometimes 'citation', sets out the title under which the Act will be cited amongst the statutes. This title is also given at the head of the Act.

(iv)   Commencement sections, indicated by the marginal note 'commencement', detail when the Act is to come into force. Since the beginning of the 1982/83 session of Parliament, commencement sections ought usually to be grouped at the end of the Act (see Anon. (1983)). It is a commonly held fallacy amongst law students that all Acts come into force on the date they receive the Royal Assent. In fact, only those statutes which contain no express provision as to commencement come into force beginning with the day on which they receive the Royal Assent. The commencement of most modern statutes is expressly postponed. Most Acts include commencement sections which may detail any number of different dates or ways in which the Act will come into force. Sometimes a particular date is named, sometimes commencement is set at the expiry of a fixed period (commonly one or two months after the date of Royal Assent), and sometimes the power to set a date for commencement – an 'appointed day' – is delegated to a government Minister. This Ministerial power is exercised through the issue of a 'commencement order', which is one of the several different types of statutory instrument (see 3.3.1). It is important to check the commencement section carefully since different sections of an Act may be brought into force at different times. Only where no provision is made for an Act to come into force, will the date of Royal Assent be the commencement date.

It is worth noting that the commencement of an Act may be considerably delayed – for example, not one section of either the Easter Act 1928 or the Employment of Children Act 1973 has, at the time of writing, been brought into force, and substantial parts of the Control of Pollution Act 1974 and the Financial Services Act 1986 are not yet in force either; much of the Reservoirs Act 1975 was only brought into force in 1986 and 1987 by statutory instruments issued over 10 years after the Act received the Royal Assent.

Since the early 1980s Parliamentary counsel, who have the task of drafting Government Bills, have adopted more clearly standardised practices for the grouping and identification of commencement provisions, and the adoption of specific commencement dates in Acts (see Anon. 1983). Nevertheless, finding, understanding and applying the information about commencement within an Act of Parliament is an important legal research skill to master.

(v)   Extent sections, indicated by the marginal note 'extent', detail the geographical area to which the Act applies (either England and Wales, Scotland, Northern Ireland individually or in any combination, or the United Kingdom as a whole). There is a presumption that statutes passed by the Parliament of the United Kingdom extend to the whole of the United Kingdom unless parts of the United Kingdom are expressly excluded by the 'extent' section.

(i)   Schedules – at the end of the Act will be found one or more schedules (abbreviated to 'Sch.') containing detailed provisions dependent on one or more of the preceding sections, rather like appendices at the back of a book.

3.2.2A4   Publication and general availability

Public General Acts are published by the Queen's Printer, currently the Controller of Her Majesty's Stationery Office (HMSO). The paper copies on sale to the public are known as Queen's Printer's copies and are accepted as evidence in courts of law. As well as copies of single Acts published separately by HMSO, a number of official and unofficial collected editions are published, which are widely available in both specialist law libraries and many general academic and public libraries.

Most Local and Personal Acts are today published by the Queen's Printer, the one exception being Acts of a very limited, personal character. Local and Personal Acts are published only as individual Acts and are not republished in collected editions. Print runs are likely to be short so unless copies are purchased shortly after the Act is published, the best means of obtaining a copy is to contact the local authority or organisation which promoted the Act. The major public library or county record office in the area to which the Act refers may be able to assist.

3.2.2A5   Citation

An Act is usually referred to by its short title, e.g., the Explosives (Age of Purchase etc.) Act 1976, though for completeness the chapter number (c. 26 in the example) may be added after the date. Prior to 1 January 1963 when the Acts of Parliament Numbering and Citation Act 1962 came into force, the official citation comprised not the calendar year and chapter number but the regnal year or years of the Parliamentary session in which the Act was passed, followed by the chapter number.

This rather complex system needs some explanation. First, what is meant by 'regnal year'? It refers to the year beginning with the date of the Sovereign's accession to the throne. For Queen Elizabeth II the regnal year commences on 6 February – she came to the throne on that day in 1952 following the death of George VI. Secondly, what is meant by Parliamentary session? It refers to the period from the opening of Parliament by the Sovereign (normally, but not always, in early November) to the ending or prorogation of Parliament, normally, but not always, about a year later (late October). However, the length of each Parliamentary session is determined by the government of the day, and if a General Election is called the session may be considerably shorter than a year.

Now, putting these two cycles, the regnal and Parliamentary, together means that an Act receiving the Royal Assent between early November and 5 February in any year between 1952 and 1962 would fall in one regnal year, whilst an Act receiving the Royal Assent between 6 February and the end of the Parliamentary session would fall in a different regnal year.

There are three further complications with this awkward system of citation. First, when an Act given the Royal Assent was to be first published, the printer might not at that time be sure the monarch would survive until his or her next accession day. So, for example, the Family Allowances and National Insurance Act 1961 received the Royal Assent on 20 December 1961, late in the 10th year of Queen Elizabeth II's reign. The printer was obliged to use the citation 10 Eliz. 2 c. 6, since he could not be sure she would survive to 6 February of the year following. But, when in due course Queen Elizabeth commenced her 11th regnal year the citation 10 & 11 Eliz. 2 c. 6 was used for the same Act. The latter citation supersedes the first.

Secondly, occasionally a Parliamentary session began and ended within a single regnal year and another started within the same year. This occurred in 1950. The Parliamentary session ran from 11 March to 26 October, wholly within the 14th year of the reign of George VI. The 39 Acts passed during that period bear the citation 14 Geo. 6 whereas the Expiring Law Continuance Act 1950, given the Royal Assent on 15 December 1950, bears the citation 14 & 15 Geo. 6, c. 1.

Thirdly, a Parliamentary session could cover the end of one Sovereign's reign and part of the first regnal year of the next. In this case both Sovereigns' names are included in the citation. For example, the 68 Acts passed in the Parliamentary session 1951/52 are styled 15 & 16 Geo. 6 & 1 Eliz. 2.

This system of citation causes particular difficulties around the year 1936. George V reigned until 20 January 1936, to be followed by Edward VIII whose brief monarchy lasted until 11 December 1936, when George VI took the throne. During 1936, Acts bear the regnal citations of either 26 Geo. 5 & 1 Edw. 8 or 1 Edw. 8 & 1 Geo. 6. The difficulties in finding statutes for this period are further compounded by the fact that up until 1940, official collections and some unofficial collections of Acts were bound in volumes containing those passed within each Parliamentary session, which in the case of 1935/6 ended in October 1936 and for 1936/7 started in November 1936. So, this means that some Acts passed only a few months apart within calendar year 1936, bear different regnal year citations and are published in different volumes based on the Parliamentary session in which they received the Royal Assent. This complicated set of circumstances affects two Acts law students are frequently required to consult: the Public Health Act 1936 (26 Geo. 5 & 1 Edw. 8, c. 49) which received the Royal Assent on 31 July 1936 and the Public Order Act 1936 (1 Edw. 8 & 1 Geo. 6, c. 6) which received the Royal Assent on 18 December 1936. They will be found in 1936 and 1937 volumes of statutes, respectively.

It is easy to see why the old system of citation was abandoned, but you will need to be familiar with it so as to correctly identify and quickly find older Acts of Parliament in the printed volumes of the period. As an aid you will find lists of the monarchs with the dates of their regnal years in the following publications:

(a)   Osborn, P.G., *Concise Law Dictionary*. 7th edition, revised by Roger Bird. (London: Sweet & Maxwell, 1983).

(b)   Pemberton, John E., *British Official Publications*, 2nd revised ed. (Oxford: Pergamon Press Ltd, 1973), pp. 120–5.

(c)   *Guide to Law Reports and Statutes*, 3rd ed. (London: Sweet & Maxwell, 1959), pp. 58–70.

3.2.2B EXPLOITATION

In most of your legal research as a student you will be concerned with Acts which are currently in force. Much of this section of the book deals with the sources and skills required to find 'live' statute law. However, occasionally you may need to look at Acts of Parliament since repealed, to trace the historical development of legislation. Two publications should be noted: first, *Statutes of the Realm*, covering statutes from 1235 (the Statute of Merton) to 1713, and published between 1810 and 1828. The texts are given in the original language of early statutes (Latin or Norman French) with translations into English where necessary. Each of the 11 volumes has a subject index with, in addition, alphabetical and chronological indexes published separately to the whole work. The second publication to note is *Statutes at Large*, containing statutes from Magna Carta (1215) onwards. The most frequently cited edition is Owen Ruffhead's, revised by Charles Runnington, and published between 1786 and 1800 in 14 volumes.

Publications containing Acts of Parliament may be divided into two groups – those published officially by HMSO and those issued by commercial publishers.

3.2.2B1 Official versions

3.2.2B1.1 Public General Acts and General Synod Measures

Sometime after the end of each calendar year all the Acts of the year are published in annual bound volumes entitled *Public General Acts and General Synod Measures*. Prior to 1940 the volumes included Acts passed each Parliamentary session rather than calendar year. From the first year of publication, 1831, until 1870 the publication was titled *Public General Statutes*. Each year's edition currently consists of two or three volumes. Each volume begins with four tables, listing the Public General Acts alphabetically and chronologically, Local and Personal Acts alphabetically and General Synod Measures chronologically. Then follow, in chapter number order, the full text of Public General Acts and General Synod Measures but *not* Local and Personal Acts. At the back of the final volume for each year, or in a separate volume, are further tables: a concordance, detailing existing legislation against each section of any new consolidating Act which replaces it and, secondly, the effect of new Acts on existing legislation – whether repealed, amended or otherwise altered.

The annual volumes of Public General Acts merely reprint Acts in the form in which they were originally given the Royal Assent. No subsequent repeals or amendments are included. To overcome this disadvantage HMSO has published two further editions of the statutes: *Statutes Revised* and *Statutes in Force*.

3.2.2B1.2 Statutes Revised

Statutes Revised has been published as numerous bound volumes in three editions, the first completed in 1885, comprising the Public General Acts in force at the end of 1878. A second edition published between 1888 and 1929 brought the revision down to 1920. Finally, a third edition, published in 1950, reprinted Acts as they were in force in 1948. Since 1940 an annual volume, *Annotations to Acts*, has been published giving instructions for copying in to the pages of *Statutes Revised* minor amendments, striking out Acts which have been repealed and sticking in gummed sheets where more substantial textual changes have occurred. Needless to say this tedious work, even if library staff have time to undertake it, makes the original publication very difficult to use with confidence.

3.2.2B1.3   *Statutes in Force*

To overcome the problems of updating created by a bound-volume format, HMSO publishes in 108 loose-leaf binders, totalling over 60,000 pages, the currently unrepealed Public General Acts of England and Wales, Scotland, Great Britain and the United Kingdom, some Acts of the Parliament of Ireland, Church Assembly and General Synod Measures and selected Local and Personal Acts. This huge work is currently arranged in 131 broad subject groups extending from agency to weights and measures. The advantage of loose-leaf publication is that new Acts can be inserted in the appropriate binder for the subject, repealed Acts can be removed and Cumulative Supplements detailing amendments and partial repeals can be inserted. Such a vast work, to be of practical use, should have:

(a)   a standard and logical arrangement,
(b)   comprehensive, yet easy to use indexes, and
(c)   a regular and timely updating service.

Regrettably, although *Statutes in Force* is the official collection of Public General Acts in force, it does not adequately fulfil these required qualities for lawyers to turn naturally to it when researching statute law. First, HMSO allows subscribers to arrange the publication as best suits their individual needs, so that there is freedom for libraries to file the Cumulative Supplements either with the subject group of Acts, or in entirely separate binders bringing all Cumulative Supplements together, regardless of subject. So, the location of this information may vary from library to library. Secondly, alphabetical indexes by the titles of Acts and chronological indexes are provided in the work, but the subject index (the approach most frequently required in legal research) is catered for in a separate publication, *Index to the Statutes*. Unfortunately, this annual publication, in two volumes, is usually at least a year out of date on publication. To use *Index to the Statutes* as a subject index follow these steps:

(a)   Look up the subject in which you are interested under the appropriate subject heading in the body of one of the volumes.
(b)   At the beginning of the entries under each subject heading is a list of the Acts referred to in more detail under the subheadings which follow. It is

important to note that this list of Acts may not be comprehensive as further Acts may be found under cross-references (the 'see' references) to other subject headings given throughout the publication.

(c) Bold typeface numbers given in brackets after the title of an Act indicate the group or subgroup in which the relevant text is printed in *Statutes in Force*.

As well as a subject index, *Index to the Statutes* can also be used as a finding list; if you know the title and year of a particular statute and wish to trace the text of it in *Statutes in Force* – here is how to do it:

(a) The pink pages at the front of volume 1 of the *Index* list statutes chronologically, and then by chapter number within each year. The title of an Act is given in bold typeface followed by the subject heading and, where appropriate, the subheading number from the body of the *Index* where the Act in question is noted. The final bold type face number/s refer to relevant sections or schedules of the Act itself. Note that some Acts cover several different topics and the text may be printed under several separate groups or subgroups of *Statutes in Force*.

(b) Look up the appropriate subject heading in the body of the *Index* and then follow steps (b) and (c), above, as if searching the *Index* by subject.

A sister publication to *Index to the Statutes,* the *Chronological Table of Statutes*, in two volumes, published every other year, consists of a list beginning with the Statute of Merton of 1235 of all Acts of Parliament, against each of which there is an entry detailing whether the Act has been repealed or amended. Unfortunately, the publication is nearly always at least a year out of date on publication, so should not be relied on for up-to-date information.

Local and Personal Acts, although not published in a collected or revised edition, are slightly better served by HMSO as far as indexing goes, for the annual publication *Local and Personal Acts Tables and Index*, published since 1948, contains alphabetical title, chronological, subject and place name indexes. In addition, there is a consolidation volume: *Index to Local and Personal Acts 1801–1947*, plus a *Supplementary Index to Local and Personal Acts 1948–1966*.

3.2.2B2 Commercial versions

The commercially published editions of Acts of Parliament reprint Public General Acts only. They fall into three distinct groups:

(a) Mere reprints of the Queen's Printer's copies of Acts.

(b) Reprints of the Queen's Printer's copies but with additional commentary or editor's notes on the meaning and effect of each Act.

(c) Reprints of the Queen's Printer's copies with additional commentary or editor's notes and a regular updating service indicating legal developments affecting earlier legislation.

3.2.2B2.1   Reprints of Queen's Printer's copies

3.2.2B2.1.1   *Law Reports Statutes*

The Incorporated Council of Law Reporting for England and Wales, a non-profit-making organisation responsible for the most authoritative reports of cases available, known as the *Law Reports* (see 3.4A1), also publishes a reprint of the Queen's Printer's copies of Public General Acts, known as the *Law Reports Statutes*. It appears in several parts each year followed by annual bound volumes of all the parts issued that year. However, the publication has limited value since it is frequently published months behind the Queen's Printer's copies and has no added value in the way of commentary or an updating service.

3.2.2B2.2   Reprints of Queen's Printer's copies with commentary

Two publications reprint the Queen's Printer's copies of Public General Acts with additional commentary and notes; these annotations have *no* official standing but can be very helpful in explaining the meaning of words or phrases and state, in relatively simple language, the relationship of the new law to existing legislation and decisions of the courts.

3.2.2B2.2.1   *Butterworth's Annotated Legislation Service*

Formerly known as *Butterworths Emergency Legislation Service*, since it was first published in 1939 with the intention of assisting practitioners keep track of the large quantity of legislation passed as a result of the outbreak of war, this publication continues to reprint *selected* Acts of more use to legal practitioners rather than academic students. Acts are reprinted with notes and detailed annotations given in a small typeface following the section to which they refer. Although the publication began as a series of loose issues in binders, for many years now new Acts are published as green coloured-bound volumes, normally with a single Act to a volume, each volume numbered, in sequence of publication, on the spine. A cumulative index is published every two or three years which lists in both title and chronological order all Public General Acts, Church Assembly Measures and certain Local and Personal Acts which have received the Royal Assent between 24 August 1939 and 1 January of the year in which the index was published. The list notes whether particular Acts have been reprinted in the series, and if so, where. Quite a few of the recent volumes have been reprinted by Butterworths as textbooks.

3.2.2B2.2.2   *Current Law Statutes Annotated*

First published in 1948, *Current Law Statutes Annotated* (CLSA) aims to perform a similar function to *Butterworths Annotated Legislation Service* but possesses a number of advantages, and is more widely used. The advantages are:

(a)   It includes all, not just a selection, of Public General Acts.
(b)   It publishes new Acts as loose-leaf pages which slip into a binder; this means CLSA is one of the first commercially produced versions of an Act to

appear after the Queen's Printer's copy. The first release of an Act in CLSA is printed on grey paper and is merely a reprint of the Queen's Printer's version, but this is subsequently replaced by a version on white paper which includes annotations and commentary. Once all the statutes of a single year have been published with annotations, the loose-leaf section is replaced by a bound volume. This three-stage process: loose-leaf grey paper, loose-leaf white paper, bound-volume white paper, means CLSA can publish legislation with annotations more rapidly than the *Butterworths Annotated Legislation Service*.

(c)   It includes amongst the editorial notes at the head of most Acts, references to where in *Hansard* debates in Parliament on the Bill which preceded the Act may be found.

(d)   It provides a cumulative subject index to the loose issues of Acts and incorporates this index at the back of each bound volume. Although limited to the statutes of a single year, it is better than the total lack of subject indexing in the Butterworths service.

(e)   It has included, since 1984, in the bound volumes, a statute *Citator* (see 3.2B2.2.3).

Each Act reprinted in CLSA on white paper usually includes editorial notes and commentary, printed in small type, in three places. The reprint of most Acts begins with a contents list, and immediately following it under the heading 'Parliamentary debates', details are given of where in *Hansard* (the verbatim reports of debates in Parliament) to find the text of what Members of Parliament said in discussion on the Bill – the draft form of the Act. In this list the HC abbreviation stands for House of Commons, followed by the volume and column number where the debates are reported; HL stands for House of Lords. The next heading, 'Introduction and general note', is the second place where commentary will be found. Under it is given a description of what led up to the legislation being presented to Parliament – an official report or policy document, for example. These references are very useful, for if you follow them up they enable you to set the legislation in context and understand why the law has developed in a particular way. The remainder of the introduction and general note consists of a summary of the main provisions of the Act. The third type of annotation is placed at the end of each section of the Act. Details are given of where to find elsewhere in the Act the definition of words used in the section reprinted above, and under the heading 'General note', the authors provide a commentary on the meaning of the section with references to earlier Acts and any court cases which relate to the new provisions.

Like the Butterworths service, some Acts and their commentary appearing in CLSA are published additionally as textbooks.

3.2.2B2.2.3   *Current Law Statute Citator and Current Law Legislation Citator*

Both the Butterworths service and CLSA have a major disadvantage: they are published as bound-volume services without a means of updating either the statements of law or the editorial annotations. The information contained in the volumes is 'frozen' at the date of publication whilst the law, in reality, continues to develop. Having said that, the publishers of CLSA have tried to overcome this disadvantage in part with the issue of two associated publications: *Current Law Statute Citator* (CLSC) and *Current Law Legislation Citator* (CLLC). There are, in fact, at least five parts to these citators, but first, what does the word '*Citator*' mean? Quite simply it is a listing of original documents, whether they be Acts, statutory instruments or cases, with details of references or 'citations' made in later Acts, statutory instruments or cases to the original documents. The statute and legislation *Citator*s are valuable tools for discovering whether a particular Act:

(a)   has come into force,
(b)   has been amended,
(c)   has had detailed rules, orders or regulations made under powers contained in it,
(d)   is still in force,
(e)   has been considered by the courts and the meaning of sections interpreted in judgments.

The oldest *Citator*, *Current Law Statute Citator*, gives details of changes to Acts which took place between 1947 and 1971 – note, it details changes to Acts dating from 1235 (the Statute of Merton) to 1971 which occurred between 1947 and 1971, not just changes to Acts which came on to the statute book between 1947 and 1971. Next, *Current Law Legislation Citator 1988* covers the period 1972 to 1988 in a single bound volume, and since then CLLC has been issued annually as a soft-covered volume covering several years. The fourth *Citator*, for the immediate past year, is currently published as a loose-leaf section in the *Current Law Statutes Annotated Service File* – a guide card marked 'Citator' will be found at the back of one of the two loose-leaf volumes. The final part of the statute or legislation *Citator* is a recent innovation – the most recent issue of *Current Law Monthly Digest* carries a table near the back (use the contents page to find the exact location) listing citations during the present calendar year.

If you are checking citations for an Act, you would start your search with the *Citator* which includes the year given in the title of the Act, and work forward through the various parts of the *Citator* until you reach the most recent issue of *Current Law Monthly Digest*. For a pre-1947 Act you would search all parts of the *Citator* service. The important point to bear in mind is to search the various parts in a *methodical order* so you pick up *all* relevant citations, rather than only using whichever part comes immediately to hand at the shelves.

How is information presented in the *Citators*?

Both CLSC and CLLC list Public General Acts in chronological order: by year and then by chapter number within the year, and against each Act note, section by section, repeals, amendments, the application of any secondary legislation such as statutory instruments (see 3.3.1) and citations to cases in which the courts have considered the provisions of the Act judicially.

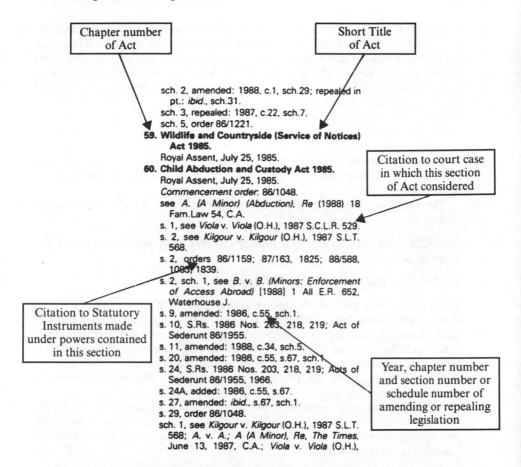

Chapter number of Act

Short Title of Act

sch. 2, amended: 1988, c.1, sch.29; repealed in
  pt.: *ibid.*, sch.31.
sch. 3, repealed: 1987, c.22, sch.7.
sch. 5, order 86/1221.
**59. Wildlife and Countryside (Service of Notices)
  Act 1985.**
Royal Assent, July 25, 1985.
60. Child Abduction and Custody Act 1985.
Royal Assent, July 25, 1985.
Commencement order: 86/1048.
see A. *(A Minor) (Abduction), Re* (1988) 18
  Fam.Law 54, C.A.
s. 1, see *Viola* v. *Viola* (O.H.), 1987 S.C.L.R. 529.
s. 2, see *Kilgour* v. *Kilgour* (O.H.), 1987 S.L.T.
  568.
s. 2, orders 86/1159; 87/163, 1825; 88/588,
  1085, 1839.
s. 2, sch. 1, see *B.* v. *B. (Minors: Enforcement
  of Access Abroad)* [1988] 1 All E.R. 652,
  Waterhouse J.
s. 9, amended: 1986, c.55, sch.1.
s. 10, S.Rs. 1986 Nos. 203, 218, 219; Act of
  Sederunt 86/1955.
s. 11, amended: 1988, c.34, sch.5.
s. 20, amended: 1986, c.55, s.67, sch.1.
s. 24, S.Rs. 1986 Nos. 203, 218, 219; Acts of
  Sederunt 86/1955, 1966.
s. 24A, added: 1986, c.55, s.67.
s. 27, amended: *ibid.*, s.67, sch.1.
s. 29, order 86/1048.
sch. 1, see *Kilgour* v. *Kilgour* (O.H.), 1987 S.L.T.
  568; A. v. A.; A (A Minor), Re, The Times.
  June 13, 1987, C.A.; *Viola* v. *Viola* (O.H.).

Citation to court case
in which this section
of Act considered

Citation to Statutory
Instruments made
under powers contained
in this section

Year, chapter number
and section number or
schedule number of
amending or repealing
legislation

Figure 3.6   Extract from *Current Law Legislation Citator 1988*.

Figure 3.6, taken from *Current Law Legislation Citator 1988*, shows part of a
page from the sequence of Acts passed in 1985. The page is split into two
columns. The chapter numbers of the Acts are given in the left-hand margin
of each column, and run from chapter 54, Finance Act 1985, to chapter 65,
Insolvency Act 1985. Take a closer look at the wealth of information given
for chapter 60, Child Abduction and Custody Act 1985. First, the date of
Royal Assent is given: July 25, 1985. Then details of the commencement order
which brought the Act into force: statutory instrument 1986 No. 1048 (see
3.2.2A3 for an explanation of 'commencement'). Next follows a reference to
a law report, *Re A (A Minor) (Abduction)* 1988, with a citation to where a
report of the case can be read in the law reports – the case mentions the Act
in general and not any particular section of it. Then follow references to
individual sections of the Act, against each of which are noted any decisions

of the courts in which the judges have considered the meaning of the section, any orders (that is, statutory instruments comprising detailed legislation made under powers given by that section of the Act) and any amendments made by later Acts to the wording of the section – see, for example, that section 9 of the 1985 Act has been amended by an Act of 1986, chapter 55 and schedule 1 of that Act (unfortunately, the short title of the amending Act is not given, but the citation is sufficient for you to find it in volumes of the 1986 Acts). If you look at another example on the same page of the citator, but not illustrated here, chapter 65, Insolvency Act 1985, you will see mention of some sections having been repealed (sections 15 to 18, for example) and rules (section 106, for example) – a slightly different type of statutory instrument – having been made.

The value of *Citators* will become even clearer in 3.2.2D, on research strategies.

3.2.2B2.3   *Reprints of Queen's Printer's copies with commentary and full updating service*

3.2.2B2.3.1   **Halsbury's Statutes of England**

The first edition of *Halsbury's Statutes* was published in 1930; the work is now in its fourth edition and is one of the key research sources you should learn to use with confidence. Copies of this publication will be found in virtually every academic library where students study law to degree level or beyond. Many large public libraries also subscribe to it, but more importantly, most firms of solicitors and barristers' chambers will contain and use *Halsbury's Statutes* as an everyday research source.

Halsbury's Statutes aims to provide up-to-date versions of *all* Public General Acts in force in England and Wales and, in addition, provides copious commentary and notes. There are six parts to the publication as summarised in figure 3.7:

(a)   *Main volumes*. Fifty Main Volumes contain an alphabetical subject-by-subject arrangement of the Public General Acts in force at the time of publication in the second half of the 1980s – the whole work was issued volume by volume over several years. Volume 1 contains the Acts relating to the topic of admiralty law and volume 50 ends with those dealing with wills. When the law on a topic has changed considerably since a Main Volume was published, a 'reissue' volume is compiled to replace the original one. Some areas of law change faster than others; for example, the original volume 12 on criminal law was replaced by a reissue volume within just four years. You can identify reissue volumes by the word and the date of publication marked on the spine. It is important to note this, as will be explained later in the section on using *Halsbury's Statutes*.

You will find editorial notes and commentary are provided in two places in the Main Volumes. At the beginning of each group of Acts relevant to a particular subject, there is a review of the development, purpose and effect of the legislation. The review is a very useful synopsis (i) highlighting earlier

50 MAIN VOLUMES	CURRENT STATUTES SERVICE	CUMULATIVE SUPPLEMENT	NOTER UP SERVICE
Subject arrangement of Public General Acts.	Six loose-leaf volumes containing the Text of recent Acts not yet included in Main Volumes.	Single bound volume issued annually — records changes affecting Main Volumes and Current Statutes Service. Up to date to end of year prior to publication.	Single loose-leaf volume — records very recent changes to Main Volumes and Current Statutes Service.

IS IT IN FORCE?	TABLES OF STATUTES AND GENERAL INDEX
Single bound volume issued annually — records exact commencement dates of all Public General Acts over previous 25 years.	Single bound volume issued annually — index to Main Volumes and Current Statutes Service.

Figure 3.7   Structure of *Halsbury's Statutes of England.*

legislation which may have been replaced by current Acts, (ii) drawing attention to government or other reports which may have shaped the content of legislation and (iii) placing particular Acts in context. Following after the review, the Acts are reprinted in chronological order, the oldest first, with notes in smaller type, giving details of (i) where to find in this or other statutes definitions of words or phrases, (ii) associated provisions in other Acts, (iii) relevant secondary legislation and (iv) cases in which the courts have considered the meaning and effect of the text of the statute. These notes are placed after the particular section of an Act to which they apply.

(b)   *Current Statutes Service.* Currently six loose-leaf volumes contain the text of recent Acts not yet included in the Main Volumes.

(c)   *Cumulative Supplement (sometimes referred to as the 'Cum. Supp.').* This single bound volume issued annually and replacing the previous Cumulative Supplement, contains details of changes which affect the information given in the Main Volumes and the Current Statutes Service. The Cumulative Supplement is usually up to date to around the turn of the year.

(d)   *Noter-Up Service.* Bridging the gap between the compilation of the Cumulative Supplement and the present is a single loose-leaf volume. Every month the publisher issues loose-leaf pages containing details of very recent developments in the law which are inserted in the binder.

(e)   *Tables of Statutes and General Index.* This single bound volume, issued annually, is the usual starting-point for research using *Halsbury's Statutes.* At the front is a list in alphabetical order by title of all the Acts reprinted in *Halsbury's Statutes*, with a subject index to the whole work, at the back.

(f)   *Is It in Force?* Another single bound volume, issued annually, records the exact commencement dates of all Public General Acts over the previous 25 years, with details of the authority (such as a statutory instrument) by which they were brought into force.

Using *Halsbury's Statutes*

The key skill to be learnt in searching *Halsbury's Statutes* is to correctly and confidently link together the use of these six parts, to ensure the law you eventually cite is up to date.

There are two ways in which *Halsbury's Statutes* can be used for research: to find information about an Act when you know its title, or to find information on a legal subject or topic. Figures 3.8 and 3.9 indicate the steps to be followed for each search.

Here are some points to note when using *Halsbury's Statutes*:

(a)   The references in the Tables of Statutes and General Index are to the volume number (in bold type) and page number (lighter type). Where (S) follows the volume number this means that the Act is to be found in the Current Statutes Service and not the Main Volume. Note the 'subject' given between (S) and the page number since each Current Statutes Service volume contains several subjects.

(b)   Main Volumes are revised and reissued when the law they contain is out-of-date. However, there can be a gap between the publication of a reissue Main Volume and an up-to-date edition of the Tables of Statutes and General Index to the whole set. So, it is important to check which issue of a Main Volume has been used from which the publishers have compiled the Tables of Statutes and General Index. This can be done quite simply by turning to the summary of titles given at the front of the Tables of Statutes and General Index, and noting which issue of the Main Volume in which you are interested has been used to compile the index entries. Compare this information with that on the spine of the relevant Main Volume itself and if the details match, then so should the entries in the Tables of Statutes and General Index and the Main Volume. If they do not as where, for example, the Tables of Statutes and General Index has been compiled from an original Main Volume but the current Main Volume is now a reissue, then you will need to look up the topic again in the index to that particular reissued Main Volume, to find the new page on which the information you require is given.

(c)   When you have found the statute or information you require in the Main Volume or Current Statutes Service, note down three elements: the *volume, subject* and *page number* of the section in which you are interested, so you can find relevant new information quickly in the Cumulative Supplement and Noter-Up. The subject is given as part of the running head across the tops of pages.

(d)   In the Cumulative Supplement and Noter-Up the volume number and subject are given as running heads across the tops of pages. The page numbers of Main Volumes to which more recent developments relate are given in the left margin. If the page number in which you are interested does not appear in the list you can assume there have been no changes to the law as stated in the Main Volume in which you originally looked. If a page number *is* given but is followed by an 'n', this indicates the change is to an editorial note on that page rather than the text of the Act itself.

The part of *Halsbury's Statutes* called *Is It in Force?* is arranged chronologically; then, within each year, the titles of Acts are printed in alphabetical order and against each is given details of when it came into force and by what authority. If you do not know the year of the Act you wish to check then, so long as you know the correct title, you can find the missing information by using the front part of the Tables of Statutes and General Index to *Halsbury's Statutes*, and afterwards consult *Is It in Force?'* Since *Is It in Force?'* is published annually it might be prudent to double-check the currency of the information it provides, by using the full *Halsbury's Statutes* service as described in figure 3.8.

3.2.2B2.3.2   Specialist subject encyclopaedias

An increasing range of loose-leaf encyclopaedias has appeared in recent years, particularly in subjects of interest to practitioners, where the law is developing or changing rapidly. Revenue law was the first area in which these were published since the law is susceptible to frequent and often unpredictable change. Most, but not all, encyclopaedias reprint Acts of Parliament with copious editorial notes and commentary and are kept up to date by publishers issuing loose pages containing new developments, which are inserted within the binder by library staff and replace old pages. These encyclopaedias are very valuable because of the greater detail given in the notes and commentary and the wide range of reprints of publications other than Acts they often contain. These characteristics are explained further in 3.7.

To discover if your library has a subject-specific encyclopaedia relevant to your enquiry, use the subject index section of the library catalogue (see 1.2.4, above) and then the classified section to find entries for books on the general area of law in which you are interested. Note any catalogue entries which have the word 'encyclopaedia' in the title or any indication after the title information that it is issued in loose-leaf format – unfortunately, not all library catalogues are designed to give this type of information. If in any doubt ask library staff for assistance. It should be emphasised that publishers only produce loose-leaf encyclopaedias in topics where they believe there is a ready market – i.e., where there is sufficient need amongst practising lawyers for a rapidly updated service. Unfortunately for students this means you will *not* find encyclopaedias in some basic legal topics such as jurisprudence, constitutional law and English legal system!

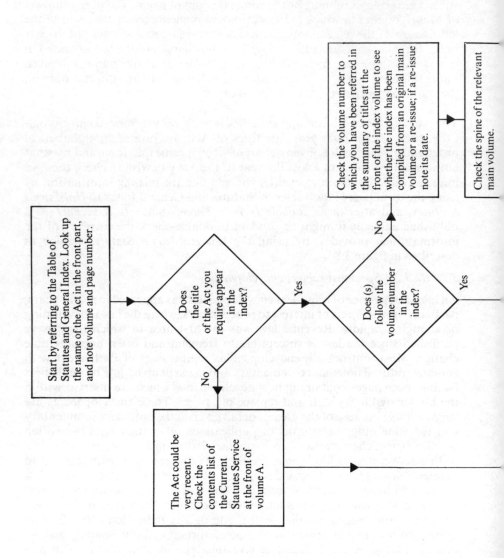

Start by referring to the Table of Statutes and General Index. Look up the name of the Act in the front part, and note volume and page number.

Does the title of the Act you require appear in the index?

No — The Act could be very recent. Check the contents list of the Current Statutes Service at the front of volume A.

Yes

Does (s) follow the volume number in the index?

No — Check the volume number to which you have been referred in the summary of titles at the front of the index volume to see whether the index has been compiled from an original main volume or a re-issue; if a re-issue note its date.

Check the spine of the relevant main volume.

Yes

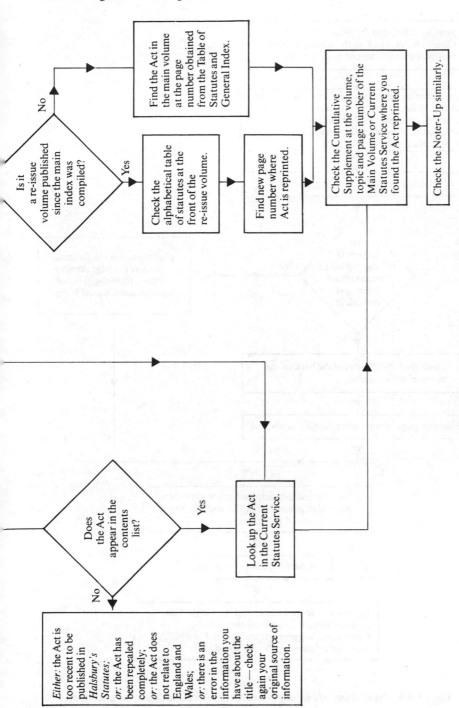

Figure 3.8 Searching *Halsbury's Statutes* for an Act by its title.

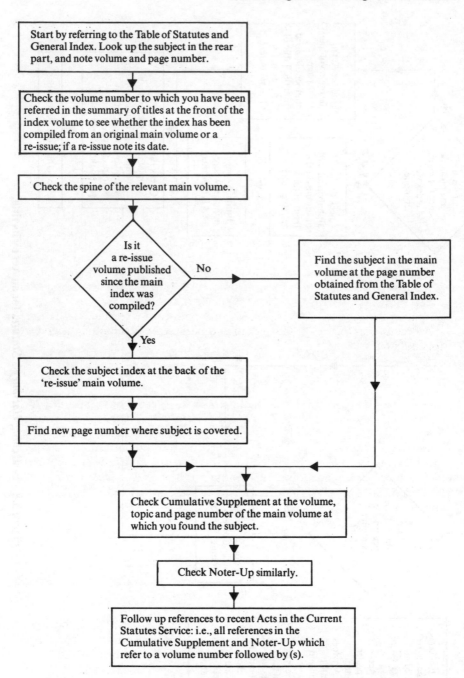

Figure 3.9   Searching *Halsbury's Statutes* for information on a subject.

3.2.2C   ELECTRONIC SOURCES

For background information on the use of electronic databases see appendix 4.

3.2.2C1   LEXIS

The on-line information retrieval service LEXIS contains the *full text* of all Public General Acts currently in force in England and Wales. The database is updated each week, but it may take several weeks between the publication of the Queen's Printer's copy of a new Act and its inclusion in the database, especially if it is a major piece of legislation effecting many changes to existing law; nevertheless, the database is reasonably well up to date. The text of every Act on LEXIS includes amendments made by subsequent legislation; the text is not merely a reprint of the Act in the form in which it received the Royal Assent.

The database is divided into libraries. The ENGGEN Library (*Eng*lish *Gen*eral) contains separate files including one devoted to statutes entitled STAT and also one for statutory instruments entitled SI, which may be combined by using the STATIS file, so that both can be searched together.

A description of the LEXIS system and basic search techniques is given in appendix 6.

3.2.2C2   Lawtel

Lawtel is an on-line *digest* of legal information – it does not contain the full text of Acts, only summaries. All Public General Acts passed since 1 January 1980 are listed alphabetically by title in two sequences – those passed between 1 January 1980 and 31 December 1983 are merely summarised; those passed since 1 January 1984 are provided with summaries and details of commencements, repeals and amendments. To obtain the statutes index select 'legislation' from the Lawtel main menu. A general description of Lawtel is given in appendix 5.

3.2.2D   RESEARCH STRATEGIES

3.2.2D1   Is this Public General Act in force? Has any section or schedule of the Act been amended or repealed by subsequent legislation?

There are several ways of undertaking this research. You will probably obtain the most up-to-date information by using the electronic sources LEXIS (3.2.2C1) or Lawtel (3.2.2C2). For LEXIS, to find if all sections of the Marine Insurance Act 1906 are in force go into the STAT or STATIS files, and type:

title (marine insurance w/5 1906)

and then press the TRANSMIT key.

Again on LEXIS, to find if section 8 of the Unfair Contract Terms Act 1977 has been amended go into the STAT or STATIS files, and type:

annotations (unfair contract w/5 1977)

and then press the TRANSMIT key.

On Lawtel, use the statutes index in which the statutes are listed alphabetically by title, with details of commencement, repeals and amendments against each entry. However, the database currently contains details for statutes passed since 1 January 1984 only.

Research using paper information sources can be undertaken in three ways, which might be described, in turn, as the 'authoritative but least up to date', the 'quick but not comprehensive' and the 'comprehensive'. They all assume you know the year of the Act – if you do not, the Tables of Statutes and General Index to *Halsbury's Statutes*, may provide the information you require.

3.2.2D1.1 *'Authoritative but least up to date'*

Assuming you know the year of the Act, consult the *Chronological Table of the Statutes* (see 3.2.2B1.3) (check the period of time covered by this publication – see title page of volume 2). Then, to cover the time gap between that publication and the present, consult recent annual issues of the *Public General Acts and General Synod Measures*: tables and index (see 3.2.2B1.1).

3.2.2D1.2 *'Quick but not comprehensive'*

Assuming you know the year of the Act, consult *Halsbury's Statutes* (see 3.2.2B2.3.1), the separate volume entitled *Is It in Force?'*. *Is It in Force?* excludes statutes more than 25 years old and, since it is published annually, also any developments in recent months.

3.2.2D1.3 *'Comprehensive'*

Two alternative research paths are available, using either the *Current Law* publications of Sweet & Maxwell or *Halsbury's Statutes* published by Butterworths.

(a) *Current Law* (see 3.2.2B2.2.3). Where you start the search depends on the date of the Act of Parliament. Figure 3.10 provides the full path available.

(b) *Halsbury's Statutes*. Follow the chart in figure 3.8. When you find the text of the Act you require, check the contents list of the Act itself for mention of a commencement section. Read the section and any notes added in small type by the editors of *Halsbury's Statutes*. For 'commencement' research and especially 'amendment or repeal' research, make sure you follow your search path right through *all* the parts of the *Halsbury's Statutes* publication, ending with the Noter-Up Service.

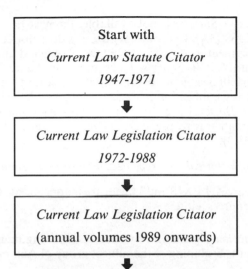

Start with
Current Law Statute Citator
1947-1971

Current Law Legislation Citator
1972-1988

Current Law Legislation Citator
(annual volumes 1989 onwards)

Current Law Statutes Annotated
Service file – *Citator* for immediate past year – located behind 'Citator' guide card at back of one of the loose leaf-volumes.

Current Law Monthly Digest – latest issue for present year – statute *Citator* located towards back of issue. (See contents page at front of monthly issue for precise location.)

Figure 3.10   How to search *Current Law*.

3.2.2D2   *Tracing Acts currently in force by subject*

This research can be conducted using either electronic or paper sources. If you are using LEXIS (3.2.2C1) you will need to take care that your search request comprehensively describes the subject in which you are interested, because the computer will be searching the full text of the Acts, not an index to them. Read appendix 6 of this book fully before you attempt this research. On Lawtel (3.2.2C2) select 'Legislation' from the main index and then 'Statutes'. Acts are listed alphabetically by title. Choose the appropriate Act and you will be taken to Commencements, Repeals and Amendments for that Act; keying the yellow number in the left margin takes you to a summary of the Act in question.

Using paper sources three research paths are available.

(a)   The best method, with superior indexing and updating, is to use *Halsbury's Statutes*. Follow figure 3.9.

(b)   If *Halsbury's Statutes* is not available, the next best alternative is to use *Halsbury's Laws* (3.4B4.1). *Halsbury's Laws* does not contain the text of Acts, but is a commentary on the whole law of England and Wales. Follow the research path for *Halsbury's Laws* given in figure 3.22. From the commentary you will be able to identify titles of relevant Acts and follow up the references in any publication to hand which gives the text of Acts.

(c)   If neither *Halsbury's Statutes* nor *Halsbury's Laws* is available, a rather poor alternative is to use *Index to the Statutes* and then *Statutes in Force* (see 3.2.2B1.3).

3.2.2D3   *Tracing historical, i.e., repealed, legislation by subject*

The electronic sources, LEXIS and Lawtel are inappropriate for this research. So, using paper sources, either:

(a)   Search *Halsbury's Statutes* by subject following figure 3.9. Read the review section at the beginning of the subject group of Acts currently in force. Or:

(b)   If legislation currently in force for the subject was published since 1947, find the text of the current Act in *Current Law Statutes Annotated* (see 3.2.2B2.2.2) and read the introduction and general note at the beginning of the reprint of the Act noting the titles and dates of earlier Acts mentioned. Or:

(c)   For references to statutes up to 1713 check the subject index to *Statutes of the Realm*, described at the beginning of 3.2.2B.

3.2.2D4   *Are there any cases on this Act or section of an Act?*

You can use either electronic or paper sources for this research. Using LEXIS (see 3.2.2C1) to find cases referring to the Unfair Contract Terms Act 1977 section 11, go into the CASES file, and type:

Unfair Contract Terms w/15 11

and press the TRANSMIT key.

If there is more than one Act with the same title in force as, for example, Employment Act, you need to include the year of the Act in which you are interested or you will get references to every Employment Act. So, in LEXIS, to find cases referring to section 20 of the Employment Act 1984, go into the CASES file, and type:

Employment w/4 1984 w/15 20

On Lawtel, select 'decisions' from the Lawtel main index and then 'statute citator'. Statutes are listed alphabetically by title. Against each section of an Act, a number is given in the right-hand column of the screen. Select the appropriate number and details of relevant cases will appear on the next screen.

As an alternative to electronic sources, two paper sources may be used. Experience suggests that the editors of *Halsbury's Statutes* and the *Current Law* publications employ different criteria by which they select cases for inclusion in their publications. This may be due to (a) the subjective judgment required to determine whether a court has judicially considered a particular section of an Act and (b) whether decisions of courts below the High Court have precedential value. To obtain a full answer to this type of research query it is advisable to check *both* publications rather than rely on one only.

(a) *Halsbury's Statutes*. Follow figure 3.8. Read the editorial notes in small type attached to the section of the Act in which you are interested. Make sure you follow the chart to its end, and finish your research by using the Noter-Up Service.

(b) *Current Law*. See 3.2.2B2.2.3, above. Where you start the search depends on the date of the Act of Parliament. Figure 3.10 provides the full path available.

3.2.2D5 Have any statutory instruments been made under this Act?

You can use either electronic or paper sources for this research.

In LEXIS (see 3.2.2C1), to find all statutory instruments made under the Merchant Shipping Act 1983, go into the SI or, preferably, the STATIS file and type:

authority (merchant shipping w/6 1983)

and press the TRANSMIT key.

In Lawtel (see 3.2.2C2), select 'legislation' from the Lawtel main index and then 'statutory instrument index'. Acts are listed in alphabetical order by title, with details of the statutory instruments made under each section of the Act. However, the database is limited because it only includes statutory instruments made since July 1983.

There are three alternative ways of searching paper sources for answers to this research query, using *Halsbury's Statutes, Current Law* publications or *Index to Government Orders*.

(a) *Halsbury's Statutes*. Follow figure 3.8. Read the editorial notes in small type attached to the section of the Act in which you are interested. Make sure you follow the chart to its conclusion, and finish your research by using the Noter-Up Service.

(b) *Current Law*. See 3.2.2B2.2.3, above. Where you start the search depends on the date of the Act of Parliament. Figure 3.10 provides the full path available.

(c) *Index to Government Orders*. This publication is described in 3.3.1B1.4. Find a reference to the Act in which you are interested in the table of statutes, printed on green paper, at the front of volume 1. Note the information given below the entry: it tells you under which subject heading in the body of the *Index* you will find details of orders made under the Act. Note that in some instances, information about a single Act is split over several subject headings to be found in different parts of the body of the *Index*. Look up the appropriate subject heading and the subheading number indicated. Since the *Index to Government Orders* is published only every other year, check if a supplement has been published during the intervening period and look for any new developments noted in the supplement, under the page number you consulted in the bound volumes.

3.2.2D6   Have any case notes or articles been written about this Act?

The best method of answering this research question is to use one or a number of periodical indexing publications, fully described in 3.8 below.

3.3   SECONDARY LEGISLATION

The last two hundred years have witnessed great changes in life and society. The continued growth and diversity of industry, commerce and technology, the creation and administration of the welfare state, are just a few of the many developments which have increased the legislative burden on Parliament. However, Parliamentary time is limited and the complexity and detail of legislation have been in conflict with the need for proper debate and scrutiny of proposals. Therefore, by the inclusion of a so-called 'enabling' section in an Act of Parliament, responsibility for drawing up details of the operation of the principles laid down in an Act can be conferred on a body outside Parliament. The bodies involved are Ministers of the Crown, local authorities, public corporations and the General Synod of the Church of England. The secondary legislation made by them falls into four categories: statutory instruments, codes of practice, by-laws and Measures of the General Synod. All statutory instruments and Measures of the General Synod must be laid before Parliament for approval before they can take effect. Most codes of practice must also receive Parliamentary approval, but some codes, along with local authority and public corporation by-laws, are subject only to confirmation by a Minister of the Crown, and not Parliament. Unlike the procedures followed by a Bill passing through Parliament, those for secondary legislation are of no direct relevance to the development of legal research skills and are therefore not dealt with here.

As a law student you are likely to use statutory instruments and probably codes of practice during your course, but this will depend largely on the areas of law you study. By-laws have been an important source of local authority law from the Municipal Corporations Act 1835 onwards and impinge on several areas of law affecting the work of solicitors. You are unlikely to be required to use Measures of the General Synod during your course and rarely, if ever, in legal practice. So, the description of research skills and techniques which follows concentrates on statutory instruments, codes of practice and by-laws.

3.3.1 Statutory instruments

3.3.1A DESCRIPTION

3.3.1A1 Definition

The term 'statutory instrument' (often abbreviated to SI) was introduced in the Statutory Instruments Act 1946. It is one of the few instances where the definition, Parliamentary procedure and publication of a legal document are governed by an Act of Parliament. Even so, confusion still arises when undertaking legal research with SIs, because the term is generic and applies to a variety of documents which may contain in their individual titles the words 'regulation' or 'rule' or 'order' or 'scheme'. Lawyers in everyday practice are more likely to refer to these documents by their individual title rather than the collective term, and yet they are published, both officially by HMSO and commercially, in volumes with 'statutory instrument' in the title, not regulation, rule, order or scheme. So, if you are referred by a lecturer or in your reading to one of these individual forms of secondary legislation, you will need to consult volumes of 'statutory instruments' and not a separate collection of, for example, 'regulations'.

Statutory instruments can be made by Ministers or by the Queen in Council – in the latter case they are known as Orders in Council. The most substantial group of Orders in Council relate to Northern Ireland. There appears to be no particular significance in the use of an Order in Council rather than an order made by a Minister, though it obviously indicates the matter is of some importance. These Orders in Council must not be confused with Orders in Council which are a form of primary legislation made by Royal decree, and are usually restricted to the affairs of dependent territories, and not classed as a statutory instrument.

Before the Statutory Instruments Act 1946, the variety of secondary legislation called rules, orders, warrants and schemes was subject to the requirements of the Rules Publication Act 1893 and was collectively known as statutory rules and orders (abbreviated to SR & O). Very occasionally you will need to consult these older documents, for some are still in force.

Over the last 40 years an average of 2,000 statutory instruments have been passed each year. In 1955 the total length of all instruments published by HMSO was about 3,240 pages; by 1988 the figure had risen to 9,048 (Bennett, 1990). As at 31 December 1989 some 17,674 SIs published by HMSO were still in force, and the number was rising annually (see Bates, 1986). Concern is sometimes expressed that too much use is made of statutory instruments by Ministers, and the chairman of the Parliamentary Joint Committee on statutory instruments has commented that 'the trouble is that a lot of statutory instruments today no longer deal with means but with principles' (cited in Bates 1986).

There are two broad classes of statutory instrument: local or general. The distinction is analogous to that between a Public General Act and a Local and Personal Act and has implications for publication and general availability (3.3.1A4 below). Ministers are required to determine whether a statutory instrument is local or general before sending it to the Queen's Printer (HMSO).

In legal research one group of general statutory instruments is of particular importance: commencement orders. As their title suggests, they fix the date for the commencement or bringing into force of provisions in an Act of Parliament. They will be noted in 3.3.1A3, below.

3.3.1A2 Origin

See 3.3.1A1, above

3.3.1A3 Structure

Figure 3.11 reproduces the whole of one SI, though to make reproduction in this book easier, the explanatory note given on the back of the original has been moved to a space at the front. Only a minority of SIs fit on to a single sheet of paper, some run to hundreds of pages and are thicker than many Acts of Parliament.

A statutory instrument comprises nine parts:

(a)   Citation – SIs are numbered consecutively by the Statutory Publications Office, roughly in the order in which they are received from Ministers, following Parliamentary approval. The sequence of numbers starts at 1 at the beginning of each calendar year. The citation is composed of the calendar year and the sequence number. Some SIs bear a letter (either C, L or S) and numbers in brackets after the sequence number. Those with a C are commencement orders, bringing an Act or part of an Act into operation, and the number which follows is the sequence number for commencement orders issued during the particular year. The letter L signifies the SI is an instrument relating to fees or procedures in courts in England and Wales, again followed by the sequence number for that series, and SIs bearing the letter S are instruments which apply to Scotland only.

(b)   Subject-matter – this word or phrase describes the subject of the SI and is the same word as will be used in the indexes to SIs published by HMSO (see 3.3.1B1.3 to 3.3.1B1.5).

(c)   Short title – this is the title by which the SI is generally known.

(d)   Statements of progress – section 4(2) of the statutory instruments Act 1946 requires that every SI must bear on its face a statement of the date on which it came or will come into operation, and either a statement of the date on which copies were laid before Parliament or a statement that copies are to be laid before Parliament. In addition, it is usual practice for SIs to also bear the date on which they were made.

(e)   Preamble and enabling powers – the text of the SI commences with a recital of the statutory authority and powers under which the instrument is made.

(f)   Main text – an SI is divided into a series of numbered divisions which may be subdivided. The name given to the divisions is determined by the title given to the SI. If the SI is titled XYZ Order then the divisions are called articles; if it is titled XYZ Regulations then the divisions are called

STATUTORY INSTRUMENTS

① **1989 No. 1674**

② **PENSIONS**

③ The Superannuation (Valuation and Community Charge Tribunals) Order 1989

④
Made - - - -	*4th September 1989*
Laid before Parliament	*15th September 1989*
Coming into force	*6th October 1989*

⑤ The Treasury, in exercise of the powers conferred by section 1(5)(c) and section 1(8)(a) of the Superannuation Act 1972(**a**) and now vested in them(**b**), hereby make the following Order:—

1. This Order may be cited as the Superannuation (Valuation and Community Charge Tribunals) Order 1989 and shall come into force on 6th October 1989.

⑥ **2.** Employment by a valuation and community charge tribunal is hereby removed from the employments listed in Schedule 1 to the Superannuation Act 1972 with effect from 1st May 1989.

Kenneth Carlisle
Nigel Lawson
Two of the Lords Commissioners
of Her Majesty's Treasury

⑦ 4th September 1989

⑧ EXPLANATORY NOTE

(This note is not part of the Order)

Employment with a valuation and community charge tribunal was on 1st May 1989 added to the employments listed in Schedule 1 to the Superannuation Act 1972 ("the 1972 Act") by the Local Government Finance Act 1988 (c.41), section 136 and Schedule 11, paragraph 6(6), and so falls within those employments to which the Principal Civil Service Pension Scheme and the Civil Service Additional Voluntary Contribution Scheme (made under section 1 of the 1972 Act) may apply. This Order removes employment by a valuation and community charge tribunal from the employments listed in that Schedule. Under the power conferred by section 1(8)(a) of the 1972 Act the Order takes effect from 1st May 1989.

A valuation and community charge tribunal will be a "scheduled body" for the purposes of the Local Government Superannuation Regulations 1986 (S.I. 1986/24) with effect from 1st May 1989 by virtue of the Local Government Superannuation (Valuation and Community Charge Tribunals) Regulations 1989 (S.I. 1989/1624).

① Citation (a) ② Subject Matter (b) ③ Short Title (c)
④ Statements of Progress (d) ⑤ Preamble and enabling powers (e)
⑥ Main Text (f) ⑦ Signatures (g) ⑧ Explanatory Note (i)

(Letters in parentheses refer to paragraphs in text where discussion on the elements of a SI occur.)

Figure 3.11 A statutory instrument.

regulations; if the SI is called Rules then the divisions are called rules. A subdivision of an article, regulation or rule is called a paragraph. In lengthy SIs the articles, regulations or rules may be grouped into numbered parts but the structure is not as uniform as with Bills or Acts (see appendix 3). There are four special types of articles etc. of which you should be aware; they are indicated by a heading printed in bold type. The 'short title' or 'citation' article etc. sets out the correct title by which you should refer to the SI; the 'commencement' article etc. gives the date on which the SI is to come into force (which should be the same date as given in the statements of progress); the 'extent' article etc. details the geographical area to which the SI applies; and, finally, the 'interpretation' article etc. gives the meaning of particular words or phrases used in the SI. Not all SIs include all these four, and some SIs roll citation and commencement together under one heading, throwing in, for good measure, an article etc. headed 'revocation', which states which earlier SIs are replaced by the new SI.

(g)   Signatures – this is the name/s and title/s of the Minister/s making the SI, and the date the SI was made.

(h)   Schedules – at the end of many SIs will be found one or more schedules containing detailed provisions dependent on one or more of the preceding paragraphs of text, rather like appendices at the back of a book.

(i)   Explanatory note – because of the complexity of many SIs, an explanatory note is added to aid the understanding of the provisions. The note is prefaced by a warning that it does not form part of the instrument. In the example illustrated in figure 3.11 the explanatory note is longer than the text of the SI itself!

3.3.1A4   Publication and general availability

As was noted in 3.3.1A1, there are two classes of SI: general or local. General instruments are published and sold by HMSO, several separate instruments appearing each working day. Between 50 per cent and 60 per cent of all SIs are general. The remainder are local instruments; examples include those relating to a particular local authority area. They are exempt from printing and sale unless the Minister concerned requests otherwise. As a law student you will be concerned with general instruments, but should you eventually practise in local authority law, the difficulties in tracing local instruments will become apparent (see Morris 1990).

Some Acts of Parliament require a draft SI to be laid before Parliament. Draft instruments are published by HMSO but lack the citation details (year and running number) and, of course, the date on which they were made.

Most self-respecting law libraries will collect loose, separate SIs as they are published, but some may only subscribe to the bound annual volumes (see 3.3.1B1.1), and so will not have copies of the most recent instruments in stock.

3.3.1A5   Citation

Statutory instruments are cited quite simply: the short title followed by the abbreviation 'SI', the year, followed by a slash '/' and then the running number. If the year and running number are very similar, confusion can be avoided by substituting the abbreviation 'No.' for the slash, but since the calendar year should *always* be cited *before* the running number the confusion is only in the mind of the reader. Here is the correct way of citing the instrument illustrated in figure 3.11:

Superannuation (Valuation and Community Charge Tribunals) Order 1989 SI 1989/1674.

3.3.1B EXPLOITATION

There are a number of official and commercially produced publications which reprint SIs or assist your researching them.

3.3.1B1 Official publications

These may be divided into publications which reprint SIs (3.3.1B1.1) and those which merely list them (3.3.1B1.2 to 3.3.1B1.5).

3.3.1B1.1 Statutory Instruments 19–

At the end of each calendar year, annual volumes entitled *Statutory Instruments*, containing reprints of general instruments, are compiled by HMSO. Unfortunately publication is frequently delayed by up to two years. The texts of only those instruments in force at the end of the year are included – this is significant because some instruments have only temporary application. The final volume of each annual set contains a subject index and numerical lists of all the SIs printed and sold by HMSO during the year, whether reprinted in the annual volumes or not. A classified list of all *local* instruments is also given.

From 1890 to 1960 the annual volumes of instruments were arranged by subject, but since 1961 they have been printed in numerical order.

Three editions of the official, revised edition of instruments have appeared, giving the text of all general instruments in force at a particular date. The latest edition, *Statutory Rules and Orders and Statutory Instruments Revised to December 31st 1948*, was published in 25 volumes between 1949 and 1952. The arrangement is alphabetical by subject.

3.3.1B1.2 Daily List of Government Publications from HMSO

Every working day HMSO publishes a list containing brief details (really little more than the citation) of the documents it has issued that day – it is known as the '*Daily List*'. SIs are included and for lawyers the list has two benefits:

(a)   By the Statutory Instruments Act 1946, section 3, the inclusion of an SI in this list is conclusive evidence of publication – there have been one or two court cases which have turned on this point, for if there is not appropriate evidence that a particular SI had been published or published on a particular day, then an action concerned with compliance with the requirements of the instrument can fail.

(b)   Although most HMSO publications are included in the *Monthly* and *Annual Catalogues* of HMSO publications, SIs are not. So, the entries in the *Daily List* are the only official means of knowing that an SI has been published, until the separate monthly *List of SIs* (3.3.1B1.3) appears. There is no index to the *Daily List*, so to find the entry for a particular SI it is necessary to scan the copies of the *Daily List* around the time you think the SI you want was published. The *Daily List* is best used as an 'alerting' publication – that is, to give warning, day by day, of the publication of new material. Whenever you can, use the monthly *List of SIs* in preference.

3.3.1B1.3   List of statutory instruments

This is a useful index for tracing relatively recent SIs; although published monthly it is usually a few months in arrears. At the year end it is replaced by an annual list which is similarly delayed. The main body of the monthly list arranges brief details about each SI published that month, under the same subject headings as are printed at the top of the SI itself. At the back of the list is an alphabetical subject index, cumulated throughout the calendar year, the December issue acting as an interim annual subject index until the annual list proper is published. There is also a list of SIs issued during the month in question, arranged in order by the sequence running number.

3.3.1B1.4   Index to Government Orders

In effect, this two-volume publication is a subject index to all statutory instruments in force. The main body of the *Index* arranges under subject headings and subheadings, brief details of Acts and the orders made under them. At the front of volume 1, printed on green paper, is a list of Acts in chronological order, with information against each of the subject heading in the body of the *Index* under which details of orders made under each Act are given. Consult these green pages first as a way into the body of the publication. Unfortunately, the *Index* is published only every other year and can be a year out of date on publication. A supplement is issued during the intervening period, and you should always check to see if one is available and note any new developments since the bound volumes were published. The supplement is arranged according to the page number of the bound volume to which the new information applies.

3.3.1B1.5   Table of Government Orders

This is a chronological listing of all instruments falling within the definition of statutory rules given in the Rules Publication Act 1893 and statutory instruments as defined in the Statutory Instruments Act 1946, and certain Orders in Council made under the Royal Prerogative (i.e., primary legislation). The list starts with an Order in Council of 1671 and gives year by year the serial number for each instrument, its title and an indication of whether it is still in force (noted in bold type) or no longer in force (noted in italic type), with brief details of why it is no longer in force. So if you know the year and serial number of a statutory instrument, you can use the *Table* to check whether it is still in force. However, the *Table* does not contain very current information. It is published annually with a Noter-Up supplement published during the year, but the information in the annual volume can be up to 18 months old by the time of publication.

3.3.1B2   Commercial publications

Like the official publications noted above, the commercial ones may be divided into those which reprint SIs (3.3.1B2.1 to 3.3.1B2.3) and those which merely list them (3.3.1B2.4 and 3.3.1B2.6).

3.3.1B2.1   Halsbury's Statutory Instruments

Halsbury's Statutory Instruments reprints a large number, but not all, SIs of general application, currently in force in England and Wales; the remainder are summarised. The decision by the editors of the publication to reprint or merely summarise an SI is based on their assessment of the general importance of an SI, set against the likely requirements of subscribers to the service. This is an occasional, but not major, disadvantage, and is more than compensated for by the superior indexing and the system for keeping the statement of law up to date.

Halsbury's Statutory Instruments consists of three parts:

(a) *Main volumes.* The whole publication has recently undergone a revision and comprises 22 grey-coloured volumes in which reprints or summaries of SIs are arranged under 97 broad subject headings (called 'titles' in the publication). Each title may be subdivided. At the beginning of each title there is a chronological list of instruments and a table of instruments no longer in operation. Then follows a preliminary note describing the scope of the title and, if the title is subdivided, there are introductory notes to each part. Finally there follows the text or a summary of each SI relevant to the title.

When the law stated in a Main Volume becomes considerably out of date, a reissue volume is published to replace the original volume. The word 'reissue' is printed at the foot of the spine and on the title page. On the page following the title page, is given the date to which the law is stated in the volume. This is important information because the Consolidated Index to the whole set is published annually, and there may be short periods when the page information given in the annual index refers to an original volume and not the recently published reissue volume to hand. If that happens it is necessary to check again the subject you want in the index to the reissue volume to find the new page number.

(b) *Service binders.* Two loose-leaf binders contain information which assists you using the Main Volumes and keeps them up to date. The Main

Service Binder contains a number of indexes: first, a list of statutory instruments in date order included in the Main Volumes with references to the volumes in which they will be found; secondly, a table of enabling statutes, i.e., statutes under which statutory instruments included in the publication were made and are now having effect, and thirdly, a list of recent commencement and appointed day orders, i.e., statutory instruments specifying the dates on which statutory provisions are to come into force. The rest of the Main Service Binder and the whole of the second loose-leaf volume, entitled 'Additional Texts', contain information which updates that given in the Main Volumes, starting with the Annual Cumulative Supplement, which is arranged in the same order as the Main Volumes, and provides details of changes which have been made since each Main Volume title was issued. The Annual Supplement is followed by the Monthly Survey, which contains updating information since the last Annual Cumulative Supplement was issued, and is in two sections: the summaries section gives brief details of recent statutory instruments, the whole section arranged in SI number order (i.e., the order in which they were originally issued) *not* in the subject groups employed in the rest of the *Halsbury* service. The second section, the Monthly Survey key, performs the function of listing the titles of recent statutory instruments under the appropriate subject title heading used in the Main Volumes of the service, with details of any amendments and revocations made to earlier statutory instruments. Right at the back of the first binder is a subject index to the Monthly Survey. The second loose-leaf binder contains the full text of selected statutory instruments awaiting inclusion in reissued Main Volumes. These additional texts are arranged in SI number order, not the subject order employed in the Main Volumes.

(c) *Consolidated index etc.* The third part of *Halsbury's Statutory Instruments* is a thick paperback index volume, replaced annually, which is in three sections: a list of the Main Volumes and their dates of issue from which the indexes have been compiled; a subject index (called the Consolidated Index) and, lastly, a list of SIs included in the publication in alphabetical order by their title (called the Alphabetical Index). The majority of entries in the subject index will provide references to the volume and page number in the Main Volumes where relevant information on the subject will be found, but where a statutory instrument is still only available in the Annual Supplement in the first loose-leaf binder, a letter S in bold type is given, instead of the volume and page number, followed by the SI citation.

Using *Halsbury's Statutory Instruments*

Because the information presented in *Halsbury's Statutory Instruments* is set out in several different parts and sometimes in different sequence orders within these parts, you may find use of the publication a little bewildering at first. However, if you remember that the general arrangement of the publication is by subject, that where this is not so indexes are provided to help you find the information you require, and that to carry out a fully up-to-date piece of research you must also use the loose-leaf binders, you should not go far wrong.

There are three different ways of using *Halsbury's Statutory Instruments* for research:

(a) Finding SIs on a subject – follow figure 3.12.
(b) Finding an SI when all you know is its title – follow figure 3.13.
(c) Tracing whether an enabling power has been exercised and the instruments made under it – follow figure 3.14.
(d) Finding an SI when all you know is its citation – follow figure 3.15.

All the research steps outlined suggest using the various indexes to the whole publication as a way of finding information. This is by far the best method to adopt when you are first learning how to use the publication. However, once you have become familiar with the presentation of material in *Halsbury's*, and especially the contents of the subject titles into which it is divided, you may wish to start your research by browsing over the spines and selecting the most appropriate of the 22 Main Volumes from the shelves and using the index and lists in that volume to guide you to the information you require. The danger to the uninitiated is that unless you use the Consolidated Indexes to the whole publication you can never be sure (a) you are checking the correct volumes for the information you require and (b) if you do not find what you are seeking, that it does not appear somewhere else in *Halsbury's*.

3.3.1B2.2 Specialist subject encyclopaedias

Many specialist law encyclopaedias reprint SIs relevant to their topic area. Although the subject coverage of particular encyclopaedias may be narrow, the greater detail included in their subject indexes, together with the rapidity with which they are updated (most are loose-leaf publications), and the fact that SIs are reprinted with explanatory notes and annotations by the encyclopaedia's editorial staff in addition, makes them a very valuable source for SIs.

3.3.1B2.3 Knight's Local Government Reports

First published in 1903 and appearing monthly, this publication includes the full text of SIs relevant to the work of local government. However, there is no subject index, nor are there annotations, and neither are the texts updated as amendments and revocations occur.

3.3.1B2.4 Current Law Monthly Digest

Summaries of a selection of SIs are given in *Current Law Monthly Digest* and *Current Law Yearbook*. You can trace where these summaries are printed by using the Alphabetical Table of Statutory Instruments found in both publications, which lists SIs by title. For SIs of the current calendar year use the list in the latest issue of *Current Law Monthly Digest* which will provide a reference to the paragraph number and monthly issue in which the summary is given. In *Current Law Yearbook* the reference is to the paragraph in the body of the *Yearbook* itself.

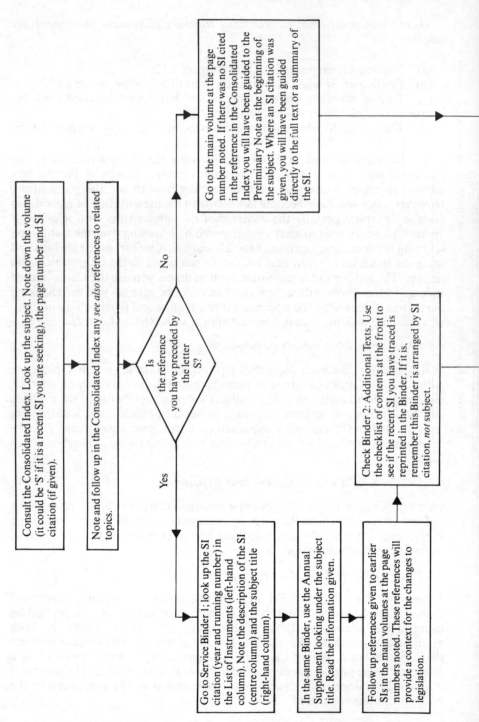

Consult the Consolidated Index. Look up the subject. Note down the volume (it could be 'S' if it is a recent SI you are seeking), the page number and SI citation (if given).

Note and follow up in the Consolidated Index any *see also* references to related topics.

Is the reference you have preceded by the letter S?

Yes

No

Go to Service Binder 1; look up the SI citation (year and running number) in the List of Instruments (left-hand column). Note the description of the SI (centre column) and the subject title (right-hand column).

In the same Binder, use the Annual Supplement looking under the subject title. Read the information given.

Follow up references given to earlier SIs in the main volumes at the page numbers noted. These references will provide a context for the changes to legislation.

Go to the main volume at the page number noted. If there was no SI cited in the reference in the Consolidated Index you will have been guided to the Preliminary Note at the beginning of the subject. Where an SI citation was given, you will have been guided directly to the full text or a summary of the SI.

Check Binder 2: Additional Texts. Use the checklist of contents at the front to see if the recent SI you have traced is reprinted in the Binder. If it is, remember this Binder is arranged by SI citation, *not* subject.

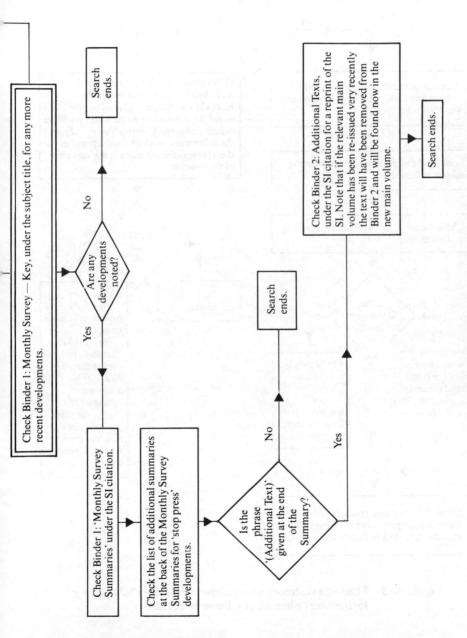

Figure 3.12 Searching *Halsbury's Statutory Instruments* by subject.

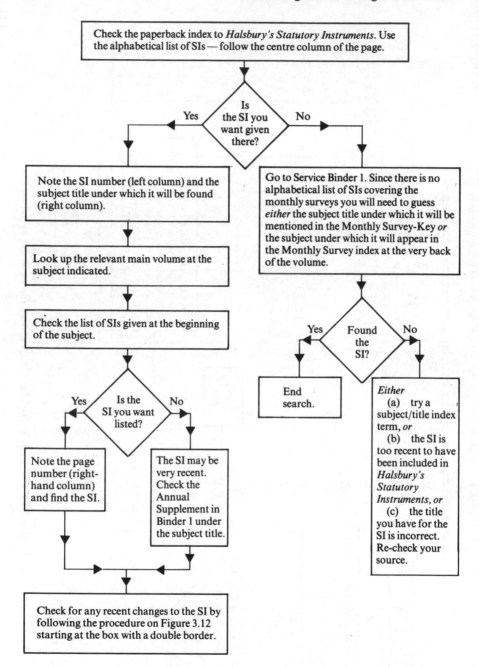

Figure 3.13   Finding a statutory instrument in *Halsbury's Statutory Instruments* when all you know is its title.

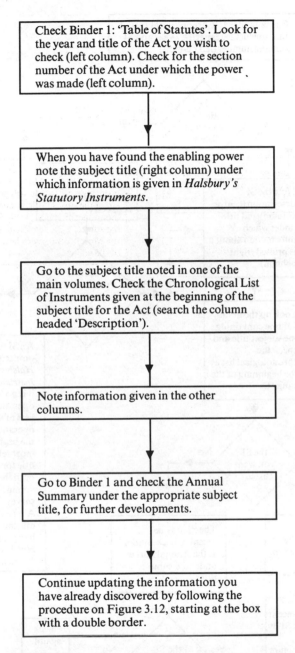

Check Binder 1: 'Table of Statutes'. Look for the year and title of the Act you wish to check (left column). Check for the section number of the Act under which the power was made (left column).

When you have found the enabling power note the subject title (right column) under which information is given in *Halsbury's Statutory Instruments*.

Go to the subject title noted in one of the main volumes. Check the Chronological List of Instruments given at the beginning of the subject title for the Act (search the column headed 'Description').

Note information given in the other columns.

Go to Binder 1 and check the Annual Summary under the appropriate subject title, for further developments.

Continue updating the information you have already discovered by following the procedure on Figure 3.12, starting at the box with a double border.

Figure 3.14   Tracing whether an enabling power has been exercised and details of the statutory instrument made under it, using *Halsbury's Statutory Instruments*.

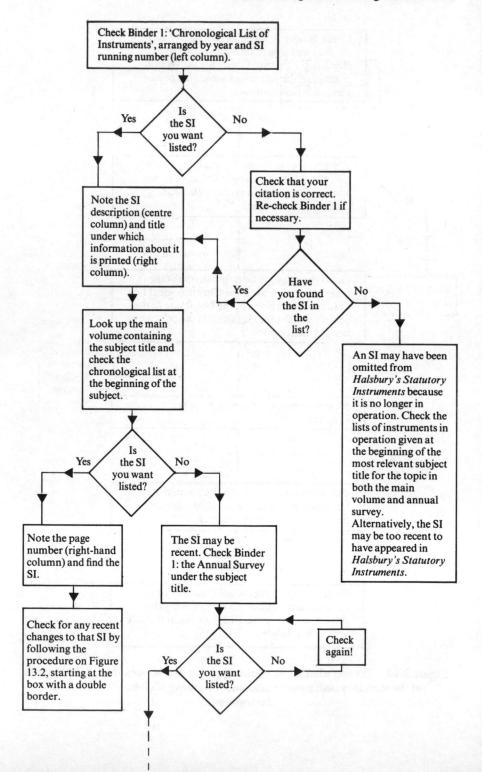

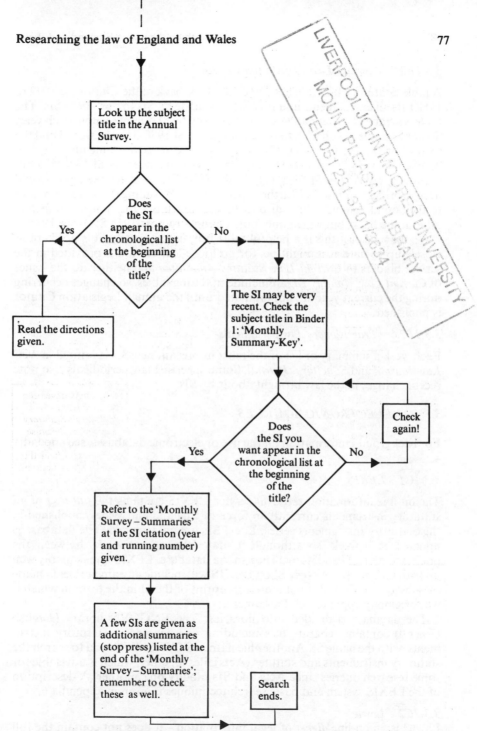

Look up the subject title in the Annual Survey.

Does the SI appear in the chronological list at the beginning of the title?

Yes

No

Read the directions given.

The SI may be very recent. Check the subject title in Binder 1: 'Monthly Summary-Key'.

Check again!

Does the SI you want appear in the chronological list at the beginning of the title?

Yes

No

Refer to the 'Monthly Survey – Summaries' at the SI citation (year and running number) given.

A few SIs are given as additional summaries (stop press) listed at the end of the 'Monthly Survey – Summaries'; remember to check these as well.

Search ends.

Figure 3.15 **Finding a statutory instrument in *Halsbury's Statutory Instruments* when all you know is its citation.**

3.3.1B2.5   *Current Law Legislation Citator*

A table 'Statutory Instruments Affected' at the back of the Citator for 1972 to 1988 lists all amendments and revocations made by SIs to post-1946 SIs. The table is arranged by year and then numerically by SI number within each year. So, for example, if you wish to trace changes to SI 1980/541 you would find the section of the list for 1980, the entry 541 and discover 'amended 81/575; revoked 85/1218', meaning the instrument was amended by SI 1981/575 but eventually revoked by SI 1985/1218. If the SI had not been revoked, you would need to bring your research further up to date by consulting the annual updates to the bound volume, which also include a 'Statutory Instruments Affected' table at the back, but which only note changes to post-1946 SIs since 1988.

On the face of it this is a helpful table but, unfortunately, it is not kept as closely up-to-date as it might be, for no loose-leaf version is provided in the service binders to *Current Law Statutes Annotated* and neither do the issues of *Current Law Monthly Digest* include updating tables, so changes occurring during the current year are not tabulated until the annual Legislation Citator is published.

3.3.1B2.6   *Practitioners' law periodicals*

Each week a summary or list of the most important new SIs is printed in *New Law Journal* and *Solicitors' Journal*. Some specialist law periodicals also note recent changes in the law brought about by SIs.

3.3.1C   *ELECTRONIC SOURCES*

For background information on the use of electronic databases, see appendix 4.

3.3.1C1   *LEXIS*

The on-line information retrieval service LEXIS contains the *full text* of all statutory instruments currently in force in England and Wales, published in the Statutory Instruments series. Local SIs are *not* included. The database is updated each week, so although it may take several weeks between the publication of a SI and its inclusion in the database, LEXIS is reasonably well up to date. The text of every SI on LEXIS will include any amendments made by subsequent SIs and is not merely a reprint of the SI in the form in which it was originally approved by Parliament.

The database is divided into libraries. The ENGGEN library (*Eng*lish *Gen*eral) contains separate files including one devoted to statutory instruments, with the name SI. Another file named STATIS allows you to search the statutory instruments and statutes (Acts) files together, which is advisable for some research queries since Acts and SIs modify one another. A description of the LEXIS system and basic search techniques is given in appendix 6.

3.3.1C2   *Lawtel*

Lawtel is an on-line *digest* of legal information – it does not contain the full text of SIs, only certain pieces of information about them, such as the title and section of the Act under which they were made, the year and SI number, title of the SI, date on which the SI came into force, whether it has been repealed or amended and the geographical area to which the SI applies. The database includes all general SIs listed by HMSO since July 1983. To obtain the Statutory Instruments Index, which is arranged in alphabetical order by the title of the enabling Act, select 'Legislation' from the Lawtel main menu. A general description of Lawtel is given in appendix 5.

3.3.1C3 SI-CD (Statutory Instruments CD-ROM)

Context Ltd, in cooperation with HMSO, markets on a single compact disc the full text of all SIs published by HMSO since 1 January 1987 and a short-form reference (no text) of SIs published by HMSO and local SIs, from 1980 to 1986. The disc runs in a CD drive attached to a personal computer. A printer can be attached to the equipment. A search request is typed into the personal computer keyboard and may consist of a word or combination of words which the computer will search for in the full text of SIs on the compact disc. The computer will report the number of occurrences of the specific word or words it finds, and the selected items can be displayed on the computer screen. The search is similar, in part, to a LEXIS search in that it is conducted on the full text of SIs, but in contrast it is also conducted on only limited data for a large number. As quick and convenient as the service appears to be, there are two drawbacks: first, the discs are updated at six-monthly intervals, so it is not possible to search for the most recent SIs (remember that several are published each working day); secondly, for technical reasons, anything in an SI that is set out in tabular form is not included on the disc.

3.3.1D RESEARCH STRATEGIES

3.3.1D1 *You know the title of an SI but not the year or running number. How do you trace a copy of it?*

There are several ways of undertaking this research. Given the volume of SIs published each year and the possibility of titles being very similar, care should be taken to ensure any SI you find is the one relevant to your research. If the SI title includes the title of the enabling Act under which it was made, it will be possible to use the electronic database, Lawtel (see 3.3.1C2); use the Statutory Instruments Index, which arranges details of SIs in alphabetical order by the title of the enabling Act, but remember that the database goes back only to July 1983. On LEXIS (see 3.3.1C1) you would go into the SI file, and if, for example, you were searching for the text of the Mental Health Review Tribunal Rules, you would type:

title (Mental Health Review Tribunal)

and then press the TRANSMIT key.

In SI-CD (see 3.3.1C3) you would search in the 'heading' field for the title required, but bear in mind the database only goes back to 1 January 1980.

Using paper sources there are several research routes, but quite a few publications, especially those officially produced, do not include indexes to SI titles but are based on the SI year/running number or the subject. In the circumstances, therefore, the following paths are suggested:

(a) *Halsbury's Statutory Instruments* (3.3.1B2.1) – use figure 3.13. *Halsbury's* is the only source to comprehensively index SIs in force in this way.

(b) · *Current Law Monthly Digest* (3.3.1B2.4) – use the Alphabetical Table of Statutory Instruments in the latest monthly issue, the December issue of any year for which *Current Law Yearbook* is not available, and each *Current Law Yearbook*. Having found the SI year/running number you should then turn to a full-text source for the SI, such as *Statutory Instruments 19*– (3.3.1B1.1). A tedious task, made more so by the way titles are grouped under subject headings in the *Yearbooks*.

(c) *Index to Government Orders* (3.3.1B1.4, above) – if the title you have includes the title of the enabling Act under which it was made, it is possible to trace the year and running number, and thus a copy of the SI itself, using *Index to Government Orders* – consult the green pages at the front of the index first, and remember to look for a supplement covering the intervening year of this biennial publication. If the title of the SI gives some clue to the subject matter it may be possible to use *Index to Government Orders* by going straight into the body of the publication and searching under relevant subject headings.

(d) Specialist subject encyclopaedias (3.3.1B2.2) – another research method would be to select a specialist subject encyclopaedia and search either its subject index or any tables of SIs, for a reference which matches the title you have and, if successful, look up the reprint of the SI in the encyclopaedia.

3.3.1D2   Is this SI, the title, year and number of which you know, in force?

Using electronic sources, Lawtel (3.3.1C2) will only provide this information if you also know, or can gauge from the title of the SI, the title of the enabling Act under which it has been made; go into the Statutory Instruments Index and search for the title of the enabling Act. The detailed screen of information on that Act will tell you whether the SI is in force. If you are using LEXIS (3.3.1C1) for your research you would go into the SI file and do a title search like the one in 3.3.1D1, noting the information given near the top of the SI on its date of 'coming into force'. A search of SI-CD (3.3.1C3) could be undertaken following the procedure given in 3.3.1D1, but do note that the discs are updated only every six months, so recent SIs are not included.

Using paper sources there are several alternative approaches. The *Table of Government Orders* (3.3.1B1.5) could be consulted under the relevant year and number; ensure you check the Noter-Up supplement, if available, for the latest developments. Since the *Table* and its supplements are updated rather tardily, a better method would be to use *Current Law Legislation Citator* (3.3.1B2.5) or *Halsbury's Statutory Instruments* (3.3.1B2.1) using either figure 3.13 or figure 3.15. Specialist subject encyclopaedias (3.3.1B2.2) may also be used.

3.3.1D3   Has this SI been amended?

Using electronic sources, Lawtel (3.3.1C2) will provide the answer only if you know the title of the enabling Act. Follow the procedure given in 3.3.1D1. The advantage of Lawtel is that the database is updated daily so it includes the very latest developments. LEXIS (3.3.1C1) incorporates into the text of SIs all amendments made up to the date the file is current (i.e., the date given on the screen displaying the files available). Repealed or spent provisions are not available on LEXIS. So, to answer this research query for, say, the Mental Health Review Tribunal Rules, you would type:

title (Mental Health Review Tribunal)

and then press the TRANSMIT key.

Within the text of the SI displayed amendments will be represented in three ways:

(a)   where words have been substituted and new words have been added or new words are to be added, square brackets [ ] will be used;

(b)   where words have been repealed or revoked or amend or repeal earlier legislation, three dots . . . will be found;

(c)   where words are prospectively repealed or repealed with savings, they will be contained between *R*** and ***R*.

At the end of each of the documents retrieved by your search request, a list headed 'Annotations' will give details of the Acts or SIs under which the amendments have been made.

SI-CD (3.3.1C3) is not an entirely appropriate database to use for this query because its SI texts are in their original and not amended form. Searches could be conducted either under the title of the SI in the heading field to uncover an amending SI with the same title, or under the title of the enabling Act to discover all SIs made under it and note any which amend the particular SI in which you are interested, or, finally, a subject search in the heading field to retrieve SIs on the same topic (though not necessarily with the same title) to see if they amend the SI in question.

Using paper sources it is important to select a publication which is regularly updated so that you can be sure of checking for the possibility of very recent amendments. The *Table of Government Orders* (3.3.1B1.5) is only updated every six months and that service appears after some delay – it should not be your first choice if other publications are available. If a specialist subject encyclopaedia (3.3.1B2.2) covers the subject, the greater frequency with which it will be updated counts in its favour – consult the list of SIs printed in the encyclopaedia to find the reprint of the SI you wish to check, and note any remarks in the text of the SI or the editorial commentary.

Two further alternative strategies are to use either *Current Law Legislation Citator* (3.3.1B2.5) or *Halsbury's Statutory Instruments* (3.3.1B2.1) using figure 3.13 or figure 3.15.

3.3.1D4   Which SIs have been made under this Act?

Using electronic sources, Lawtel (3.3.1C2) will provide the answer but lists only SIs made since July 1983; follow the procedure in 3.3.1D1, above. In LEXIS (3.3.1C1) select the STATIS file, which combines the statutes and statutory instruments files. The reason for doing this is that Acts and SIs frequently modify one another. Supposing the Act in which you were interested is the Merchant Shipping Act 1983, type:

authority (Merchant Shipping w/6 1983)

and then press the TRANSMIT key.

The question can be researched using SI-CD (3.3.1C3), but since the database only goes back to 1980, and is updated only every six months, your answer may not be comprehensive.

Several printed publications may be used for this research. If *Halsbury's Statutes* (3.2.2B2.3.1) is available, follow figure 3.8. When you have found the Act in the Main Volumes or Current Statutes Service, check the editorial notes attached, and follow any recent developments through the Cumulative Supplement and Noter-Up.

A quicker method is to use *Halsbury's Statutory Instruments* (3.3.1B2.1) following figure 3.14. The authoritative *Index to Government Orders* (3.3.1B1.4) could be consulted, but it is perhaps less easy to use and certainly less up-to-date than *Halsbury's Statutory Instruments*. Specialist subject encyclopaedias (3.3.1B2.2) may also be used.

3.3.1D5   Is this SI still in force?

Using electronic sources, Lawtel (3.3.1C2) will provide an answer if you know the title of the enabling Act under which the SI was made. Follow the procedure in 3.3.1D1. Lawtel has the advantage of being updated daily so the information given is current. LEXIS (3.3.1C1) contains the text of only those SIs currently in force at the date to which the file is current. So, to answer this research query you would undertake a title search, as in 3.3.1D1, and if the SI is in force, LEXIS will trace it. If it is not, LEXIS will either declare it has found nothing or if it has been revoked by an SI of the same title it will retrieve the new SI.

The research can be undertaken on SI-CD (3.3.1C3) but in view of the poor currency of the information – the lists are updated every six months – the answer will not take account of recent developments. Several paper sources are available for this research. Using *Halsbury's Statutory Instruments* (3.3.1B2.1), follow figure 3.13 or 3.15. Alternatively, use *Current Law Legislation Citator* (3.3.1B2.5). The *Table of Government Orders* (3.3.1B1.5) may be used but, because it is not updated so frequently, it is less safe to rely on for the latest developments. Specialist subject encyclopaedias (3.3.1B2.2) may also be used.

3.3.1D6   Has this SI been considered by the courts?

Electronic or paper sources can be used for this research.

Lawtel (3.3.1C2) can be used if the statutory instrument is the principal topic with which the case is concerned, as it will then appear in the appropriate subject index, e.g., Matrimonial Causes Rules; Industrial Tribunal Rules.

If you are using LEXIS (3.3.1C1), select the CASES file, and supposing you wished to check for cases on the Social Security Benefits Up-Rating Regulations, you would type:

Social Security Benefits Up-Rating Regulations

and then press the TRANSMIT key.

If there is any possibility of there having existed several SIs with the same title, the search request could be made more specific by adding the date of the particular SI in which you are interested:

Social Security Benefits Up-Rating Regulations w/4 1981

Paper sources offer two research routes. The editorial notes to instruments included in *Halsbury's Statutory Instruments* (3.3.1B2.1) mention cases where the meaning and effect of the SI have been judicially considered. *Law Reports Index* (3.4B1.1) carries a table of statutory instruments etc. judicially considered, but appears to restrict coverage of cases to those mentioned in the handful of law reports it indexes. *Halsbury's Statutory Instruments'* coverage appears more catholic, particularly amongst the specialist law reports.

3.3.1D7   Have any notes or articles been written in periodicals about this SI?

There are two ways of following up this research query – either using an electronic source: LEXIS, or a paper source: *Legal Journals Index*. Because of the larger number of publications included in *Legal Journals Index* as opposed to the LEXIS database, the paper source is more likely to yield information.

However, if you wish to use LEXIS (3.3.1C1), you would select the ENGGEN library and the UKJNL file which contains the full text of a handful of law periodicals, two from 1986 to the present but most from more recent dates. If you were searching for notes or articles on the Mental Health Review Tribunal Rules, you would type:

title (Mental Health Review Tribunal)

and then press the TRANSMIT key.

Since LEXIS will search the full text of these publications you may find that some of the times where the rules are mentioned it is merely in passing, and of no great value to you.

Legal Journals Index indexes the contents of over 160 legal periodicals and is fully described in 3.8B1. Of the five separate indexes in each monthly issue of *Legal Journals Index* you would select the legislation index for this particular research query.

3.3.2   Statutory codes of practice

3.3.2A   DESCRIPTION

3.3.2A1   Definition

There is no official definition, and this is one of the difficulties faced by the researcher and user of statutory codes of practice. Although Parliament, through provisions in an Act, gives a government department, or in some cases an outside body, the power to prepare a code, the code may not be subject to approval by Parliament (as is a statutory instrument) but by a Secretary of State, or a Minister, or even the outside body itself, depending on what the Act stipulates. Further, some codes are intended merely to provide guidance or to be a statement of accepted good practice, whilst others have a legal effect and may be used in civil or criminal proceedings as tending to establish or negate liability. There has been concern amongst lawyers and Parliamentarians at:

(a)   the uncertainty of the legal effect of failure to comply with codes of practice,
(b)   the lack of a standard procedure for the approval of codes of practice, and
(c)   the nature of the content of some codes, which could and should have been included in an Act or in regulations.

These concerns led to a debate in the House of Lords on 15 January 1986 and the subsequent issue, in 1987, by HM Government, of a note: 'Guidance on Codes of Practice and Legislation' (reprinted in [1989] Stat LR 214). The aim of the guidance note is to secure consistency and legal certainty in future legislation. Nevertheless, between 1973 and 1986, 25 statutes have come into force under which 48 codes of practice may be made (per Lord Renton, HL Deb (1985-86) 469 col. 1086), and a considerable number of those which were made during that period are of particular value to law students, and embody the qualities the guidance note seeks to correct. Some statutes confer duties on regulatory authorities, such as the Director General of Fair Trading, to encourage private organisations to prepare and disseminate codes of practice. These 'voluntary' codes are dealt with in section 3.5 on extra-legal sources since they are not legally enforceable in their own right and may rely on non-legal sanctions.

3.3.2A2   Origin

The oldest and no doubt the best known statutory code of practice is the Highway Code. By the Road Traffic Act 1930, section 45, the Minister of Transport was empowered to issue directions for the guidance of road users. Clearly, the statute could not deal with all the details relating to proper conduct on the road, so the code of practice was created. Similarly, the Industrial Relations Act 1971 provided for the issue of an Industrial

Relations Code of Practice by the Secretary of State, covering a wide range of matters such as employment policies, collective bargaining, grievance and disputes procedures. But it was the spate of legislation commencing with the Health and Safety at Work etc. Act 1974, and the Control of Pollution Act 1974, quickly followed by the Employment Protection Act 1975, Sex Discrimination Act 1975 and Race Relations Act 1976 and later, the Employment Act 1980, Child Care Act 1980, Police and Criminal Evidence Act 1985 and Housing Act 1985 which led to the concerns noted in 3.3.2A1. Codes under many of these Acts are likely to feature in your reading as a law student.

3.3.2A3   Structure

Since each code may be designed for a different purpose and addressed to a different audience, including the general public as well as local authority officers, trade union representatives, police officers etc., there is no common structure for statutory codes of practice. However, one feature is common: they are meant to be read by lay people, not lawyers, and so frequently use simple, intelligible language rather than the stilted or obscure language of statutes. They are, therefore, much easier to understand!

3.3.2A4   Publication and general availability

Again, there is no common practice though many, like the Highway Code, are published by Her Majesty's Stationery Office (HMSO). Some, like the codes prepared by the Equal Opportunities Commission for the elimination of discrimination in employment, are published by the organisation which prepared them. The note of guidance on codes of practice (see 3.3.2A1) suggests authorities should consider arranging for sale through HMSO or include the code in a relevant annual report. So, the picture remains rather confused. Many academic law libraries will keep individual copies of the major codes of practice a student will need to consult – the best way to track them down, so long as you know either the correct title or the name of the issuing authority, is through the library's catalogue. If you are not sure of either the title or 'author' try one of the methods outlined in 3.3.2B.

3.3.2A5   Citation

There is no standard form of citation but, for clarity, codes of practice should usually be referred to by their full title, the date of publication (especially if more than one edition or a revision has been published) and the name of the authority which has prepared the code.

3.3.2B   EXPLOITATION

Invaluable assistance in tracing codes of practice can be obtained by using law encyclopaedias. A check of a general encyclopaedia like *Halsbury's Statutes*, either by the title of the Act under which the code was made, or by the subject matter, should lead to an editorial footnote at the appropriate section of the Act, which will give details of the title and issuing authority for the code (follow figures 3.8 and 3.9 on how to use *Halsbury's Statutes*). *Halsbury's* will not reprint the code itself and the summary provided may be very brief, but with the correct title and issuing authority you can now try the library catalogue with more confidence. However, a better strategy is to consult a specialist law encyclopaedia covering the subject area with which the code deals. Specialist subject encyclopaedias (see 3.7) are a valuable resource for they:

(a)   are frequently well and fully indexed making searching for information easier,
(b)   may even bring similar types of publication, such as codes of practice, together in one section,
(c)   are usually published in loose-leaf format and so the information they contain is updated frequently by the publishers – if a revision to a code of practice has been made, it will be included with very little delay.

So, for example, a number of the codes of practice relating to industrial relations law are reprinted complete, with the addition, in some cases, of footnotes by the encyclopaedia editors, in the following specialist titles:

(a)   *Encyclopedia of Labour Relations Law* (published by Sweet & Maxwell).
(b)   *Encyclopaedia of Employment Law and Practice* (published by Professional Publishing).

In addition some textbooks will reprint codes of practice as appendices, and in the area of industrial relations law, one textbook is published in loose-leaf format and includes several codes: *Harvey on Industrial Relations and Employment Law* (published by Butterworths).

For codes of practice in which local authorities may be interested, covering subjects such as housing or control of pollution, the Local Government Library series of specialist encyclopaedias published by Sweet and Maxwell may be of help.

3.3.2C   ELECTRONIC SOURCES

At the time of writing no electronic sources include either the full text or summaries of codes of practice.

3.3.2D   RESEARCH STRATEGIES

See the discussion under 3.3.2B.

3.3.3 By-laws

3.3.3A DESCRIPTION

3.3.3A1 Definition

By-laws are a form of secondary legislation (i.e., detailed rules or regulations) made by a local authority or public authority (such as British Rail or a water authority) under powers given by an Act of Parliament. The by-laws have to be confirmed or approved by the Minister of the government department nominated by Parliament in the Act which grants the power to make the by-laws. By-laws differ from other types of secondary legislation in two ways: first, whilst Parliament defines the content, the responsibility for drawing up the by-law rests with an authority outside central government; secondly, by-laws are not approved by Parliament but by a Minister.

3.3.3A2 Origin

Although by-laws may be made by local or public authorities, it is those made by local authorities which you are more likely to need to be aware of both as a student and later, particularly if you decide to practise in local government law. The discussion which follows therefore concentrates on local authority by-laws.

By-laws existed long before the period of great municipal reform in the early 19th century, but it was the need to tackle the physical and social problems of the rapid growth and expansion of industrial towns and cities that led Parliament to give local authorities powers to make by-laws which had far-reaching effect for 'good rule and government' (Municipal Corporations Act 1835, section 90) and the 'prevention and suppression of nuisances' (Public Health Act 1875, sections 182 to 188), for example. To assist local authorities, the Local Government Board (set up under the Local Government Board Act 1871) began to issue model by-laws, providing guidance on what was likely to be confirmed by the Board and to ensure some degree of uniformity amongst local authorities. However, during the 20th century, despite these models, it was difficult to achieve adequate uniformity and gradually local by-laws were replaced by Ministerial regulations (i.e., statutory instruments). The Local Government Act 1972, which reorganised local government, provided an opportunity for a thorough review of the accumulated mass of 'local' law. As a result each new local authority was required to submit a Private Bill to Parliament incorporating all the powers under Local Acts and by-laws it had inherited from predecessor authorities, and which it wished to retain. Model clauses for the Private Bill were prepared by government departments to give authorities guidance on what was considered acceptable and desirable. Parliament then had the opportunity to scrutinise each Private Bill and amend it as necessary before it became law as a Local Act. Any legislation not included in these Local Acts ceased to have effect. This review therefore considerably tidied up the 'local' statute book and means that the large number of Local Acts dating from the late 1970s and early 1980s entitled '—shire County Council Act' are the *first* place to look when researching by-laws. However, these recent Local Acts are not the only place to look for by-laws, because Parliament has continued to include within Public General Acts powers for local authorities to make local by-laws on a number of matters, for example, the regulation of pleasure boats (Local Government, Planning and Land Act 1980, section 185), and the regulation of acupuncture, tattooing, ear-piercing and electrolysis (Local Government (Miscellaneous Provisions) Act 1982, sections 14 to 16). A list of principal powers to make by-laws is given in Cross and Bailey (1986, pp. 625–31).

3.3.3A3   Structure

There can be variety in the structure of by-laws, but they usually comprise a series of numbered sections, rather similar to an Act.

3.3.3A4   Publication and general availability

According to the Local Government Act 1972, section 236, copies of local authority by-laws must be available for inspection at the offices of the local authority by whom the by-laws were made, and the by-laws should be available for sale to the public at a cost of not more than 20p per copy. Similar requirements may exist for public authority by-laws; for example, copies of the British Railways Board by-laws are available for inspection at station ticket offices.

Academic law libraries are unlikely to stock by-laws made by either local or public authorities, but the larger public libraries may keep copies of those for the local authority in whose area they are situated, possibly as part of the local history collection, if not as part of the reference library.

3.3.3A5   Citation

No generally accepted method of citation exists.

3.3.3B   EXPLOITATION

See 3.3.3A4.

3.3.3C   ELECTRONIC SOURCES

By-laws are not included on electronic databases.

3.3.3D   RESEARCH STRATEGIES

See 3.3.3A2 and 3.3.3A4.

3.4   CASE LAW

3.4A   DESCRIPTION

3.4A1   Definition

There is no official definition of what constitutes a law report, the name given to a single, published decision of the courts. In the plural, the term law reports refers to the publication/s containing collections of decisions. However, to research this important source of law effectively you need to appreciate two basic characteristics of the system which makes law reports available:

(a)   There is no official series of law reports in this jurisdiction – there is no case-law equivalent of the Queen's Printer's copy of an Act, which forms an official, authentic record of what the courts have determined in every case. Law reporting has traditionally been in private hands and, although Her Majesty's Stationery Office (the government printer) is responsible for publishing reports of cases in revenue law (*Reports of Tax Cases, Value Added Tax Tribunal Reports*), immigration law (*Immigration Appeal Reports*) and social security law (decisions of the Social Security Commissioners), the great majority of reports of cases are published by over 20 different, often competing, private publishers;

(b)   whilst the courts hear and decide over 200,000 cases each year in England and Wales alone, only about 2,500 (or 1.25 per cent) are published, or as lawyers say, reported. The rest remain either as unpublished (un-reported) transcripts or go totally unrecorded.

Keep these two points in your mind whenever you research case law and you will be able to make some order of what, at first sight, appears to be a rather complex and bewildering system. In contrast with the other major sources of law, such as Acts and statutory instruments both of which are published by the authority of Parliament, there is no official, authoritative version of all case decisions.

Let us explore some of the implications of these characteristics a little further.

Since there are so many different law report publications, what constitutes an authoritative report? First, it has been a long established but unwritten rule, that to be accepted by a court as authority, the report must have been prepared by and published under the name of a barrister. Some law report publications, such as *The Times, Current Law* and *Estates Gazette* have been criticised in judicial statements from the 1880s down to the 1950s because it appears that even though the reports were compiled or edited by barristers, their names did not appear against the reports. Secondly, whilst there is no official series of law reports, the courts have accorded greater respect and authority to some publications over others. From about 1785 some report publications became recognised as 'authorised' or 'regular'. Their authority stemmed, in part, from the assistance the judges gave the particular reporters in revising oral judgments and providing copies of written notes before publication. During the early 19th century an 'authorised' reporter was attached to each of the higher courts and their reports published in collected volumes under the personal name/s of the reporters, for example, Phillips, *Chancery Reports*, Adolphus and Ellis, *King's Bench Reports*. By 1865 there were 16 individual reporters compiling and publishing 'authorised' reports, as well as a considerable number of barristers producing reports which were not authorised, either issued under their own names or in the columns of the increasing number of law journals. In that year the mantle of these 16 authorised reports passed to a new, single series of reports entitled the *Law Reports*. The series is still active today. The judgments published in this title have been checked by the bench before publication, and because of this greater authority, the rule of 'exclusive citation' has developed, whereby should a case be reported in several publications including the *Law Reports*, the version in the *Law Reports* should be cited to the court and no other. For this reason you may find both in your reading and during lectures that the *Law Reports* are cited most frequently.

However, whilst the *Law Reports* possess great authority they only report around 175 or about 7 per cent of the 2,500 cases published annually. Further, it seems the price of accuracy is delay in publication, and the *Law Reports* frequently take nine months from the date of the decision to the date of publication. Those cases not included in the *Law Reports* are scattered through about 50 different titles of lesser authority. Also, some titles aim to publish brief reports of the latest decisions as quickly as possible. For example, about 10 per cent of all cases reported in *The Times* are reported the day after the judgment was given, but the report, when compared with later versions in other publications, is often very much shortened. Unfortunately, not all reports of cases which appear in *The Times* or other 'advance' series such as *Solicitors' Journal* and *New Law Journal* are selected by other law report publications for full reporting. In 1985, for example, nearly one in eight of the cases published in *The Times* was never printed as a fuller report in another series of reports (Clinch 1989). If barristers rely on these brief versions the authority of their argument can be weakened for, as recently as 1983, Lord Roskill in a House of Lords judgment in *Export Credits Guarantee Department* v *Universal Oil Products Co.* [1983] 1 WLR 399 considered a case briefly and only reported in *Solicitors' Journal* to be 'virtually unreported'.

This brings us to consider the second implication of the way the law reporting system in England and Wales is organised – who selects the cases to be reported and on what criteria?

As strange as it may seem, whilst the courts make decisions on the law they play no part in ensuring those decisions are made available to the profession and public at large. The process of selecting which of the 200,000 or so cases heard in court each year should be reported, and so formally become part of the law of this jurisdiction, is in the hands of the editors of the 50 or so different law report publications currently active. Different series may employ different selection criteria, dependent on the editor's perception of the needs of the market the particular law report publication is intended to serve. For example, some series of reports (such as the *All England Law Reports* or the *Weekly Law Reports*) set out to serve the needs of general practice, whilst others are aimed at particular groups of lawyers (such as *Justice of the Peace Reports* or *Solicitors' Journal*) or compiled on special subjects (such as *Butterworth's Company Law Cases, Family Law Reports* or *Criminal Appeal Reports*). According to Paul Brown (1989), publishing director of Butter-worths, six basic selection criteria are used by the editors of the *All England Law Reports*. A case will be reported if:

(a) it *makes new law* by dealing with a novel situation or by extending the application of existing principles;

(b) it includes a *modern judicial restatement* of established principles;

(c) it *clarifies conflicting decisions* of lower courts;

(d) it *interprets legislation* likely to have a wide application;

(e) it *interprets a commonly found clause*, for example in a contract or will;

(f) it *clarifies an important point of practice or procedure.*

So, for example, cases of narrow specialist interest, such as decisions in intellectual property or criminal sentencing, might fall outside these criteria, and are in fact rarely reported by the *All England Law Reports*, but left to such specialist titles as *Reports of Patent, Design and Trade Mark Cases* and *Criminal Appeal Reports (Sentencing)*, respectively.

But what of those cases which are *not* selected by any law report publication? Before 1980 and the advent of LEXIS, the computerised legal information retrieval service (see appendix 6) which includes thousands of reports in its database, most unreported cases would remain largely undisturbed on court files or the shelves of the Supreme Court library or the files of the private firms of shorthand writers whose employees sat in court taking the judgments down. Assiduous textbook or periodical article writers or exceptionally industrious barristers would occasionally unearth an unreported decision and cite it in support of their argument. The *Report of the Law Reporting Committee* (Lord Chancellor's Department (1940), p. 20) considered that after the law report editors had selected cases for inclusion in their publications, 'What remains is less likely to be a treasure-house than a rubbish heap in which a jewel will rarely, if ever, be discovered'. LEXIS has made the search of the 'rubbish heap' much easier but in 1983 the courts took fright of being 'bombarded' with cases 'which contained no new law', and 'hoped that a good deal of discretion would be used in citing such cases.' (Donaldson MR in *Stanley* v *International Harvester Co. of Great Britain Ltd* (1983) *The Times*, 7 February 1983). Just eight days later the House of Lords, in *Roberts Petroleum Ltd* v *Bernard Kenny Ltd* [1983] 2 AC 192 took a much stronger and unorthodox line in henceforth prohibiting the citation of transcripts of unreported judgments of the Civil Division of the Court Appeal without special leave having been gained to do so. The rulings gave rise to considerable discussion on the use of both unreported cases and online database services, including a cogent review by Nicolas Harrison, then managing director of Butterworth (Telepublishing) Ltd, the firm which markets LEXIS in the United Kingdom (Harrison 1984).

There are two further points to consider: first, do all courts contribute decisions to the body of case law, and secondly, what of those decisions made not in open court, but in the judges' chambers?

Since the operation of the principle of precedent relies on a hierarchical arrangement of courts it might follow that the higher a court is in the structure, the more likely its decisions will be reported. Very little empirical work has been done on this, but the rather limited results available (Clinch 1989 p. 350) appear in part to support this hypothesis. In practice virtually every decision of the House of Lords is reported, and in the single year (1985) studied, over 70 per cent of the decisions of the Court of Appeal (Civil Division) were also reported. A little over a third of the decisions of the Family Division of the High Court, and 29 per cent and 22 per cent of the Queen's Bench and Chancery Divisions respectively were reported, but under 10 per cent of the decisions of the Court of Appeal (Criminal Division) appeared in law reports. In some areas of law such as social welfare, industrial relations, landlord and tenant, immigration, and VAT, tribunals have been created to resolve disputes. Comparatively few of the cases they hear are reported. One particular group of tribunal decisions must be highlighted for it forms a very important part of the law of a specialised area: the decisions of the Social Security Commissioners. Of the 2,000–3,000 decisions made each year, well under 100 are published – the selection of decisions for reporting is made by the Chief Commissioner after consultation with Commissioners. At Crown Court or county court level only a handful of decisions are reported each year (somewhere around one or two in every 10,000 heard). So broadly speaking, the lower the court in the hierarchy the less chance there is of its decisions being available in law reports.

Some cases are heard and determined not in open court but in judges' private rooms or chambers. This practice is most frequently found in divorce-related cases (Pearson 1986). It is traditional that only decisions given in open court may be reported, and there are instances where a judge has heard a case in chambers but decided, because issues or concerns have been raised deserving wider dissemination, to give his judgment in open court (see, for example, *Re Y (A Minor)* [1985] FLR 294, *M* v *Lambeth Borough Council (No. 2)* [1985] FLR 371, *Re PB (A Minor) (Application to Free for Adoption)* [1985] FLR 394 and *Re C (Adoption Application: Legal Aid)* [1985] FLR 441.

As the foregoing discussion shows, the courts have been concerned with two matters: the adequacy of the record and the value of the decision as a precedent. Therefore, a definition of a law report must highlight these essential elements, and the following, by a respected law reporter, expresses it succinctly:

> an adequate record of a judicial decision on a point of law, in a case heard in open court, for subsequent citation as a precedent (Moran 1948 p. 13).

Since there is no official published record of the decisions of the courts, and most law libraries will have access to both reported and, via LEXIS, unreported decisions, when you research case-law sources you will need to ask yourself:

(a)   Is the record of the decision the most authoritative available?
(b)   Is it sufficiently full for the point of law that was decided to be stated clearly and unambiguously?
(c)   Are there alternative and fuller versions of the same case?
(d)   Does the decision, particularly if it is unreported, really extend, clarify or interpret the law, or does it merely restate previously established principles?

3.4.A2   Origin

During your legal studies you will need to refer not only to recent law reports but also decisions made in the 18th and 19th centuries and, perhaps, earlier still. The brief historical survey of the development of law reporting which follows concentrates on those factors which affect the way you research case law of different periods.

3.4A2.1   The Year Books

The medieval equivalent of the law reports are the Year Books. They commence in 1272 and cease in 1535. They were compiled anonymously and were probably intended for the personal use of individual members of the legal profession. They are mainly handwritten in law French, though some were amongst the first books to be available in the new printing technology of the late 15th and early 16th centuries. The individual case reports are very brief and concentrate on the pleadings, (the arguments, claims and counter-claims put forward by either side), and often omit all reference to the judgment. Rarely are Year Books cited in present-day courts and, unless you are studying English legal history, you are unlikely to need to consult them. Modern reprints with English translations alongside have been made during the 19th and 20th centuries, in the Rolls Series, and volumes published by the Selden Society and the Ames Foundation.

3.4A2.2   The nominate reports

After a short break, the period of the nominate reports commences with the publication in 1571 of Edmund Plowden's *Commentaries*. This formative period in law reporting, with collections of cases published under the name of the individual responsible for compiling them (hence the collective term, 'nominate reports'), lasted until the founding of the *Law Reports* in 1865. The earliest collections were never intended for publication, being notes of cases prepared for personal use, and were frequently published posthumously. Up to 1750 very little in the way of a *system* of law reporting may be traced. But in the second half of the 18th century three developments took place which laid the foundations of the system which has evolved to the present:

(a)   the setting of accepted standards in the technique of reporting;
(b)   the appointment of authorised reporters;
(c)   the publication of reports with the minimum of delay.

Between 1765 and 1786 three reporters, James Burrow, Henry Cowper and Sylvester Douglas, established standards for the technique of law reporting and the layout of reports. During the same period, probably after 1782, judges became willing to revise reports of their judgments or even make written copies of them available to particular reporters. The judges also took part in the appointment of a particular reporter to the court. Thus developed the concept of the 'authorised' report, accurate and authentic. If there were two reports of the same case, that of the 'authorised reporter' was taken as 'the deliberate expression of the judge's opinion' (Pollock, 1896, p. 292). The third breakthrough was the reduction in the delay with which reports were published. In 1786 two reporters: Charles Durnford and Edward East began publishing their reports of King's Bench cases 'within a short time after each term' (Durnford and East 1786, preface) – hence the popular name for their publication, '*Term Reports*'. The venture was immediately successful and followed by reporters in other courts. Delay was even further reduced from 1822 onwards with the advent of the monthly publication *Law Journal*, which carried law reports. In 1830 a weekly publication, *The Legal Observer*, commenced, followed in 1837 by *The Jurist* and in 1843, *The Law Times*. This was the age of free trade and the principles also applied in law report publishing: all that was required was a barrister to write the reports of cases he had heard and a publisher willing to print them. The 'authorised reports' accounted for only a small number of the cases reported, and since many of the reporters also carried on business as practising barristers, representing and advising clients, they were often slow to publish and expensive! So a huge industry of competing reports developed – multiple versions of the same case, each trying to undercut the other in terms of the number of cases published and the speed with which they were made available. In 1863 the situation became intolerable and the Bar formed the Council of Law Reporting (later the Incorporated Council of Law Reporting for England and Wales), which began publication of the *Law Reports* in 1865, a series designed to replace the authorised reports, make reports available quickly, and cheaply, but above all, still ensure they were accurate. So, the nominate reports died, but many of the weekly and monthly periodical publications survived; including one to this day: *Solicitors' Journal* (founded 1857).

Over 500 different publications containing law reports were published between 1571 and 1865. Although some libraries will have modest collections of some of these reports in their original, published form, most libraries may have none at all, but either rely on reprint collections, of which there are three, or on a photographically reduced version of the originals. The three reprint series are the *English Reports*, the *Revised Reports* and the *All England Law Reports Reprint*. The *English Reports* are widely found and the most comprehensive set of the three, covering over 170 report titles. They comprise 176 volumes of verbatim reprints of the most significant decisions up to 1865. Two further volumes (177 and 178) are an alphabetical index to the main work, arranged by the names of cases. The *Revised Reports* reprint cases from a selection of about 140 report titles from the period 1785 to 1865 only. Whilst there is quite a large measure of duplication with the *English Reports*, several 19th century report titles are only reprinted in the *Revised Reports*. The third reprint source is the *All England Law Reports Reprint*, quite widely available in law libraries. Published between 1957 and 1968, it reprints a selection of cases from 1558 to 1935, which were considered by the editors still to be of value. The final source for pre-1865 cases is the Readex Microcard Reprint of pre-1865 cases, held by a few libraries. A large number of reports, some not appearing in any of the reprint sources, have been photographically reduced and printed on to thick card. The photographic image can only be read through special viewing equipment which requires some patience and good eyesight to use, and it is virtually impossible to take copies from the images; consequently it is not popular!

3.4A2.3   Modern reports

Two trends evident before 1865 have become more marked since. First, the division of law report publications into the 'general' series, attempting to report cases on points of law of wide interest, and the 'specialist' series, selecting cases of particular interest to lawyers in a discrete practice area. Secondly, the division of law report publications into those which report cases in a brief, edited form, but as rapidly as possible, referred to by some lawyers as 'advance reports' (using terminology from the United States), and those publications which report judgments verbatim but are subject to some delay. The relationship between these two categories is illustrated in figure 3.16.

	Advance	Full-text
General	All subjects. Edited reports.	All subjects. Full reports.
Specialist	Selected subjects. Edited reports.	Selected subjects. Full reports.

Figure 3.16   A typology of modern law reports.

Amongst the 'general' series will be found those like *The Times* newspaper, which publishes brief reports of a very large number of cases, about 10 per cent of which appear the day following the judgment was given. Two other generalist publications, the *Weekly Law Reports* and the *All England Law Reports*, normally publish full-text reports but, on average, about five months after the judgments were handed down. The most highly respected series of law reports, the *Law Reports*, the text of which is checked by the judges before publication and also includes summaries of the arguments of counsel, takes between 10 and 14 months, on average, to report cases. A similar pattern will be found amongst the specialist reports: in criminal law, for example, *Criminal Law Review* publishes brief reports of cases but with a delay of about four and a half months on average, whilst *Criminal Appeal Reports* prints the full text but takes nearly nine months on average.

The problem for the legal researcher is that because law reporting is presently in the hands of over 20 different publishers, each employing different criteria for the selection of cases (see 3.4A1), it does *not* follow that every briefly reported case will be reported eventually in one of the full text services. In one study of law reporting (Clinch 1989) about a third of all cases reported during a selected year were reported only once, and 129 or 16 per cent of these appeared in *The Times*. On the other hand, there is also a very high degree of duplication of reports between the 50 or more titles currently published: in the same study nearly 25 per cent of all cases were reported in between five and 10 different law report titles, and one case had the dubious distinction of being printed in 15 different publications!

Add to these difficulties the question of unreported decisions available on electronic databases, such as LEXIS (explored in 3.4A1), and it becomes even more apparent why case law research causes students so much difficulty, and why it is important to ask yourself the questions posed at the end of 3.4A1 when you are gathering material to answer a legal problem.

3.4A3   Structure

Since there are so many law report publishers attempting to serve the differing needs of the profession, it is not surprising that there is a variety in both the different pieces of information (or elements) each publication includes in its reports of cases, and the order in which they are presented. Fifteen different elements are found in law reports of the English jurisdiction but no report publication includes them all. The basic elements found in virtually all modern law reports are marked * in the list which follows. The illustration in figure 3.17 is an extract from a case taken from the *All England Law Reports*.

(a)   *Names of parties*.* Individual cases are identified and referred to by the names of the parties involved. In civil actions the name of the person bringing the case (the plaintiff) is given first, followed by the name of the defendant; for example, *Smith* v *Jones*. The 'v' separating the parties means 'versus' but when spoken becomes 'and': 'Smith and Jones'. In criminal actions, the single letter '*R*' (standing for the Latin words *Rex* or *Regina* (King or Queen)) comes first, indicating the State's role as prosecutor; the accused person, the defendant, is named after the 'v', for example, '*R* v *Smith*'. However, when spoken, a criminal case name becomes 'the Crown against Smith'. Unfortunately, there are differences in the practice of citing criminal cases, and you may find cases referred to in law reports and textbooks with the 'R v' omitted, and cited merely as, for example, 'Smith'.

These simple, straightforward rules are subject, however, to a number of variations:

(i)   In shipping cases the case name is frequently subtitled with the name of the ship involved and this shorthand case title is sufficient on most occasions to find the case in textbooks and *Citators*. So, for example, *Overseas Tankship (UK) Ltd* v *Morts Dock and Engineering Co. Ltd (The Wagon Mound)* [1961] AC 388 may be referred to simply as: *The Wagon Mound*.

(ii)   In some property and family cases the report may be headed either '*In re Smith*' or in modern cases '*Re Smith*'. *Re* means 'in the matter of' or 'concerning'. Similarly, some cases may be titled '*Ex parte Smith*' meaning that Smith is the name of the party on whose application the case is heard. In some actions the identity of the people involved is protected by using only the initial letters: '*In re S*', '*Ex parte S*' or '*S* v *J*'.

(iii) Where the court is being asked to judicially review the administrative actions of, for example, a government department, or a lower court, the case title is usually in the form, '*R* v *Secretary of State for the Environment, ex parte Jones*'.

(iv) Some criminal prosecutions may be commenced by one of the government's law officers: the Attorney-General or the Director of Public Prosecutions. Where this occurs the official's title (sometimes abbreviated to A-G or DPP) appears in place of the Crown as prosecutor, for example:

Attorney-General v *British Broadcasting Corporation*
Director of Public Prosecutions v *Goodchild.*

Occasionally, the Attorney-General may obtain the opinion of the Court of Appeal on a point of law. The title in such cases is given as, for example, *Attorney-General's Reference (No. 2 of 1983).*

Further details of these and some archaic forms of case title you may come across in Year Books and other older reports are given in: University of London, Institute of Advanced Legal Studies, *Manual of Legal Citations*, part 1, The British Isles, (London: The University, 1959), pp. 14–24.

It might be thought that the names of parties to an action would be a good enough identifier for the researcher trying to trace a case in indexes. Unfortunately this is not always so, because there appear to be wide variations in the practice of law reporters identifying parties to an action or, more technically speaking, formulating the style of cause to an action. The House of Lords recognised the problem as long ago as 1974, and issued a *Practice Direction* [1974] 1 WLR 305, requiring the title of cases brought before it to carry the same title as that used in the court which first heard the case. Other courts have not made any similar ruling. Actual examples of some of the most common difficulties encountered are noted below, but a fuller list, based on a large-scale study is given in Clinch (1990).

(i) Local authority names:

Westminster City Council v *British Waterways Board*
also styled as
City of Westminster v *British Waterways Board.*

Newham London Borough v *Ward*
also styled as
London Borough of Newham v Ward

Cahalne v *London Borough of Croydon*
also styled as
Cahalne v *Croydon LBC*

Bentley-Stevens v Jones and others

CHANCERY DIVISION

PLOWMAN J

15th, 18th MARCH 1974

Company — Director — Removal — Resolution to remove director — Interlocutory injunction to restrain company acting on resolution — Quasi-partnership — Irregularity in convening meeting — Irregularity capable of being cured by going through proper processess — Whether director entitled to interlocutory injunction.

The defendant company was a wholly-owned subsidiary of another company, H Ltd, of which the plaintiff and the first and second defendants, J and H, were the three directors. They were also three of the four directors of the defendant company. J and H held between them 58 per cent of the issued share capital of H Ltd. They wished to remove the plaintiff from the board of the defendant company, under s 184 of the Companies Act 1948, and on 27th January 1974 J sent the plaintiff a letter notifying him of a board meeting of H Ltd to be held the next morning at which it was to be resolved that H Ltd should convene an extraordinary general meeting of the defendant company for the purpose of removing the plaintiff from the board. The plaintiff did not receive the letter until after (i) J and H had met and passed the resolution, (ii) H Ltd had requisitioned the extraordinary general meeting and (iii) J, as a director of the defendant company, had called an extraordinary general meeting of that company for 26th February. The notice convening that meeting purported to be given by order of the board but no board meeting of the company was held. The extraordinary general meeting was held on 26th February and the votes of H Ltd were cast in favour of removing the plaintiff from the board. The plaintiff brought an action against the defendants and applied for an interlocutory injunction restraining them from acting on the resolution on 26th February.

Held — The plaintiff was not entitled to an interlocutory injunction for the following reasons—
    (i) The court would not grant an interlocutory injunction in respect of irregularities which could be cured by going through the proper processes. If, for example, the proceedings that followed the board meeting of 28th January were invalid because proper notice had not been given, the invalidity could be cured by the giving of a valid notice (see p 655 *f* to *h*, post); dictum of Lindley LJ in *Browne v La Trinidad* (1887) 37 Ch D at 17 applied.
    (ii) Assuming that the plaintiff was a quasi-partner he could still be expelled; the defendant company had a statutory right to remove him from its board and his only remedy was to apply for a winding-up order on the ground that it was just and equitable for the court to make such an order (see p 655 *f* and *j*, post); *Ebrahimi v Westbourne Galleries Ltd* [1972] 2 All ER 492 explained.

Notes
For convening of meetings of a company, see 7 Halsbury's Laws (4th Edn) 330-334, paras 560-566; and for cases on the validation and waiver or irregular notice, see 9 Digest (Repl) 604, 4000-4004.
    For the Companies Act 1948, s 184, see 5 Halsbury's Statutes (3rd Edn) 255.

Cases referred to in judgment
Browne v La Trinidad (1887) 37 Ch D 1, 57 LJCh 292, 58 LT 137, CA, 9 Digest (Repl) 604, 4003.
Ebrahimi v Westbourne Galleries Ltd [1972] 2 All ER 492, [1973] AC 360, [1972] 2 WLR 1289, HL.

(9) **Case also cited**   *a*
   Bainbridge v Smith (1889) 41 Ch D 462, CA.

(10) **Motion**
   By notice of motion dated 26th February 1974 Charles Edward Bentley-Stevens, the
   plaintiff in an action commenced by writ issued on 26th February 1974 against the
   defendants, (1) D Gareth Jones, (2) Gerald S J Hyam and (3) Sloane Nursing Home *b*
   Ltd, sought an order restraining the defendants and each of them until the trial of the
   action or further order from acting on the resolution purported to have been passed by
   the defendant company at a purported extraordinary general meeting thereof held at
   9.30 am on 26th February 1974 removing the plaintiff as a director of the defendant
   company. The facts are set out in the judgment.

                                                                                           c
(11) *Allan Heyman QC* and *M K I Kennedy* for the plaintiff.
   Ralph Instone for the defendants.

(12) **PLOWMAN J**. The notice of motion which is before me asks for an order on behalf of
   the plaintiff—
                                                                                           d
      'restraining the Defendants and each of them until the trial of the action or further
      order from acting upon the resolution purported to have been passed by the
      Defendant Company at a purported Extraordinary General Meeting thereof held at
      9.30 a.m. on the 26th February 1974 removing the Plaintiff as a Director of the
      Defendant Company.'

      . . .

      For these reasons the plaintiff is not, in my judgment, entitled to the relief which he
   seeks on this motion, and I must dismiss it.
                                                                                           e
   Motion dismissed.

(13) Solicitors: *A Kramer & Co* (for the plaintiff); *Norton, Rose, Botterell & Roche* (for the
   defendants).
(14)   Jacqueline Metcalfe Barrister.

(1) Names of Parties (a) (2) Name of Court (c) (3) Name of Judge (d)
(4) Date/s of hearing and judgment (e) (5) Catchwords (f)
(6) Headnote (g) (7) Commentary or notes (h) (8) List of cases cited in
judgment (i) (9) List of other cases cited in argument (j) (10) Details of
proceedings (k) (11) Names of counsel (l) (12) Judgment (n) (13) Names
of solicitors (l) (14) Name of law reporter (o)

(Letters in parentheses refer to paragraphs in the text where the elements of a
report are discussed.)

Figure 3.17   A law report.

(ii)   Rotation of names of parties:
 (1)   Single actions:
Cornish v *Midland Bank*
also styled as
Midland Bank plc v *Cornish*

(this was an appeal in an action in which Cornish was the plaintiff, reported under different styles).
 (2)   Consolidated appeals:
Carver v *Duncan* and *Bosanquet* v *Allen*

(consolidated appeals, also reported with *Bosanquet* v *Allen* first).

 (iii)   Anonymity lost!

L v *K*
also styled as
Kane v *Littlefair*

AR v *Avon County Council*
also styled as
Ashley-Rogers v *Avon County Council*

 (iv)   Entirely different names!

Re C
also styled as
Re a Baby

Council of Civil Service Unions v *Minister for the Civil Service*
also styled as
R v *Secretary of State for the Foreign and Commonwealth Office, ex parte the Council for Civil Service Unions*

Frampton and another (Trustees of Worthing Rugby Football Club) v *Inland Revenue Commissioners*
also styled as
Worthing Rugby Football Club v *Commissioners of Inland Revenue*

Fox v *Chief Constable of Gwent*
also styled as
R v *Fox*

Anderton v *Ryan*
also styled as
Chief Constable for Greater Manchester v *Ryan*

In every instance the variations in styles of cause would result in the entries for these cases in an index falling at quite different parts of the alphabetical sequence. In a few cases the form of an alternative style of cause can be guessed from elements in the one available, but in most cases, unless the index is well constructed and includes entries under both styles, a researcher could draw a blank. If you are unsure whether the case you have found under an alternative style of cause is the same as the one you require, check whether the court in which it was heard and the dates of hearing and/or judgment accord with information you may have.

(b) *Official court roll or docket number.* Only a few of the publications of the Incorporated Council of Law Reporting provide this information: *Chancery, Queen's Bench* and *Weekly Law Reports,* for example.

(c) *Name of the court in which the case was heard.** This is now a universal and very important feature of case reports, for without this information a system of precedent, which depends on a hierarchical court structure, cannot exist.

(d) *Names of the judges, with abbreviations for their rank.** Early law reports omit this detail. The status and rank of judges can influence the weight of the decision.

(e) *Date/s of hearing and judgment.** Without this information, often lacking in early law reports, it is virtually impossible for a system of precedent to develop.

(f) *Catchwords.* They provide a succinct summary of the subject of the decision. There can be several paragraphs of catchwords, each dealing with a different issue considered in the case. The catchwords are compiled by the law reporter and have no official standing with the court. Some law reports, such as *Housing Law Reports, New Law Journal* and *Trading Law Reports,* do not provide them.

(g) *Headnote.* The headnote is a summary of the facts of the case, the questions of law and finally, after the word 'Held' frequently printed in a bold type, the decision of the court. In the USA a headnote is called a 'syllabus'. Like the catchwords, it is compiled by the law reporter and although it is a useful guide to the main issues, it should not be relied on as a sole source of information about the case. Read the whole report. Some law reports, such as *Building Law Reports, Criminal Law Review* and *Estates Gazette,* do not provide headnotes.

(h) *Commentary or notes.* A minority of law reports, all specialist, provide a commentary to place a particular case in context. *All England Law Reports* provide notes referring to Butterworths' other publications, *Halsbury's Laws* and *Halsbury's Statutes of England,* and *The Digest,* where further information on the subject may be found.

(i) *List of cases cited in judgment.* Quite a few law reports provide this list, and helpfully provide a number of alternative citations for each case, so that finding reports of these cases is made much easier.

(j) *List of other cases cited in argument.* This is used to check that relevant cases were cited to the court even if they were not referred to in the judgment.

(k) *Details of the proceedings.* This note, compiled by the law reporter, gives a short history of the case.

(l)   *Names of counsel and solicitors.* Omitted from many specialist reports, such as *Criminal Appeal Reports (Sentencing), Housing Law Reports.*

(m)   *Argument.* Only the *Law Reports* and, in a minority of cases, *Reports of Tax Cases,* give a résumé of the arguments of counsel.

(n)   *Judgement.** All law reports give details of the judgment of the court (called in the House of Lords, individual 'opinions'), but the fullness of the report varies considerably between different law report publications. As a student learning the law you should, whenever possible, use full-text reports rather than brief-note versions. The list below shows the general-coverage law reports divided into full-text and brief note categories.

Full-text	Brief-note
All England Law Reports	All newspaper law reports
Appeal Cases	Law Society's Gazette
Chancery	New Law Journal
Family	
Queen's Bench	Solicitors' Journal
Weekly Law Reports	

(o)   *Name of reporter.* May be given as a full name or just initials, most frequently at the end of the individual case report.

The foregoing description of the structure of a law report does not apply to the specialised decisions of the Social Security Commissioners. Initially, these decisions are published as *individual* case reports, not collections, by Her Majesty's Stationery Office. They do not carry the names of parties. In most other respects, however, there are similarities in the structure of the report.

3.4A4   Publication and general availability

Most academic libraries where law is taught to degree level will have at least one set of each of the full-text general-coverage modern law reports, and some, if not all, of the brief-note general reports. They will subscribe to a selection of the 40 or more specialist law report publications, depending on the subjects taught.

As for older law reports, you should find academic law libraries will keep a set of the *English Reports* (1220–1865) or at least the *All England Law Reports Reprint* (major cases 1558–1935). Some of the larger academic libraries will also have a selection of the nominate reports in their original form, and copies of some of the defunct Victorian weekly periodicals which published law reports, such as *Law Journal Reports* and *Law Times Reports.*

Unreported cases are obviously more difficult to trace. A useful article by Cole (1988) gives details. The computerised legal information retrieval service LEXIS (see appendix 6) contains, since 1 January 1980, the transcripts of English unreported cases from the House of Lords, Privy Council and Court of Appeal (Civil Division), along with selected decisions of the High Court and some tribunals.

Some libraries may have purchased the set of over 2,000 microfiche of the transcripts of 13,613 Court of Appeal (Civil Division) judgments (1951–80), published by HMSO in 1985 indexed by plaintiff, defendant and judge. Unfortunately there is no subject index to this huge collection.

Public libraries do not normally keep or subscribe to law report publications, but it is worth checking at the central public library of your nearest city.

3.4A5   Citation

The majority of the information given in this subsection applies to all reports of cases. However, the decisions of Social Security Commissioners are cited quite differently and a note on this is provided in 3.4A5.2.

3.4A5.1   General practice

Cases are referred to by the names of parties to the action (see 3.4A3). In addition, because there may be several versions of a case reported, the case name is followed by a sequence of numbers and letters which identify where the report is published. Here is how the case illustrated in figure 3.17 would be cited:

Bentley-Stevens v *Jones* [1974] 2 All ER 653.

The citation comprises four elements: a date, a volume number, an abbreviation for the title of the publication in which the case is published, and the page number. This apparently simple system of reference is qualified by a number of conventions:

(a)   *The date* is the year in which the case was *reported* and is given in square brackets. If, however, the publication in which the case is reported is identified by volume numbers running sequentially from the first volume to the present, then the date will be the year the judgment was *given* and will be printed in round brackets (parentheses).
For example:

(1986) 130 *SJ* 785
(1986) 83 *LSGaz* 2919.

(b)   *The volume number:* if the date preceding is given in square brackets and the publication is issued in more than one volume during that year, then a volume number will be given. Some law reports are published in only one volume each year so the volume number is omitted. If the date preceding is given in round brackets, the volume number – not the date – is what you should be looking for on the spine or on the cover of the law report publication. A case may have been judged one year but reported the next; a date in round brackets indicates this is information *not* relevant to finding the case in the particular law report publication cited.

(c)   *Abbreviations* for the names of many law publications abound. Although many publishers of modern law reports give details of the preferred style of citing their law reports (a note will usually be found on the title page or introductory pages near to it), hybrid abbreviations are in common use.

For example, the *All England Law Reports*, properly abbreviated by All ER may be found cited as AELR or AER or All Eng. The problem is even worse with old reports: *Railway and Canal Cases* (published 1840–55) has 24 different citation abbreviations attributed to it! Confusion can also arise amongst the nominate reports where reporters with commonly occurring surnames are cited without the inclusion of forenames or initials. Sometimes an abbreviation may be too concise to distinguish between different series, for example, B & A could refer to Barnewell & Adolphus or Barnewell & Alderson or Barron & Arnold or Barron & Austin. Sometimes references to pre-1865 cases do not include the abbreviation of the original series of reports in which they were published, but the abbreviation to the reprint collection, such as the *English Reports* (ER) instead (see 3.4A2.2, above).

However, help in expanding fully the abbreviation of the title of the law report, is available in the following publications:

(a)   Raistrick, D., *Index to Legal Citations and Abbreviations* (London: Professional Books, 1981). (This is the most comprehensive of all the indexes here listed.)

(b)   *Guide to Law Reports and Statutes*, 3rd ed., (London: Sweet & Maxwell, 1959).

(c)   Osborn, P.G., *Concise Law Dictionary*, 7th ed., revised by Roger Bird (London: Sweet & Maxwell, 1983).

(d)   University of London, Institute of Advanced Legal Studies, *Manual of Legal Citations*, part 1, The British Isles (London: The University, 1959).

(e)   *Halsbury's Laws of England*, vol. 1 (London: Butterworths).

(f)   *The Digest*, vol. 1(1) (London: Butterworths).

(g)   *Current Law Case Citator*, (London: Sweet & Maxwell), any issue.

(h)   *Legal Journals Index*, (Hebden Bridge: Legal Information Resources Ltd), any issue.

(d)   *the page number* refers to the page on which the case begins. Sometimes in periodicals and textbooks, authors wish to draw attention to a later section of the report whilst still giving the proper form of citation for the case. This is achieved by giving the number of the first page of the report followed by the word 'at' and then the page number of the particular section to which attention is drawn, for example:

Fox v *P.G. Wellfair Ltd* [1981] 1 Lloyd's Rep 514 at p. 521

This citation practice is peculiar to law; in other subjects references would be given to the page where the particular text of interest is given, and would not include the number of the first page in the chapter.

3.4A5.2   *Decisions of the Social Security Commissioners*

The decisions of the Social Security Commissioners differ from all other series of law reports in the form of citation they use. The names of parties are not given in the report at all. Anonymity is preserved as far as possible. The decisions are referred to by a system of letters and numbers. Reported decisions carry the letter R followed, in brackets, by letters indicating within which of the benefit series of commissioners' decisions the case falls. The full list of series (as presently published) is as follows:

R (A) Attendance allowance
R (F) Child benefit
R (FIS) Family income supplement
R (G) General – miscellaneous: maternity benefit, widow's benefit, death grant etc.
R (I) Industrial injuries benefit
R (IS) Income supplement
R (M) Mobility allowance
R (P) Retirement pensions
R (S) Sickness and invalidity benefit
R (SB) Supplementary benefit
R (SSP) Statutory sick pay
R (U) Unemployment benefit.

The citation of unpublished decisions is prefaced by C rather than R, followed by letters not in brackets, indicating the benefit series. Within each series, whether reported or not, decisions are cited by the report number and the year. So, for example, R (S) 2/82 Incapacity for work, is the second reported decision in the sickness and invalidity benefit series for 1982, while CS 69/58 Incapacity for work, is the 69th unreported decision in the sickness and invalidity benefit series for 1958. This system of citation operates for all reported decisions since the beginning of 1951. Prior to that date decisions which become reported retained their original decision number on publication with the addition of the suffix 'KL' (Key Law). As a result reported decisions for the years 1948 to 1950 are not consecutively numbered. In addition some decisions given up to the end of January 1950 bear the suffix 'K' which indicates that the decision was of limited value and did not establish any new principle of law.

Since the beginning of 1987, revisions have been made to the way in which the commissioners make decisions available. Decisions which are of more general significance are 'starred' – these are the decisions the commissioners think should be published. Decisions which are not starred should remain unreported. A starred case prior to publication is cited in the same manner as illustrated above, except that the year is given in full, e.g., CS 2/1982. On being published this decision would become R (S) 2/82. If, however, it was not starred then it would be cited as CS 2/82.

Starred and unreported decisions can be inspected, and copies made on payment, at the London and Edinburgh offices of the Social Security Commissioners.

3.4B EXPLOITATION

There are four different types of publication which will help you find cases:

(a)   indexes to law reports
(b)   indexes with brief summaries of cases
(c)   *Citators*
(d)   commentaries.

3.4B1   *Indexes*

3.4B1.1   *Individual law report publications*

Some individual law report publications publish not only annual indexes but also indexes to the cases they have reported over much longer periods of time. The *All England Law Reports* publishes a *Consolidated Tables and Index* covering the period from 1936 to the present, but it only indexes the 300 to 400 cases reported each year in the *All England Law Reports*. The *Law Reports* has published an index since it commenced in 1865, but it is the set of 'red books' published since 1951, each covering up to a ten-year period, supplemented by 'pink books' published quarterly, which is of the most use in present-day research. Not only do these volumes index the *Law Reports* themselves but also a number of other law report publications such as the *Weekly Law Reports, All England Law Reports, Industrial Cases Reports, Knight's Local Government Reports, Tax Cases, Lloyd's Law Reports, Criminal Appeal Reports* and *Road Traffic Reports*. Each red or pink book includes up to nine separate indexes, the main ones being an alphabetical list by the name of the case, to all those cases reported in these publications, with citations to where the report may be found. An alphabetical subject index with a paragraph of catchwords for each case, and indexes of statutes and cases considered by the courts in these cases, are also included.

The index to the *Law Reports* is a valuable starting-point for research on cases in the absence of the more sophisticated publications (see later parts of this sub-section) which are updated regularly and contain more substantial summaries of cases or commentary.

Many textbooks include, at the beginning of the publication, tables of cases discussed in the work and can be a valuable starting-point for research on a subject.

3.4B1.2   **Legal Journals Index**

First published in 1986 and issued monthly since, *Legal Journals Index* (LJI) is an index to the contents of over 160 legal periodicals published in the UK, including journals such as *New Law Journal, Solicitors' Journal* and *Law Society's Gazette*, which include brief reports of cases on a wide range of subjects, and *Criminal Law Review, Family Law* and *Construction Law Journal* which carry brief reports of cases of specialist interest. There are five separate indexes in each monthly issue of LJI, including a subject index and a list of cases by name. An advantage of LJI is that not only does it include references to where a case was originally reported in one of these periodical titles, but also provides references to articles and case notes (i.e., commentary on the cases) appearing in any of the 160 or more titles indexed. LJI is compiled and published with speed, so it is useful for tracing recent cases and comment. Monthly issues are cumulated quarterly and then, in turn, annually, to make searching over a long period of time easier.

3.4B2 Indexes with summaries

3.4B2.1 Daily Law Reports Index

Daily Law Reports Index began publication in 1988 and is issued fortnightly in loose parts. These parts are replaced every quarter by a bound volume, which in turn is replaced shortly after the end of each calendar year, by a further bound volume. It indexes the 1,500 or so cases reported annually in the daily newspapers, including *The Times, Financial Times, Independent, Guardian* and *Daily Telegraph*. The index is in four parts: a case index, in which entries are arranged in alphabetical order by the name of the case, with details of which newspapers carried a report, plus an abstract or summary of the facts and decision; a keyword index, which lists relevant cases under subject headings; a legislation index, which lists statutes which have been considered by the courts in the cases indexed; and, finally, a case report index, which appears in the quarterly cumulation and lists cases alphabetically by their title, with details of where they have been subsequently fully reported in the main general series of law reports, such as the *Law Reports, All England Law Reports* and *Weekly Law Reports*.

The value of this publication is the speed with which it indexes recent decisions and the full and helpful subject indexing, making tracing a recent decision, perhaps only partly remembered from an aside by a lecturer or a news item on TV, much easier to achieve. However, it is worth pointing out that the index covers only those law reports in the newspapers which are accredited to a barrister, and does not list 'news reports' of court cases compiled by journalists.

3.4B2.2 Current Law Monthly Digest

Current Law commenced in 1947 and provides a monthly digest or summary of changes in the law. The summaries are arranged under broad subject headings and include details of recent cases as well as many other sources of legal information. It digests cases from most series of law reports, but is very selective amongst the briefer reports which appear in the daily newspapers or law journals. It is neither as up to date nor has it as wide a coverage of the brief reports as *Daily Law Reports Index* or *Legal Journals Index*. Towards the back of each monthly issue are two indexes, one a cumulative table of cases summarised in the publication so far during the calendar year, arranged alphabetically by case name; the other index is a cumulative index to subjects. In both indexes the reference against each entry refers to the monthly issue and paragraph at which a brief summary of the case will be found.

During the summer of each year, the *Current Law Yearbook* for the previous calendar year is published, and cumulates the monthly parts into single sequences. The case summaries are edited in the light of events which may have occurred since the case was noted in a monthly issue, and arranged in a single sequence rather than 12 separate ones. The table of cases summarised is given at the *front* and the index to subjects at the *back* of the *Yearbook*. The references in both indexes against each entry refer to the paragraph in the *Yearbook* where the case summary is to be found.

The organisation of *Current Law Yearbook* is not entirely straightforward. The summaries for the first five years, the period 1947–51, are reprinted in a very thick single volume entitled *Current Law Consolidation* volume. At five-year intervals since then, up to and including the *Yearbook* for 1971, individual issues have been designated 'Master Volume', and are marked as such on the spine. These thicker volumes for 1956, 1961, 1966 and 1971 cumulate, in a single sequence, all the summaries for the preceeding four *Yearbooks* and the monthly parts of the fifth year. However, by 1976 so much material was being summarised in *Current Law* that only the subject index at the back of the *Yearbook* was cumulated, and this covers the period 1947 to 1976. The 1986 *Yearbook* index covers the period 1972 to 1986 and the latest volume presently available (1990), 1986 to 1990.

This arrangement means that to carry out a thorough search of *Current Law Yearbook* from 1947 to date requires the use of the indexes at the back of the volumes for 1976, 1986 and the latest annual volume. The lack of a single, cumulated index covering the whole period is a handicap, and use of *Current Law Yearbook* for case research over long periods of time can be laborious.

There are two further drawbacks to using *Current Law Monthly Digest* and *Current Law Yearbook* to research cases:

(a)   The subject terms used are frequently rather broad so it is possible to end up looking at a large number of references to cases which do not cover the specific topic in which you are interested.

(b)   The subject index refers not only to summaries of cases, but also all the summaries of Acts and statutory instruments as well. References to cases are not specially or separately indicated in the subject index so, again, you can be led to summaries which are irrelevant to your research needs.

Current Law Monthly Digest's strength, however, is in keeping regular readers of the monthly issues up to date with new legal developments, a technique covered in more detail in chapter 5.

References in the indexes of *Current Law Yearbook* are of two types. Volumes which cover the period 1947–51 may contain against index entries a series of numbers without a slash dividing them, such as 3588 or 11062. These are references to the paragraph numbers of summaries in the very thick *Current Law Consolidation* volume. Most references, however, will be of the second form, a series of numbers separated by a slash such as 56/2302 or 61/5914 or 71/7837. The two numbers in front of the slash indicate the year of the *Current Law Yearbook* referred to (1956, 1961, 1971), followed by the paragraph number where relevant information within that *Yearbook* will be found.

3.4B2.3   *The Digest*

The first edition of *The Digest* (it was known until recently as *The English and Empire Digest*) was published in 47 volumes between 1919 and 1932. Since then it has been replaced by a second edition, known as the blue band edition because of the coloured band on the spine, and is now into a third edition, known as the green band edition. The current edition is in about 60 volumes which divide into six parts, see figure 3.18.

MAIN VOLUMES	CONTINUATION VOLUMES	CUMULATIVE SUPPLEMENT
Over 50 volumes containing summaries of over 250,000 cases drawn from over 1,000 different series of law reports.	Occasionally published bound volumes containing summaries of recent cases not included in Main Volumes.	Annual bound volume containing summaries of recent cases not included in Main or Continuation Volumes.
CONSOLIDATED TABLE OF CASES	CONSOLIDATED INDEX	
Alphabetical list of cases summarised in Main and Continuation Volumes.	Subject index.	

Figure 3.18   Structure of *The Digest* (formerly *The English & Empire Digest*).

(a)   *Main Volumes.* The largest part of *The Digest* comprises over 50 Main Volumes which provide short summaries of the whole case law of England, together with a selection of cases from the courts of Scotland, Ireland, Canada, Australia, New Zealand and other British Commonwealth countries. The summaries are arranged within a very detailed subject classification which, as far as possible, follows the subject arrangement in *Halsbury's Laws of England* (see 3.4B4). Each subject title, and several may appear in a single volume, begins with a table of contents or a synopsis showing how the cases are arranged. Then follow case summaries arranged under each subject heading and subheading in chronological order. Immediately following each major heading, cross-references are provided to *Halsbury's Statutes of England* (3.2.2B2.3.1) and *Halsbury's Laws of England* (3.4B4). English cases are summarised first under each heading and are printed in ordinary size type, cases from other jurisdictions are printed in a smaller type following the English ones. Each individual case summary ends with a citation to where the case was originally published in law reports. Where appropriate, following the case summary and citation, details are provided of subsequent decisions of the courts in which an opinion on the earlier case has been given. This concise history of judicial comment on the original decision is a valuable feature of *The Digest*.

When the law on a subject has changed considerably since the Main Volume was originally published, the publishers produce a so-called reissue volume which replaces the out-of-date original volume. The 'reissue volume' incorporates summaries of new cases as well as retaining relevant older cases. In some subjects, so many changes have occurred since the original Main

Volumes began to appear from 1971 onwards, that even the first reissue volumes have been replaced by second reissue volumes. If a volume has been reissued the word 'reissue' appears on the spine, and if it is a second or subsequent reissue, the word 'reissue' is preceded by 2nd, 3rd etc.

(b) *Continuation Volumes.* The Continuation Volumes include summaries of recent cases, and decisions affecting earlier cases, which have occurred since the Main Volumes were published. The summaries are arranged under appropriate subject headings corresponding to those used in the Main Volumes. An additional Continuation Volume is published every three or four years.

(c) *Cumulative Supplement.* This bound volume is published annually and contains summaries of the most recent cases, and indicates where amendments to the text of the Main Volumes have occurred. The Cumulative Supplement is usually up to date to 1 November of the year before publication.

(d) *Consolidated Table of Cases.* These volumes are a list of cases included in *The Digest*, arranged in alphabetical order by the names of parties. The reference given against each entry is to the Main Volume number and subject heading (given in an abbreviated form) within that volume where the case will be found. To find the precise location of the summary for the case in which you are interested you will need to look up the case name again in the list of cases at the front of that particular Main Volume. Depending on the age of that Main Volume, you will be referred either to a page number, or in more recently published volumes, a case summary number.

(e) *Consolidated Index.* This single volume is a subject index to the whole of *The Digest*. It is probably the most frequent point at which to start research using *The Digest*. It is an alphabetical list of subjects against each of which is the Main Volume number, the subject heading (in abbreviated form) and the relevant case summary numbers. Because of the frequency with which Main Volumes are reissued with extra, new case summaries, there are always times when some of the summary numbers in the Consolidated Index refer to superceded Main Volumes and the index and summary numbers do not match. If this occurs, carefully follow the instructions given below on using *The Digest*.

Using *The Digest*

There are three different ways in which research can be carried out using *The Digest*; the steps to follow are given in figure 3.19: (a) search by subject, a general review of a wide subject area; (b) search by subject, a highly specific subject enquiry; (c) search by case name. The last search method should be used when you have an incomplete or incorrect citation to a case, and you have been unable to trace the case in the *Current Law Case Citators* (see 3.4B3). *Current Law Case Citators* contain references to English cases reported from 1947 onwards and major pre-1947 cases cited since then. *The Digest*, on the other hand, is valuable for tracing citations to less well known, pre-1947 English cases and cases from outside the English jurisdiction.

(a) *Search by Subject* — a general review of a wide subject area.

Consult list of Main Volume titles at front
of Cumulative Supplement.
↓
Consult Main Volume indicated; use contents
pages of that volume to discover subject
arrangement and page numbers.
↓
Consult Continuation Volumes and
Cumulative Supplement for up-dating material.

(b) *Search by Subject* — a highly specific subject enquiry.

Consult Consolidated Index for relevant
Main Volume number, subject and case numbers.
↓
Consult contents pages at front of
Consolidated Index to see from which issue of the
Main Volume the index you require has been compiled.
↓
Consult Main Volume, check spine to see it is same
issue as used to compile the Consolidated Index. If it is,
look up subject and case numbers. If it is not, use
Reference Adaptor at back of Main Volume to
convert old case numbers to re-issue case numbers.
Take care to use the correct Reference Adaptor —
there are often two: one for English cases, one for
other jurisdictions. Look up subject and case numbers
in body of Main Volume.
↓
Consult Cumulative Supplement for up-dating
material and, if necessary, Continuation Volumes,
guided to them by entries in Cumulative Supplement
(noted as: See Continuation Vol, followed by the volume letter).

(c) *Search by case name*

Consult Consolidated Table of Cases
for volume number and subject.
↓
Consult case name index at front of
relevant Main Volume.
↓
Consult Continuation Volumes and
Cumulative Supplement for up-dating material.

Figure 3.19   Step by step research using *The Digest*.

Here are some points to note when using *The Digest*:

(a)   Main volumes are revised and reissued when the law they contain is out-of-date. However, there can be a gap between the publication of a reissue Main Volume and an up-to-date Consolidated Index to the whole set. So it is important to check which issue of the Main Volume has been used from which to compile the index. This can be done by comparing (a) the information given in the contents pages at the front of the Consolidated Index under the volume you wish to consult, to see whether the word 'reissue' is given against it, with (b) the 'reissue' information on the spine of the Main Volume itself or its publication date. If the index was published *after* the Main Volume, then the references it contains should match the case numbers in the Main Volume. If the index was published *before* the Main Volume, then the references it contains may not match the case numbers in the reissued Main Volume; in this instance you will need to use the reference adaptor printed at the back of the reissued Main Volume, to convert the case numbers given in the Consolidated Index to their new equivalents in the latest reissue volume.

(b)   Unfortunately, during the publication of the green band edition of *The Digest*, the publishers have changed their policy on two details which can result in users becoming quite confused when researching. First, the earliest issues of the Main Volumes, some of which are still current, carry contents pages where the references given are to *page* numbers; later reissues carry references to *case* numbers. Secondly, early issues of the Main Volumes contain two separate sequences of case numbers: one for English cases, the other for non-English. In addition, the case number in the non-English sequence carries a distinguishing asterisk. Later reissues, on the other hand, have a single sequence of case numbers throughout, without asterisks, regardless of the origin of the case.

3.4B2.4   Social Security Case Law. Digest of Commissioners' Decisions

This two-volume loose-leaf work compiled by Desmond Neligan, and frequently referred to as '*Neligan's Digest*', contains brief summaries of a large number of the reported and some unreported decisions of the Social Security Commissioners. The two volumes are divided into 31 chapters (though, currently, chapters 20 to 29 are not yet used). Each chapter commences with a contents list of the subjects covered and then follow case summaries under each subject heading in chronological order. At the back of volume 2 is a general index – an alphabetical subject index to both volumes – with references to where in the body of the digest the appropriate decision summaries will be found. The digest is useful for identifying relevant decisions through its subject indexing and arrangement, but the summaries should not be relied on solely, since references ought be followed up in the full versions of commissioners' decisions.

3.4B3   Citators

3.4B.3.1   Current Law Case Citator

Current Law Case Citator is a unique and valuable publication. It is an alphabetical list by case name of cases reported between 1947 and the present with:

(a)   A comprehensive list of references to where the case was originally reported in the law reports.

(b)   A judicial history of each case detailing reported appeals to a higher court.

(c)   Details of whether courts in later cases have applied, considered, approved, disapproved, followed or referred to the original decision.

(d)   Details of where the case is summarised in the sister publication of *Current Law Yearbooks*.

These four characteristics are illustrated in figure 3.20.

Some points to note when using the *Citator*:

(a)   It lists not only cases *reported* since 1947, but also major pre-1947 cases *cited* since 1947 with, usually, a single citation to where the original case might be found in law reports, and a reference to where in the relevant *Current Law Yearbook* the summary of the case in which it was cited, will be found.

(b)   It includes not only English cases but also those from the courts of Northern Ireland, Scotland and the European Communities which have been summarised in *Current Law Monthly Digest*.

(c)   It is published in several volumes:

(i)   *Current Law Case Citator 1947–1976:* a bound volume covering cases reported or cited between those dates;

(ii)   *Current Law Case Citator 1988:* a bound volume supplementing the above;

(iii)   *Current Law Case Citator 1989–90* and each year subsequently: a paperback supplement covering the period from 1989;

(iv)   *Current Law Monthly Digest:* the cumulative table of cases at the back of the current issue lists, in ordinary type, new cases which have been summarised in *Current Law Monthly Digest* during the current year, and in italic type, cases which have been judicially considered, overruled by statute, or been the subject of an article or case note.

From the 1991 issue of the *Case Citator* onwards the content has been rearranged slightly. The *Citator* is in two parts: part I contains the English *Citator* and part II contains cases digested or referred to in the Scottish section of *Current Law Yearbook*, together with cases appearing in *Scottish Current Law*. Make sure you are referring to the correct part in the *Citator*!

It is essential when researching the history of a particular case to use *all* the appropriate volumes of the *Citator* and not, as some students do, rely on a dip into whichever of the volumes is immediately to hand at the time, otherwise the result is likely to be an incomplete piece of research.

Although at first sight you may think the *Citator* a tool to be used only in the most detailed research on a case, you will find it invaluable in day-to-day use of the law library because:

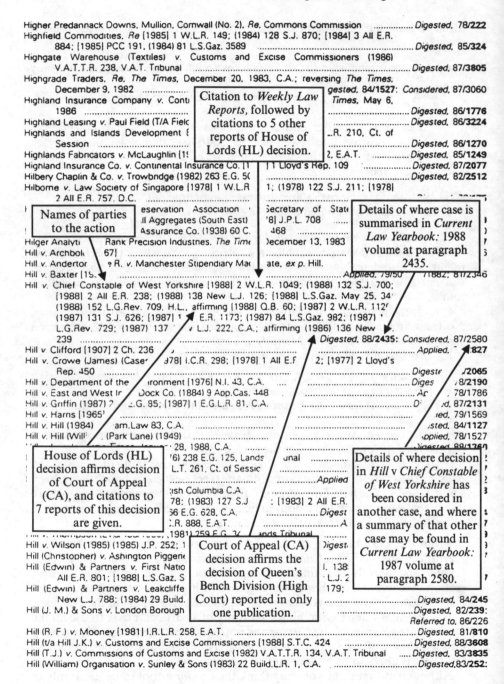

Figure 3.20   Extract from *Current Law Case Citator 1988*.

(a)   There will be occasions, especially during lectures, when you will be given the name of a case without its citation. Using *Current Law Case Citator* you can check:

(i)   whether it has been reported since 1947, and if so, where;
(ii)   if it was reported before 1947 but has been cited since, one citation will be given to where it was originally reported.

(b)   You may be competing frequently with other students for the same volume of law reports. Using *Current Law Case Citator* you can check whether the case has been reported in any other series of law reports and use that alternative version for your reading, unless the lecturer has made a special point of recommending a particular version, which won't often happen.

(c)   You may be referred in lectures and your reading to cases in law reports which your law library does not possess. Using *Current Law Case Citator* you can find the reference to the summary of the case in the appropriate *Current Law Yearbook* and read that as an alternative. It should be emphasised that whilst reading case summaries is a valuable 'safety net' when the full reports are not available in the library, it can be a recipe for disaster in essays, assignments, projects and examinations if undertaken as the sole method of reading case law.

3.4B4   Commentary

3.4B4.1   *Halsbury's Laws of England*

Halsbury's Laws of England was first published in 1907 and is now in its fourth edition. It is a key research publication and copies will be found in virtually every academic library where students study law to degree level or beyond. Many large public libraries also subscribe to it, but more important-ly, most firms of solicitors and barristers' chambers will use *Halsbury's Laws* as an everyday research source. *Halsbury's Laws* is a commentary, written by editorial staff, on the whole law of England and Wales. Unlike its sister publication *Halsbury's Statutes*, with which it should not be confused, *Halsbury's Laws* does not reprint original legal materials.

There are seven parts to the publication, as summarised in figure 3.21.

(a)   *Main volumes.* Fifty-two Main Volumes contain a narrative state-ment, arranged by subject, of the whole law of England and Wales, derived from statutes, rules, regulations and cases. The volumes have been published at a variety of dates between 1973 and 1986, when the fourth edition was completed. Volume 1 contains the law relating to the topic of administrative law and volume 50 ends with that on wills. Two further volumes (51 and 52) cover European Communities law. When the law on a topic has changed considerably since a Main Volume was published, a 'reissue' volume is published to replace the original one. Some areas of law change faster than others. You can identify reissue volumes by the word appearing near the top of the spine of these particular volumes and also on the title page. It is important to note this, as will be explained later in the section on using *Halsbury's Laws*.

Main Volumes	Annual Abridgements	Cumulative Supplement	Current Service
Narrative statement, arranged by subject, of whole law of England and Wales derived from statutes, rules, regulations and cases.	Annual bound volumes recording changes to law not yet included in Main Volumes.	Two bound volumes issued annually — record changes affecting Main Volumes and Annual Abridgements. Up to date to end of previous year.	Two loose-leaf binders: **Binder 1: Monthly Review:** details very recent changes to Main Volumes and Annual Abridgements. **Binder 2: Noter Up:** brief annotations to Main Volumes and Annual Abridgements.

Consolidated Table of Statutes	Consolidated Table of Cases	Consolidated Index	
Alphabetical list over 2 volumes, of Statutes (Acts) occupying both volumes, and Statutory Instruments (towards back of second volume).	Alphabetical list of cases noted in Main Volumes only, not the Annual Abridgements.	Two volume subject index.	

Figure 3.21   Structure of *Halsbury's Laws of England*.

(b)   *Annual Abridgements*. These volumes record changes to the law in any one year not yet included in the Main Volumes and provide brief summaries of cases and legislation.

(c)   *Cumulative Supplement* (sometimes referred to as the 'Cum. Sup.'). Two bound volumes, issued annually and replacing the previous Cumulative Supplement, record changes affecting the Main and Annual Abridgements, and are up to date to late in the year prior to publication.

(d)   *Current service*. Two loose-leaf binders contain the Monthly Review, a booklet published monthly which provides brief summaries of recent cases and legislation, and in the second binder, the Noter-Up Service, which includes citations to new court decisions and legislation arranged under subjects in the same order as in the Main Volumes and Cumulative Supplement.

(e) *Consolidated Index*. A two-volume alphabetical list of references to subjects included in the Main Volumes.

(f) *Consolidated Table of Statutes*. Alphabetical list by title of the statutes referred to.

(g) *Consolidated Table of Cases*. Alphabetical list by title of the cases referred to.

Using *Halsbury's Laws*

The key skill to learn in searching *Halsbury's Laws* is to correctly and confidently link together the use of the seven parts to ensure the law you eventually cite is up to date.

There are four steps in research using *Halsbury's Laws*, as figure 3.22 shows.

Four step search: Index ➡ Main Volume ➡ Cumulative Supplement ➡ Current Service

INDEX

Look up the statute, case or subject in the appropriate volume of the consolidated indexes. Note the volume and paragraph number to which you are referred. If the statute, case or subject is too recent to be included in the main work index, consult the index at the back of the Cumulative Supplement and the index at the back of the Current Service volume. These will guide you to the appropriate part of the work for the latest information.

MAIN VOLUME

Compare the date of issue of the Consolidated Index with the date at which the Main Volume states the law – this is given a couple of pages after the title page. If the Main Volume pre-dates the index find the relevant paragraph number noted from the Consolidated Index. If Main Volume has been published after the Consolidated Index look up statute, case or subject in the index to the re-issued Main Volume itself. Then find relevant paragraph number.

CUMULATIVE SUPPLEMENT

If you have not been guided by the indexes to the Cumulative Supplement volume refer to it under the relevant Main Volume, subject and paragraph numbers.

CURRENT SERVICE

Check the Noter-Up in Binder 2 under the appropriate volume, subject and paragraph number to trace latest developments. Short summaries of these developments can be read in the Monthly Review in Binder 1. Use the Key to Monthly Reviews, set out at the beginning of Binder 1, to trace where the summaries are located.

Figure 3.22   Step by step research using *Halsbury's Laws of England*.

Here are some points to note when using *Halsbury's Laws*:

(a)   Research should normally start with one of the consolidated indexes, which one will be determined by the information sought: about a subject, a particular statute or a case. Each reference in the index consists of two groups of figures: a bold number indicating the volume, followed by a number in a lighter type indicating the paragraph number – note: not the page number. An alternative approach, not recommended, is to browse over the spines of the Main Volumes or glance through the list printed towards the back of the *Halsbury's Laws of England User's Guide* booklet, and select the title volume most relevant to the subject of enquiry. Then look up the topic in the index to that particular volume. The danger of this procedure is that there can be several possible titles relevant and you will not take advantage of the work of the indexer in bringing mention of them together in the consolidated index.

(b)   Main volumes are revised and reissued when the law they contain is out-of-date. However, there can be a gap between the publication of a reissue Main Volume and an up to date edition of the consolidated tables or consolidated index to the whole set. So it is important to check which issue of the Main Volume has been used to compile the tables and index. This can be done by comparing the date given on the title pages of the tables and index with the date up to which the law is stated in a Main Volume. If the tables and index were published *after* the Main Volume then the references they contain should match the paragraphs in the Main Volume. If the tables and index were published *before* the Main Volume then the references they contain may not match the paragraphs in the reissued Main Volume; in this case you should look up the topic you require again in the index to the particular reissued Main Volume to discover the new paragraph number at which it is discussed.

(c)   When you have found the information you require in the Main Volume, note three elements: the *volume, subject* and *paragraph number* of the section in which you are interested, so you can find relevant new information quickly in the Cumulative Supplement and Noter-Up. The subject is given as part of the running head across the tops of pages.

(d)   In the Cumulative Supplement and Noter-Up the volume number and subject are given as running heads across the tops of pages. The paragraph numbers of Main Volumes to which more recent developments relate are given in the left margin. If the paragraph number in which you are interested does not appear in the list you can assume there have been no changes to the commentary in the Main Volume in which you originally looked.

(e)   Research using *Halsbury's Laws* may be completed by using the relevant Annual Abridgement volumes to trace summaries of the cases and legislation to which you have been referred by the Main Volumes. This is a useful step for a busy solicitor or barrister, but as a law student you should try to avoid depending on case summaries until you are fully conversant with the structure and principles of a legal topic, otherwise, you may have difficulty relating one case decision effectively to another. Whenever possible consult full-text versions of cases, as originally published.

3.4C ELECTRONIC SOURCES

For background information on the use of electronic databases see appendix 4.

3.4C1 LEXIS

The on-line information retrieval service LEXIS contains the *full text* of virtually all reported cases since 1945, plus *Tax Cases* reports since 1875 and, since 1 January 1980, transcripts of a large number of unreported cases of the Court of Appeal (Civil Division), some from the High Court and selected tribunals. The database is updated each week, but it may take several weeks between a judgment being given and its inclusion in the database, for only the fullest version of the decision is carried, not the brief or edited report.

The database is divided into libraries. The ENGGEN Library (*English General*) contains separate files including one devoted to law reports entitled CASES.

A description of the LEXIS system and basic search techniques is given in appendix 6.

3.4C2 Lawtel

Lawtel is an on-line *digest* of legal information – it does not contain the full text of cases, only summaries. Cases have been added to the database since 1 January 1980 and new cases are added as soon as a newspaper law report or the transcript of the case is to hand. When a fuller report of a case is published in the printed law reports Lawtel provides citations to these reports. Case summaries may be found by one of three routes from the Lawtel main menu: either by selecting 'Subjects A–Z' and then selecting from the alphabetical list of subjects in the directory of subject indexes, or by selecting 'Decisions', which will provide an alphabetical list by the names of parties of all the cases in the database, or by searching the Statute Citator.

A general description of Lawtel is given in appendix 5.

3.4C3 Justis

Justis is a database which contains the full text of the following law reports:

(a) *Weekly Law Reports* (January 1985 to date)
(b) *Independent* newspaper law reports (October 1987 to date)
(c) *The Times* newspaper law reports (December 1989 to date).

It also contains the text of the following indexes:

Law Reports index (1981 to 1986)
Criminal Appeal Office index of judgments (1982 to date)

Although a useful database, the value of Justis is rather limited when compared with the far greater coverage of titles and time period available on LEXIS.

3.4C4   Justis Weekly Law CD

This is a compact disc of the full text of the *Weekly Law Reports* from January 1985 to date. The disc runs in a CD drive attached to a personal computer. A printer can be attached to the equipment. A search request is typed into the personal computer keyboard and may consist of a word or combination of words which the computer will search for in the full text of the cases on the compact disc. The computer will report the number of occurrences of the specific word or words it finds, and the selected items can be displayed on the computer monitor. The search is similar to a LEXIS search in that it is conducted on the full text of the cases, not an index to them. As quick and convenient as the service appears there are two drawbacks: first, the discs are updated at six–monthly intervals, so it is not possible to search for the most recent cases – also the database only commences in January 1985, although during 1992 the coverage of the disc will be extended. Secondly, the CD has the text of only a single series of law reports – however, in 1992, the disc is due to include the *Law Reports Index*, so references to reports other than *Weekly Law Reports* will be retrieved, but still only the text of a single series of reports will be included on the disc.

3.4C5   Magister Current Law Yearbook

At the time of writing Sweet and Maxwell have announced that the *Current Law Yearbooks* are to become available on compact disc. The first disc will contain the yearbooks for 1986 to 1990. This development could mean that many of the impediments to using the yearbooks to search for a particular type of legal source, such as cases, or for a specific detailed subject, will be overcome.

3.4D   RESEARCH STRATEGIES

3.4D1   Tracing a report of a case where only the names of parties are known

This is one of the most frequently occurring research tasks facing a law student. There are two ways of finding the information: by electronic sources or by printed sources.

Lawtel (3.4C2) is valuable because it is updated with new case summaries daily. So if you think the decision is very recent a search from the Lawtel main menu, selecting 'Decisions', will provide an alphabetical list by names of parties to the cases on the database.

LEXIS (3.4C1) is updated less rapidly than Lawtel but contains the full-text versions of cases; the database also goes much further back in time. To search LEXIS you would select the ENGGEN Library, the CASES file and, if you were interested in the case of *Candler* v *Crane, Christmas & Co.* you would type:

name (Candler w/4 Crane)

and then press the TRANSMIT key.

If one party's name is very common then, to avoid being inundated with references to cases which are not relevant, you could request the computer to look for another name, phrase, word or number in close proximity to the common name, to narrow the number of cases found and improve the chances of a hit. For example: to find *R* v *Smith*, assuming you know the subject-matter of the case, type:

name (Smith) and burglary

and then press the TRANSMIT key.

If you do not have a complete case name, for example, only the popular name for a case, and the popular name actually appears in the case title, such as '*High Trees*', then you should type

name (High Trees)

and then press the TRANSMIT key. The computer should retrieve *Central London Property Trust Ltd* v *High Trees House Ltd* [1947] KB 130.

Research using paper sources is a little more laborious; figure 3.23 illustrates the preferred sequence.

An alternative strategy, if *Current Law Case Citator* is not available, would be to substitute the *Law Reports Index* (the 'red' and 'pink' books, 3.4B1.1) or the *All England Law Reports* consolidated tables and index (3.4B1.1). Where *The Digest* is not available, substitute the *English Reports* index (3.4A2.2) or the *All England Law Reports Reprint* index (3.4A2.2), but note that neither indexes cases from outside the English jurisdiction. Where the case is thought to be recent but *Current Law Monthly Digest* is not available, substitute the latest index to the *Law Reports* (3.4B1.1), the list of cases printed in the latest issue of the *Weekly Law Reports*, and the most recent tables and index to the *All England Law Reports*. Where the *Daily Law Reports Index* is not available, substitute browsing through recent copies of *The Times* and other newspaper law reports and also check the case reports in the weekly periodicals: *Law Society's Gazette*, *New Law Journal* and *Solicitors' Journal*.

3.4D2   Has this case been considered by the courts on a subsequent occasion?

There are two ways of carrying out this research: either using electronic sources or paper sources.

Using LEXIS (3.4C1) you would select the ENGGEN library and the file: CASES. Assuming you were searching for cases citing *United Scientific Holdings Ltd* v *Burnley Borough Council* [1978] AC 904 you would type:

United Scientific w/8 Burnley

and then press the TRANSMIT key.

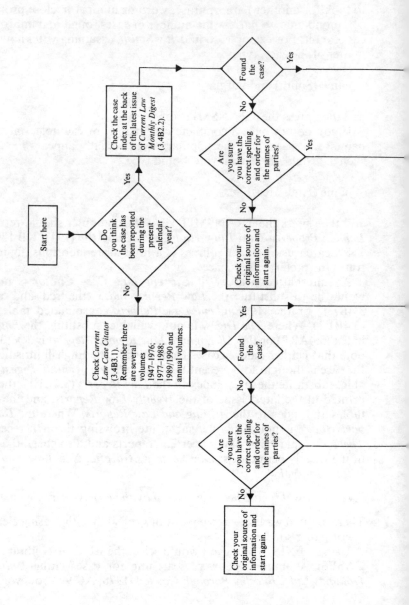

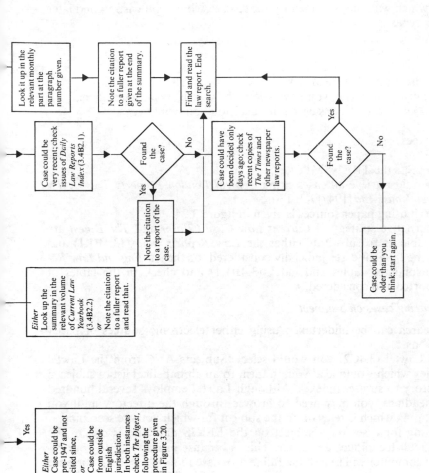

(The letter and numbers after publication names refer to the sub-section where they are discussed.)

Figure 3.23   Tracing in printed sources a report of a case when only the names of parties are known.

If the name of one of the parties to the case you are searching for is very common, such as *R* v *Smith*, to avoid retrieving from the database citations to all cases titled *R* v *Smith*, you will need to include a word, phrase or number which will uniquely identify the case to which you wish to find later citations; type:

Smith w/15 burglary

and then press the TRANSMIT key.

If the only information you have about the case is its popular name, such as '*High Trees*', to find cases citing this decision you would type:

High Trees

and then press the TRANSMIT key.

This should retrieve all cases citing *Central London Property Trust Ltd* v *High Trees House Ltd* [1947] KB 130.

Research using paper sources is given in figure 3.24.

An alternative strategy, if *Current Law Case Citator* and *The Digest* are not available, is to substitute either the *Law Reports Index* (3.4B1.1) and check in the table of cases judicially considered, or the *All England Law Reports* consolidated tables and index (3.4B1.1) and check in the tables of cases reported and considered.

3.4D3 Tracing cases on a subject

This research can be undertaken using either electronic sources or paper publications.

Using Lawtel (3.4C2) you would select 'Subjects A–Z' from the Lawtel main index which would lead you, in turn, to an alphabetical list of subjects: the directory to subject indexes. Although Lawtel employs several hundred subject headings, you may need to browse through the directory until you find a heading which is relevant to the subject for which you are searching.

Searching for cases on a subject on the LEXIS database is one of the more difficult techniques to master. This is because in response to your request the computer will search the full text of case reports for the occurrence of the words, and *only* the words, you specify. LEXIS is literal – LEXIS cannot think for you. You will need to think carefully about the words or phrases you select for your search request, for if a judge has discussed the legal concept in which you are interested but not used the precise words you specify to LEXIS, then the computer will not retrieve that document. More advice on the use of LEXIS is given in appendix 6. To search for cases by subject you would select the ENGGEN library and then the CASES file before specifying the word/s or phrases for which you wish the computer to search.

Paper sources can be used for this research and a number of alternative strategies are available. *The Digest* is arranged by subject and figure 3.19 shows how a search by subject can be carried out. *The Digest* will provide

case summaries and covers non-English case law as well as English. However, because there is no loose-leaf updating service it does not feature the
very latest decisions. *Halsbury's Laws of England* is also arranged by subject
and figure 3.22 shows how to search for information by subject. Whilst *Halsbury's* does not contain case summaries, nor does it include cases from outside the English jurisdiction, it does provide a commentary on the law and,
through its loose-leaf service, include the latest decisions. *Current Law Yearbook* is not easy to use for this type of research, especially if you need decisions on a very specific point of law or wish to carry out in-depth subject
research over a considerable period of years – the reasons are noted in
3.4B2.2. The *Law Reports* indexes (3.4B1.1) are useful if other sources are
not available, but since the number of different law report publications indexed is restricted – specialist subject law reports are particularly under-rep-
resented – your research results are unlikely to be comprehensive. *Legal
Journals Index* (3.4B1.2) is easy to use but is limited by both the small number of law report publications it includes and the short period of time it has
been available (1986 onwards). If all else fails, a search of the library catalogue by subject (see 1.2.5) should retrieve details of relevant textbooks
which will contain references to and commentary on the leading decisions
on a topic.

3.4D4   Have there been any case notes or articles on this case?

Electronic or paper sources can be used for this research, but this is one area
where the paper sources score heavily over the electronic for the wide variety of publications indexed.

Lawtel (see 3.4C2) indexes articles by subject, not by case name. However, it is very often obvious from the title of the article that it deals with a
particular case.

LEXIS (see 3.4C1) contains within its ENGGEN library a file entitled
UKJNL which contains the full text of a handful of periodicals, two dating
from 1986 onwards, the rest from more recent dates. To find mention of a
case such as *United Scientific Holdings Ltd* v *Burnley Borough Council* [1978]
AC 904 in these publications you would type:

United Scientific w/8 Burnley

and then press the TRANSMIT key.

Since LEXIS will search the full text of every item which has appeared in
these periodicals, the result of your search could be a useful case note or just
a passing reference in an article on a much broader topic.

Amongst the paper sources, two in particular should be used for this research. *Legal Journals Index* (3.4B1.2), indexes a very wide range of periodicals and carries in each issue a separate list of references to cases, arranged
in alphabetical order by the names of parties. You will be able to trace not
only references to the original report of a case which has appeared in one of
the 160 periodicals indexed, but also articles and case notes on it. However,
LJI only commenced in 1986, and for earlier information you will need to

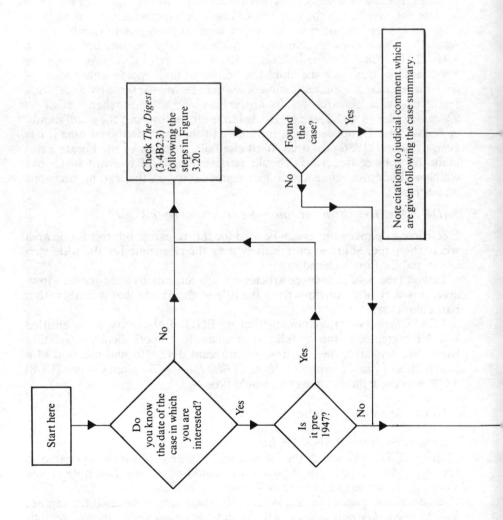

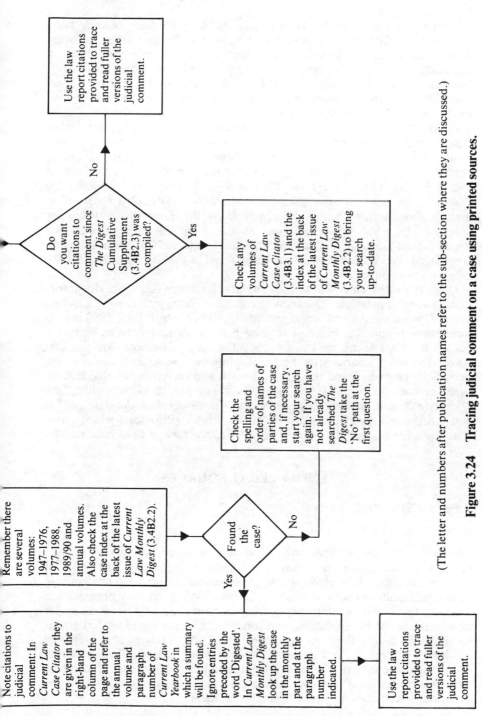

Figure 3.24   Tracing judicial comment on a case using printed sources.

(The letter and numbers after publication names refer to the sub-section where they are discussed.)

rely on *Current Law Yearbooks* (3.4B2.2). Towards the back of each *Yearbook* is a list of periodical articles which appeared during the year in question, arranged under broad subject headings (note, not case names). Searching these subject headings for relevant references to a case is rather laborious, because the references to individual articles are arranged in alphabetical order by the first word in the title of the article. You are really forced to run your eye over every entry under the appropriate subject heading to make sure you do not miss relevant material. This list only includes references to major articles on a subject – it is not an index of case notes or shorter material. If you do not have access to *Legal Journals Index* with its more helpful and sophisticated indexing to cover the period 1986 to the present you may need to use *Current Law Yearbooks* and *Current Law Monthly Digest* itself. The issues of *Current Law Monthly Digest* (3.4B2.2) arrange information about articles rather differently from the *Yearbooks*; articles are listed *not* at the back of an issue, but as one of the last entries under each broad subject heading by which information in the body of the publication is arranged. You will not find case notes indexed in *Current Law Monthly Digest*, only substantial articles.

Other less satisfactory ways of finding articles which might provide information about a particular case include checking *Halsbury's Laws of England* Noter-Up and the Annual Abridgements (3.4B4.1), which since 1990 list articles from a limited number of leading periodicals under the same broad subject headings as are used in the encyclopaedia. Case notes are not featured. The most laborious method of finding case notes is to select a few periodical titles which you think are relevant, and search their individual indexes or contents pages. If the case was important, check titles like *Law Quarterly Review, Modern Law Review* or *Cambridge Law Journal*, or if it was a decision in a specialised area of law, check periodicals which cover that topic, for example, *Journal of Social Welfare Law* or *Criminal Law Review*.

3.5 EXTRA-LEGAL SOURCES

3.5A DESCRIPTION

3.5A1 Definition

The term 'extra-legal sources' covers a variety of documents variously called codes of practice, codes of conduct, guidance or standards. The codes of practice described here differ from those discussed in 3.3.2 (collectively known as statutory codes of practice) in two ways. First, any organisation can issue them, whereas statutory codes of practice can only be issued under powers conferred by legislation, and some must be presented to Parliament for approval before they can take effect. Secondly, extra-legal sources are not legally enforceable in their own right, but either seek to influence behaviour or advise, and may rely on non-legal sanctions, such as loss of membership of a professional or trade association, to ensure conformity amongst those whose activities they are designed to influence.

3.5A2 Origin

Since 'any Tom, Dick or Harry' (Ferguson 1988, p. 12) can issue one of these extra-legal sources, it is difficult to trace an historic origin for this type of publication. Ferguson's article makes a major contribution to a better understanding of this frequently neglected type of legal literature, and has formed the basis for the discussion in this section of the book. However, some areas where extra-legal sources occur *can* be identified.

The British Standards Institution, with origins dating back to 1901, was the first national standards body in the world, and has a current catalogue of over 10,000 British Standard publications with more than 700 new or revised standards issued each year. The aim of the publications is to set generally recognised standards of quality for industry and commerce. The familiar 'kitemark' on a product, followed by a British Standard number (normally abbreviated to BS followed by a running number), indicates that the product or service satisfies the requirements of that standard. Some safety legislation, notably dealing with clothing (e.g., the Nightdresses (Safety) Regulations 1967 SI 1967/839), specifies tests for quality, included in particular British Standards, to which products should conform.

In consumer law, the Fair Trading Act 1973 placed a duty on the Director General of Fair Trading to encourage the preparation of Codes of Practice by trade associations. Nearly 30 have been introduced. They are 'designed to state the legal responsibilities of the traders supporting them and in addition consumers receive benefits in excess of the strict legal requirements' (O'Keefe 1991, division 1, para. 5065). Many codes contain conciliation and arbitration schemes. Examples include the *Association of British Travel Agents Ltd. (ABTA) Tour Operators' Code of Conduct* and *ABTA's Travel Agent's Code of Conduct* as well as the *Code of Practice for the Motor Industry* covering advertising, sales, repair and servicing of both new and used cars, prepared jointly by three trade associations including the Society of Motor Manufacturers and Traders Ltd.

Similarly, the Data Protection Act 1984 places a duty on the Data Protection Registrar to encourage trade associations to prepare and disseminate codes on compliance with data protection principles enshrined in the Act.

In business law, the Accounting Standards Committee, formed of representatives of a number of professional bodies in accountancy, has developed a number of Statements of Standard Accounting Practice (SSAP) to codify generally accepted best practice in financial accounting and financial statements in, for example, company accounts. A final area where extra-legal sources may be found is in the codes of practice or codes of ethics of professional bodies, such as the British Medical Association, as set out in its Handbook, and the Pharmaceutical Society of Great Britain, in its *Statement upon Matters of Professional Conduct*.

3.5A3 Structure

The variety of types of extra-legal source and issuing organisation means there is no common structure to these documents.

3.5A4   Publication and general availability

The lack of central control of the publication of extra-legal sources means that each organisation responsible for a code or standard etc. will adopt its own policy on publication. Whilst many academic and the larger public libraries will have complete sets of the British Standards Institution publications, and the libraries of universities, polytechnics or colleges teaching accountancy will collect Accounting Standards Committee documents, very few will include either the codes of practice of trade associations or codes of ethics of professional bodies as original documents. But codes of practice are one type of material which some of the specialist loose-leaf encyclo-paedias described in 3.7, below, provide and so prove their value. For example, O'Keefe, J.A., *The Law Relating to Trade Descriptions* (London: Butterworths, loose-leaf) gives details of where all the codes of practice made under the encouragement of the Director General of Fair Trading can be obtained; Goode, R.M., *Consumer Credit Legislation* (London: Butter-worths, loose-leaf) reprints the *Finance Houses Association Code of Practice* and the *Consumer Credit Trade Association Code of Practice*; and Chalton, S.N.L. and Gaskill, S.J., *Encyclopedia of Data Protection* (London: Sweet & Maxwell, loose-leaf) provides information on trade codes of practice.

3.5A5   Citation

The variety of types of extra-legal source means there is no standard way in which they should be cited. However, good practice would dictate that a reference should include the name of the issuing organisation, the full title of the document, the edition number or date of publication and any reference number which uniquely identifies it.

3.6   TEXTBOOKS

3.6A   DESCRIPTION

A law textbook may be defined as a systematic, narrative explanation of and commentary on the law. Five different types may be identified:

(a)   Books of authority: a few, older works written between the late 12th and mid 18th centuries, before the system of law reporting was fully develop-ed, which are accepted as reliable statements of the law of their time. Examples include Sir Edward Coke's *Institutes of the Laws of England* (1628–44), and William Blackstone's *Commentaries on the Laws of England* (1765–69).

(b)   Modern textbooks: books which collect, synthesise and critically evaluate the law.

(c)   Casebooks: books which reprint or summarise a selection of judg-ments on a subject, sometimes with editorial commentary – in recent times these publications have also included material from statutes, government reports and periodical articles, with questions and points for discussion highlighted. They are frequently published under the title: *Cases and Materials on [subject]*.

(d) Practice books: guides to practice and procedure in the courts, primarily for the use of practitioners, rather than law students. Examples include: *Supreme Court Practice* (otherwise known as the 'White Book'), *County Court Practice* (sometimes referred to as the 'Green Book'), and *Stone's Justices' Manual* (it has blue covers, but is not yet known by its colour).

(e) Precedent books: collections of forms and documents which have been found valid, effective and useful in the past, and provide lawyers with a general layout and wording accepted as standard. They are most frequently used for the preparation of documents in connection with a court action, or in conveyancing.

3.6A1 Individual categories

3.6A1.1 Books of Authority

Textbooks of all types are frequently cited in court, but although they are treated with great respect, their authority is merely persuasive. However, the small group of 'books of authority' are accorded greater respect and in the absence of any conflicting cases their statements of the law may be followed. As well as the works by Coke and Blackstone already noted, those of Glanvill, *Tractatus de legibus et consuetudinibus regni Angliae* (written between 1187 and 1189); Bracton, *De legibus et consuetudinibus Angliae* (written between 1250 and 1258); Littleton's *Tenures* (written in the late 15th century and one of the first, major legal works to be printed in England by Lettou or Machlinia in 1481 or 1482); Hawkins, *A Treatise of the Pleas of the Crown* (1716); Hale, *Pleas of the Crown* (1678); and Foster, *Discourses upon a Few Branches of the Crown Law* (1762) are generally regarded as books of authority. A detailed, yet readable account of these and many other pre-19th century books is given in chapter 9 of *The Chief Sources of English Legal History* by Percy Winfield (1925).

3.6A1.2 Modern textbooks

A customary distinction is made between practitioners' books, mostly written by and for practising lawyers, and students' textbooks, mainly written by academics, but the boundaries are blurred.

Practitioners' books, often in the past though now rarely referred to as treatises, provide a detailed treatment of a subject and are usually read selectively, and used more in the way of a work of reference. The emphasis is on an up-to-date statement and commentary on the law, its practice and procedure. However, because they are such extensive publications, often in several volumes, new editions are expensive to produce and do not appear at very frequent intervals. It is always important to check the statement of the date up to which the law is stated; this is usually printed either on the title page or in or near the preface. Where Cumulative Supplements are issued to keep the Main Volume up to date (sometimes the preface will indicate this to be the method of future updating), check that you are about to use the most up-to-date available, because out-of-date ones can sometimes be left on library shelves through an oversight by library staff. Some practitioners' books are now published as loose-leaf works, so that individual pages containing out-of-date law can be replaced with little delay, by pages giving the latest information. Examples of wholly loose-leaf works include: *Woodfall's Law of Landlord and Tenant*; *Emmet on Title*; and *Palmer's Company Law*. The original authors of some practitioners' texts may be long dead but their work has become an established publication and, although subsequently revised by others, the original author's name becomes part of the title; for example: *Chitty on Contracts*, *Rayden on Divorce*. Sometimes, in informal conversation or writing reference to such well known titles is even further shortened to just '*Chitty*' or '*Rayden*'.

Student textbooks, on the other hand, are less concerned with detail but more with describing general principles of law and identifying and commenting on areas of doubt or conflict in statute or case law. They may also provide background information establishing the social or political context within which the law has developed and note possibilities for future law reform. Some of the more established student texts such as Smith and Hogan, *Criminal Law* and Trietel, *Law of Contract* have become standard works on their subject and are occasionally cited in court. In a recent study of the law reports for 1985 Clinch (1989, p. 475) found that well over 100 different textbooks, both practitioner and student titles, were cited in judgments. New editions of student textbooks appear at frequent intervals and you should check, when using a library copy, that you are consulting the latest edition available, as many libraries retain superseded editions on the open shelves.

Also, avoid the temptation to save money by buying a student textbook secondhand, when the only edition on sale is other than the latest. It will be a false economy, for citation from out-of-date sources, unless to provide an historical perspective, will be marked down by lecturing staff.

3.6A1.3   Casebooks

At first sight the reprints or summaries of key cases and other materials contained in these publications may seem a great boon to the student faced with a heavy reading list. Eminent lawyers have gathered together in the space of a single volume the essential sources relevant to a subject. However, although this portable library may appear convenient, it does contain only extracts and is no substitute for reading the original statutes, cases and other materials. A casebook is best used as a guide to further research rather than an end in itself.

3.6A1.4   Practice books

Practice books are specialised manuals, including statutes and court rules, with copious notes of guidance on their interpretation and application to the practice and procedure of the courts. New editions are very frequently published: *County Court Practice, Stone's Justices' Manual and Blackstone's*

Criminal Practice annually, while *Supreme Court Practice*, which deals with civil procedure in the superior courts, and *Archbold's Pleading, Evidence and Practice in Criminal Cases*, are published every three years or so, with Cumulative Supplements issued several times a year.

3.6A1.5 Precedent books

Three different types may be identified:

(a) Some practitioners' books include standard forms and documents as an appendix, for example, *Rayden on Divorce*.

(b) Separate collections of forms and precedents for particular courts or topics have been published, for example, *McCleary's County Court Precedents*, and the loose-leaf series, *Precedents for the Conveyancer*. This latter title is updated six times a year in association with the journal, *Conveyancer and Property Lawyer*.

(c) Two major encyclopaedic collections, *Atkin's Encyclopaedia of Court Forms in Civil Proceedings* (known as '*Atkin's Court Forms*' or more simply still as '*Atkin*'), and *The Encyclopaedia of Forms and Precedents*.

Atkin comprises three parts: the main work, 41 volumes of forms and precedents, is arranged in subject groups. Each subject begins with an explanation of the courts and their procedure in the topic. The step-by-step procedures which must be followed in an action are set out in helpful tabular form, and followed by precedents and forms relevant to those proceedings. The second part of *Atkin* is an Annual Supplement which records changes to the Main Volumes; and the third part is an annual consolidated index to the whole set. The current, second edition was begun in 1953 and is kept up to date by the frequent issue of replacement volumes in the main work. Since a revised index is published annually, revisions provided in replacement volumes are quickly included. *Atkin* is normally used in three steps: look up the topic in the annual index, refer to the Main Volume and, finally, consult the Annual Supplement for the latest developments since the Main Volume was published.

The Encyclopaedia of Forms and Precedents is an authoritative guide to the drafting of legal documents. It is now in its fifth edition and comprises three parts. The first part has 42 Main Volumes, which, when the edition is complete, will provide a subject-by-subject presentation of forms and documents for 94 different subjects. The second part is a loose-leaf updating service, and the final part an annual consolidated index to the whole work. The research sequence is as for *Atkin*: index, Main Volume, loose-leaf updating volume. This encyclopaedia is one of the first to be available on disc for use in a personal computer, so that lawyers can call up a particular form or document for a legal transaction, amend the wording to suit particular circumstances and have the completed document printed out to word-processed standard; this is a vision of a future when new technology will more generally assist the lawyer in research and drafting.

The very practical nature of precedent books means students have, in the past, been unlikely to use these publications. However, the increasing accent on skills acquisition during all types of law course will result, in future, in more students practising how to draw up different types of document for transactions, using some of these sources.

3.6B EXPLOITATION

Information sources which help you identify if relevant textbooks exist to assist your research may be divided into two classes: sources which restrict themselves to law; and general sources. Each class again divides into sources which cover new or recently published material, and those which include titles regardless of whether or not they are still in print. The boundary of the division does become rather blurred, so below publications are arranged in a very general sequence starting with in-print sources and gradually moving towards historical listings. As a result of using some of the sources noted you may discover details of books your library does not stock – see appendix 2 for information on the inter-library loans service.

3.6B1   Sources

3.6B1.1   Publishers' or bookshop catalogues

Each of the major law textbook publishers, Butterworths, Sweet & Maxwell, Blackstone Press etc., produces a list of current publications, with summaries of contents. Some issue lists of student textbooks specifically. Two of the largest law booksellers, Hammick's Bookshop and Law Notes Bookshop, publish annual catalogues listing thousands of titles arranged under broad subject headings. But the research value of these publications is rather limited since they only cover what is in print at the time.

3.6B1.2   *Current Law Monthly Digest*

Towards the end of the subject entries in each issue of *Current Law Monthly Digest*, brief details of new books are given. These references are consolidated into a single list near the back of each *Current Law Yearbook*, but perseverance is required when checking for new or recent publications in a particular subject over a period of years, because the subject headings used are quite broad, and the list does not cumulate year on year.

3.6B1.3   *Information Sources in Law*

Although this publication aims 'to provide a bibliographical survey of the whole range of general and specialist literature which is available to those engaged in legal study and research', many of the sources discussed are textbooks. More than two thirds of the book comprises chapters evaluating and commenting on the general and subject-specific publications of English law. The reviews are authoritative and form an admirable starting-point when coming fresh to subjects such as constitutional and administrative law, revenue law, commercial law etc.

3.6B1.4   Lawyers' Law Books (2nd ed., 1985)

Subtitled 'a practical index to legal literature' this is a quite detailed subject-by-subject listing of encyclopaedias, periodicals and textbooks. Unlike *Information Sources in Law* (3.6B1.3), there is no evaluation of the sources. Most texts listed are of recent origin, but older and still useful titles are also included. The combination of an arrangement by quite specific subject categories and the inclusion of both in-print, and out-of-print, titles makes this a valuable research source, yet it could now do with updating.

3.6B1.5   Published catalogues of major law libraries

The catalogues of two of the most important academic law libraries in the United Kingdom were published in the 1970s as one-off ventures. No volumes of more recent acquisitions have been published. The two libraries are the Squire Law Library, University of Cambridge, and the Institute of Advanced Legal Studies, University of London.

The advantage of these listings lay in the wealth of historical, obscure and long out-of-print material they include. Of course, they are not very helpful for current topics.

3.6B1.6   Law Books in Print

This is an American publication published every three years, which aims to list all law books in the English language from around the world in print at the time it is published.

3.6B1.7   Law Books Published

Another American publication, but issued twice a year, to act as a supplement to *Law Books in Print* (3.6B1.6).

3.6B1.8   Law Books 1876–1981 plus supplements

A third American publication listing about 130,000 books published in English (mainly in the United States) from 1876 onwards – supplements have been issued since the original four volumes appeared, bringing the work more up to date.

3.6B1.9   International Legal Books in Print

First published in 1990, this two-volume work indexes over 20,000 English-language legal texts and treatises in print published or distributed within the UK, Western Europe and current or former Commonwealth countries. Entries are arranged by subject and some carry a brief annotation describing the content of individual publications. There are separate indexes for authors and titles.

3.6B2   General sources

3.6B2.1   Whitaker's Books in Print

Formerly known as *British Books in Print*, *Whitaker's Books in Print* is unique in providing the only British list of books in print. The paper version is published annually whilst a microfiche edition is updated monthly. It lists nearly half a million titles in a single alphabetical sequence of authors and titles. The disadvantage for research purposes is that there is no subject listing – if you look up 'tax', for example, all books in print with the word 'tax' appearing in the title will be listed, regardless, of whether they deal with law, accountancy, economics, politics etc. But if the word 'tax' does not appear in the title yet the book is about the topic, there will be no entry under 'tax'. This problem can be overcome by using the CD-ROM version (see 3.6C1).

3.6B2.2   *British National Bibliography (BNB)*

BNB lists new works published in the British Isles and received under the Copyright Act 1911 by the Legal Deposit Office of the British Library. Unfortunately for lawyers the listing is not comprehensive, for it excludes some publications of Her Majesty's Stationery Office including Bills of Parliament, Local and Personal Acts, House of Commons and House of Lords Parliamentary debates, government circulars, regulations etc. *BNB* is in three sections: the subject index, which is an alphabetical index of subjects appearing in the classified subject catalogue; the classified subject catalogue itself, which lists publications according to the Dewey decimal classification scheme (as employed by the majority of libraries to arrange their stock), and finally, an alphabetical arrangement by author. Weekly lists are published, cumulated quarterly and, finally, into annual bound volumes. The usual way to research the publication is to look up the subject in which you are interested in the subject index, note the classification number and then consult the classified subject catalogue under that number. This laborious process can pay dividends since this is the most comprehensive listing of British publications. Considerable time and effort can be saved if you can gain access to the CD-ROM version (see 3.6C2).

3.6C   *ELECTRONIC SOURCES*

For background information on the use of electronic databases, see appendix 4.

3.6C1   *Bookbank*

This is the CD-ROM equivalent of 3.6B2.1. Not only will the computer software search on book titles, but also subtitles and series titles. In addition it is possible to undertake very basic subject searches using the 'classification' search key, but the publisher advises using this in combination with title or author. The half million books detailed in the database are assigned to only 53 subjects, one being 'law and public administration', so searching solely on this key is likely to produce a long list of titles, very few of which may be relevant to your particular search enquiry.

3.6C2   *BNB on CD-ROM*

This is the equivalent of 3.6B2.2, but the database is so large it is spread over three discs, two covering British book publishing output 1950–1985, the third, 1986 to the present. A remote online version, *Blaise Line*, is also available.

3.6D RESEARCH STRATEGIES

Since there is such variety amongst the sources noted in 3.6B and 3.6C, you should read the descriptions given and select the titles most appropriate to your research needs.

3.7 ENCYCLOPAEDIAS

One definition of an encyclopaedia is 'an elaborate and exhaustive repertory of information on all the branches of some particular art or department of knowledge; especially one arranged in alphabetical order' (*Oxford English Dictionary*).

In the literature of English law there is one encyclopaedia which attempts to provide information on the whole extent of the law of England and Wales, in an alphabetical subject arrangement – *Halsbury's Laws of England* (see 3.4). Several others provide information on law and procedure as contained in particular types of publication – *Halsbury's Statutes of England* (see 3.2.2), *Halsbury's Statutory Instruments* (see 3.3.1), *Atkin's Court Forms* (see 3.6) and *The Encyclopaedia of Forms and Precedents* (see 3.6 also).

A third category takes a closely defined area of law and provides either, a commentary arranged alphabetically by topic, or reproduces all the relevant statutes, secondary legislation and extra-legal sources on the topic, with footnotes on relevant cases and additional editorial comment. Most, if not all, of the examples of this type of encyclopaedia are published entirely in loose-leaf format, which means publishers can issue 'releases' of pages containing updated information at frequent intervals, for subscribers to insert in the binders and also remove superseded material. These publications are valuable in legal research because (a) they cover a discrete legal topic in depth; (b) they include a wide range of legal source publications, including extra-legal sources which can be difficult to track down otherwise; and (c) they are regularly kept up to date.

The range of legal topics covered in encyclopaedic loose-leaf format grows every year. Tax law, for example, which changes frequently, is served by several encyclopaedias. Butterworths, Sweet & Maxwell, CCH Editions, and other major law publishers all produce encyclopaedias. Sweet & Maxwell group together a number in a series entitled 'Local Government Library', covering such topics as planning, compulsory purchase, rating, housing, environmental health, road traffic and local government law in general.

How do you discover if there is an encyclopedia available on the subject in which you are interested? First, check your law library's catalogue by subject, and watch for any entries with the word 'encyclopaedia' (which some publishers like to spell without the 'a') in the title. Secondly, if you cannot spot any from the catalogue ask the library staff for assistance or, alternatively, look in either *Lawyers' Law Books* (see 3.6B1.4) or one of the major law bookshop catalogues (see 3.6B1.1).

Before using one of these specialist encyclopaedias, check the pages at the beginning of the volume which tell you how recently the information given has been updated. If the last 'release' was more than a year ago, it is a clear indication that the updating of the work has lapsed and you should enquire with library staff. It could be dangerous to cite from a loose-leaf work which is badly out of date.

3.8 PERIODICALS

3.8A DESCRIPTION

3.8A1 Definition

Periodicals, also referred to as journals or magazines, have been a feature of legal literature since the 1760s. They are normally published as individual *issues*, which at predetermined intervals are gathered together to form a *volume* with a title page and/or index. Each issue is characterised by a variety of contents: *articles, news, notes* and *digests* of information; and a variety of contributors. The law periodicals you may need to use during your studies can be divided into five types:

(a)   Those of primarily academic interest, such as *Cambridge Law Journal, Law Quarterly Review, Modern Law Review* and the *Oxford Journal of Legal Studies*. They generally contain lengthy, analytical articles, often the product of considerable research. Notes of recent cases and legal developments are included by most, and since the periodicals are published quarterly or even less frequently, what they may lack in currency they make up for in thoroughness.

(b)   Practitioners' periodicals, for example, *Solicitors' Journal, New Law Journal* and *Law Society's Gazette*. Published approximately weekly, they contain short articles on a wide range of legal topics of interest to practising lawyers, including staff and office management, marketing and promotion, computer and information technology applications for lawyers. Case notes, digests of recent developments, practice notes, book reviews, professional news and advertisements for vacancies and services are also included.

(c)   Specialist periodicals covering particular areas of law, for example, *Criminal Law Review, Journal of Business Law, Family Law, Civil Justice Quarterly*. This is one of the growth areas in legal publishing. These titles usually include articles, case notes, notes on practice and procedure and comment on recent legal developments.

(d)   Newsletters: a recent development in law publishing, newsletters are often only a few pages long, but published frequently. They tend to contain topical information and comment rather than the more comprehensive analysis found in other types of periodical. Most are intended for use by practitioners, and include titles such as *Lloyd's Maritime Law Newsletter, Business Law Brief* or *Simon's Tax Intelligence*. A few are produced by the larger law firms, primarily for client companies and organisations, but are also made more widely available. Yet others are published by pressure groups, such as the Howard League for Penal Reform (*Criminal Justice*).

(e)   Law periodicals published abroad, particularly in other common law jurisdictions, such as the United States, Canada, Australia and New Zealand. They are the overseas equivalents of those given as examples in (a) above. Most academic law libraries will subscribe to a selection.

As well as these publications designed specifically for lawyers, useful information, particularly on the impact of law on a particular section of business, commerce or society, will be carried by non-law periodicals, e.g., titles such as *Economist, New Statesman and Society, Spectator, British Journal of Criminology* and *Town and Country Planning*.

The quality newspapers also carry regular features on legal topics.

So, the number of sources in which useful information for your essay, assignment or project might be found is vast. But as 3.8B shows, there are ways of methodically and efficiently, exploring and exploiting this literature.

3.8A2   Publication and general availability

Most academic law libraries are likely to subscribe to a wide range of academic and practitioner periodicals. The range of specialist periodicals will depend on the particular interests of the teaching department. Some newsletters may be taken, but again the titles purchased will reflect the interests of the law department. The quality newspapers should be available and some of the non-law specialist periodicals, again depending on the teaching interests of the particular university, polytechnic or college.

Public libraries, on the other hand, are likely to take only a very limited number of law titles, such as *New Law Journal* and *Solicitors' Journal*, the quality newspapers and a few of the major non-law specialist periodicals.

3.8A3   Citation

Lawyers frequently abbreviate the title of a journal in which an article they are quoting appears. There are no generally accepted standards for abbreviating titles and a wide variety of practices occur. You may frequently need to use one of the following lists of abbreviations to sort out the journal to which you are being referred:

(a)   Raistrick D., *Index to Legal Citations and Abbreviations* (London: Professional Books, 1981.

(b)   *Current Law Case Citator* (London: Sweet & Maxwell), any issue.

(c)   *Legal Journals Index* (Hebden Bridge: Legal Information Resources Ltd), any issue.

3.8B   EXPLOITATION

Many students make the mistake, when looking for periodical articles to assist preparation of an essay or assignment, of browsing through the contents pages or annual indexes of one or two of the major periodicals, in the hope of stumbling over relevant, valuable information. This method is not always productive and costs considerable time and effort. The most efficient way of finding relevant periodical articles is to use an indexing publication: a commercially produced index to the contents of tens if not hundreds of periodicals, with references to each article arranged under appropriate subject headings. *Legal Journals Index, Current Law* and *Index to Legal Periodicals* are the three indexing services relevant to the law of England and Wales. But, as a law student, you may occasionally need to research subjects related to law, such as criminology or social control, so publications including *Criminology and Penology Abstracts* and *Sociological Abstracts* are briefly noted below. Finally, newspapers often contain useful background articles on recent legal developments, or publish journalistic reports of notable court cases, which may never appear as authentic law reports. Examples include instances where sentencing policy or the level of awards of damages are in question or where the reliability of original forensic evidence is now doubted. Therefore a description of newspaper indexes, including *The Times Index*, and the *Clover Newspaper Index* is also provided.

3.8B1   *Legal Journals Index*

Legal Journals Index or LJI was first published in September 1986 and has appeared monthly since. It has quickly established itself as the foremost law periodical indexing service for the English jurisdiction for three reasons:

(a)   It indexes a very large number of periodicals – over 160 different titles, covering not only law as such but also topics such as the legal profession, education, training, computers and information technology generally.

(b)   It arranges entries under quite detailed and specific subject headings with frequent 'see' references from words or headings *not* used by the indexers to preferred headings.

(c)   Each issue contains five separate indexes: a subject index, author index, case index, legislation index and a book review index.

Further, to make LJI easier to use, the publishers cumulate the index entries every quarter, and at the year end an annual bound volume is issued.

Figure 3.25 shows the layout of several typical subject index entries with an explanation of the components.

The subject headings under which information is gathered are given in bold type, the main subject heading being in capital letters and any more detailed subject headings provided in upper and lower-case letters. All the entries in the subject index are in alphabetical order according to the subject headings. Below the subject heading, in smaller type, is the title of the periodical article or case note, or if the information relates to an original law report in a periodical, the names of parties. If the title of the periodical article does not make clear what the article is about, the compilers of LJI include in brackets a helpful summary of the subject-matter. Next follows the name/s

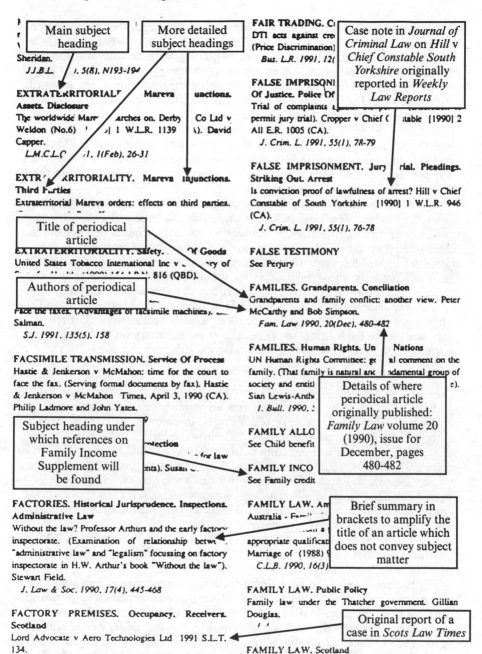

Figure 3.25 Extract from subject index of *Legal Journals Index*, March 1991.

of the author/s of the article. For a case note or law report the case citation is provided. Finally, in italic typeface, details are given of where the article or case note was originally published, beginning with an abbreviation for the title of the periodical, and then the year, volume, issue number and page number/s. You will need to use the list of abbreviations given at the front of each issue of LJI to expand the periodical title fully. Only when you have the full title of the periodical can you check the periodical holdings list of your library, to see if the periodical is in stock, and so find and read the article or case note you have discovered by using LJI. If the periodical is not in the stock of your library you will need to use the inter-library loan service (see appendix 2), and your request for this service must include the full title of the periodical you require.

As well as the subject index you will probably find the case and legislation indexes valuable. The case index arranges, in alphabetical order by the names of parties to an action, references to not only original reports of the cases when they appeared in law periodicals, but also case notes or commentaries, which will help you understand the meaning and effect of the court's decision. Similarly, the legislation index arranges references, in alphabetical order by the title of the Bill or Act of Parliament or secondary legislation, to articles explaining its meaning and effect. This index is especially useful when you are seeking guidance on the likely effect of a current Bill or recently passed Act of Parliament, for explanatory commentary on such recent developments is likely to be found only in periodicals.

3.8B2   Current Law Monthly Digest

Current Law Monthly Digest or CL has been published monthly since 1947, and at the end of each year index entries are cumulated into a single, bound volume, *Current Law Yearbook* (CLY). CL, in contrast to LJI, indexes a more restricted range of periodicals since it is concerned only with the law as such. Also, the subject indexing is not so detailed and user friendly, and there are no brief descriptions added by the compilers in instances where the title of the original article indexed is not self explanatory. However, CL's strength is in the range of different legal sources indexed, for apart from periodical articles it also indexes textbooks, new Acts, statutory instruments, cases and major government publications.

Information is arranged in CL under very broad subject headings. Where an article is noticed by the compilers it is mentioned in one of the final entries under each subject heading.

The presentation of the same information in *Current Law Yearbook*, the annual cumulation, is quite different. References to articles are removed from the main sequence in the body of the yearbook and arranged in a separate sequence towards the back of the volume, but still under broad subject headings. References to individual periodical articles are arranged under each subject heading in alphabetical order by the first word in the title. This arrangement is not very helpful. Let us take an example and discover why. Suppose you are looking for articles on the subject of 'medical negligence'. The illustration in figure 3.26 is taken from *Current Law Yearbook* for 1988.

Publication access in public libraries: 151 L.G.Rev. 984.

Race relations and local authority contracts (R. Ward): 152 L.G.Rev. 804.

Rate refund paid under a mistake of law: 152 L.G. Rev. 484.

Recent review of case law (P. Cooling): 152 L.G.Rev. 507.

Redress possible against council delays (W. Birtles): [1987] L.G.C. November 20, 12.

Responsibility without power—social worker's dilemma (R. Marr): 1988 S.L.T. (News) 333.

Review of recent case law (P. Cooling): 152 L.G.Rev. 43.

Review of the year—case law '87 (C. Cross): [1988] L.G.C. February 26, 11.

Sex establishment licensing in Soho: (C. Manchesten: 152 L.G. Rev. 663.

"Sex establishments" and determining the validity of a licensing authority decision 3.Rev. 124.

General subject heading

uthority publicity: 152

Sub c/ racts: councils' legal position (C. C .s): [1987] L.G.C. December 11, 12.

Symb /: and meaningless legislation (Local Go / nment Act 1988, s.28) (K. Norrie): (1' s) 33 J.L.S. 310.

War / nip, judicial review and local authorities (Holgate): 152 L.G.Rev. 585.

W' er remedy for aggrieved councils? . Crawford): [1988] L.G.C. August 5, 9.

MEDICINE

AIDS: adapting the law (A. Orn): 13⁵ /ew L.J. 3⁰⁰

Assistei

Title of periodical article

(s in

Engla

Compe aganas): 16 Anglo-Am. 117.

Controlling AIDS: some legal issues (R. Wacks): 138 New L.J. 254.

Damages for sterility (M. Puxon and A. Buchan): 138 New L.J. 80.

Demarcation in medical practice: the extended role of the nurse (D. Kloss): (1988) 4 P.N. 41.

Doctors with AIDS: dilemmas of confidentiality (J. McHale): (1988) 4 P.N. 76.

Expert evidence in medical negligence actions or forensic blind man's-buff (L. Mulcahy): (1987) 3 P.N. 187.

Further reflections on medical causation (A. F. Phillips): 1988 S.L.T. (News) 325.

Gold, Kay and the limits of medical liability (J. Keown): (1988) 4 P.N. 1.

Mental health review tribunals (A. Khan and D. Murgatroyd): 132 S.J. 682.

Negligence and Wilsher (J. Tingle): 132 S.J. 910.

New development in professional negligence handwriting and the duty of care (D. Feldman): (1988) 4 P.N. 68.

Parallel importation of pharmaceutical products in the Common Market (C. Morcom): [1988] 2 E.I.P.R. 47.

Procedural fairness and the General Medical Council (D. Feldman): (1987) 3 P.N. 155.

Proof of causation in medical negligence cases (J. Logie): 1988 S.L.T. 25.

Radiation: proving the causal link with cancer (D. Branams): 138 New L.J. 570.

Selective reduction of multiple pregnancy (J. Keown): 137 New L.J. 1165.

Selective reduction of pregnancy (D. Branams): [1988] L.S.Gaz. January 6, 25.

Social security adjudication and occupational lung diseases

Author of periodical article

Sterilisation and Pearh: [1987]

Sterilisation of mentally handi ped children (considering Re B. [1987] .L.Y. 2533) (J. Thomson): 1988 S.L.T. (N vs) 1.

Surrogacy: giving it an unde pod name (D. Morgan): [1988] J.S.W.L. . ⁵.

Transplantation, the fetus an the law (D. Branms): 138 New L.J. 91.

Treatment and mental handicap (Gunn): 16 Anglo-Am. 242.

Update on medical negligence (A. Samuels): 131 S.J. 1500.

MENTAL H TH

Abuse of ₹ old and vulnerable (I. Young): [1988] L Gaz. February 24, 25.

Enduring ₣ ers of attorney and statutory wills (D. n): [1988] L.S.Gaz., March 9, 38.

EPAs as ord ry powers? (R. Oerton): 131

Details of where periodical article originally published: Solicitors' Journal, volume 131, page 1500

s (A. Khan and 2.

and the courts ¹1, 100.

Mental Health ¹.L.R. 660.

Sterilisation of mentally handicapped children (considering Re B. [1987] C.L.Y. 2533) (J. Thomson): 1988 S.L.T. (News) 1.

Treatment and mental handicap (M. Gunn): 16 Anglo-Am. 242.

MINING LAW

Extracting taxation facts (J. Both): 966 Est. Times 14.

Figure 3.26   Extract from *Current Law Yearbook 1988*.

First, there is no entry in the subject heading list for this topic, and no 'see' reference to guide you to where the indexer has chosen to place information on medical negligence. You have to work out for yourself that medical negligence is indexed twice, under both the broad subject headings of 'medicine' and 'negligence'. Other subjects can be buried under headings you might not expect. Articles on computer hacking, for example, are listed under the heading of criminal law! Secondly, the references to individual periodical articles listed under each subject heading are arranged alphabetically by the first word the author happens to have selected for the title of the article. The illustration shows the entries under the heading 'medicine' and you can see that two articles happen to be titled 'medical negligence' and appear at 'M' in the sequence but there are other articles on the topic at 'E' (Expert evidence in medical negligence actions . . .), 'G' (Gold, Kay and the limits of medical liability . . .), 'P' (Proof of causation in medical negligence . . .) and 'U' (Update on medical negligence . . .). So, to search *Current Law Yearbook* fully for periodical articles you will need to scan the *whole* list of articles under the most relevant heading you can find – a rather laborious business! Thirdly, where the titles of articles are enigmatic or too brief to give much of an idea of the content of the article itself, there are no helpful summaries, as in *Legal Journals Index*, to assist you decide whether the item is going to be worth the effort of finding it in the original publication.

As with LJI, references in CL and CLY to periodical titles are abbreviated, so you will need to use the list of abbreviations, printed elsewhere in the publication, to expand the title fully, before you can check your library's periodical holdings list to see if the original periodical is in stock.

CL offers only a single index to periodical articles and does not include case or legislation indexes which LJI has.

3.8B3 *Index to Legal Periodicals*

Index to Legal Periodicals or ILP has been published since 1908. It is an American publication, issued 11 times a year, with quarterly and annual cumulations. It indexes over 450 periodical titles and, as you might expect, they are mainly United States publications but it also includes major titles published in Canada, Australia, New Zealand, Ireland and Great Britain. It is valuable for the references it contains to overseas writing on English law, and on occasions when you need to compare practice and procedure in English law with that in another common law jurisdiction (when you are studying comparative law).

There are four separate indexes in each issue: a combined subject and author index, which is the one you will probably find most useful, an index to periodical articles or notes on cases (the majority are to non-English cases), an index to articles on statutes (again, mainly non-English) and, finally, an index to book reviews.

The layout of the combined subject and author index is helpful, as figure 3.27 shows. Just beneath some subject headings a 'see' reference guides you to the preferred heading used by the indexer for a topic. Some subject headings have lists of 'see also' reference which guide you to entries on related subjects, elsewhere in the publication. These 'see' and 'see also' references are especially useful because, being an American publication, it uses transatlantic terminology. For example, there are no entries under 'murder' but the index will guide you to the preferred term 'homicide'.

As with the other periodical indexing services discussed above, the titles of individual periodicals indexed are much abbreviated and to expand the title you will need to consult the list printed at the front of each issue.

For a periodical article to appear in ILP it must be at least five 'ordinary' pages or two folio pages in length. This means the short articles in practitioners' periodicals are not included. So, coupled with its distinctive American bias, ILP is not the first periodical indexing service to consult when undertaking legal research, except if you specifically require material for comparative law.

3.8B4   Halsbury's Laws of England – Noter-Up and Annual Abridgements

Since 1990, articles from a limited number of the leading practice and academic periodicals have been indexed in the Noter-Up and Annual Abridgements under broad subject headings, which correspond to those used in the arrangement of information in the Main Volumes of this encyclopaedic work. The most recent articles are listed in the loose-leaf Noter-Up binder. At the end of the year they are incorporated in the Annual Abridgement volume. Only longer articles seem to be included; case notes are excluded. The arrangement of individual articles under a subject heading is by the first word in the title chosen by the author, so searching can be tedious. There are no cross-references to ensure readers are guided to the most appropriate heading for their query. However, since Halsbury's Laws is so widely available in libraries it is a valuable stand-by, but not the first publication to consider using for research on the periodical literature.

3.8B5   Criminology and Penology Abstracts

Criminology and Penology Abstracts or C & PA was first published in 1961 under the title Excerpta Criminologica; in 1969 it changed to Abstracts on Criminology and Penology and in 1980 adopted its current title. Although a Dutch publication, it is an international abstracting service which includes references to articles on criminal procedure and the administration of justice. Over 250 periodicals covering sociology, criminology, medicine, psychology as well as law are included in the quarterly issues. C & PA is an abstracting service so each entry includes more information than that appearing in an indexing service. In addition to the details of where to find the original article, the compilers provide a brief, descriptive summary of each article ('the abstract') which helps you to decide whether the article is relevant to your research, before spending time tracing the original in the library.

3.8B6   Sociological Abstracts

Sociological Abstracts, SA, an American publication, began in 1953 and is published six times a year. Its coverage is international and entries are

SUBJECT AND AUTHOR INDEX **419**

Subjects and authors inter-filed in a single alphabetical sequence

Note American spelling

Subject heading under which references on labor arbitration will be found

Subject heading

Kupperman, Joel J.
Relations between the sexes: ti
25 *San Diego L. Rev.* 1(

Kuroda, Kenji
Beware of Japanese negotiation style: how to ›tiate with Japanese companies; by D. Zhang, K. da. 10 *Nw. J. Int'l L. & Bus.* 195-212 Fall '89

Kurtz, Maxine
Report of the public employee relations committe M. Kurtz, S. Levitan, J. Toole. 21 *Urb. Law.* 94 Fall '89

Kurucza, Robert M.
Securities and investment advisory activities of banks; by R. M. Kurucza, R. G. Ballen, N. H. Diana. 45 *Bus. Law.* 1919-29 Je '90
Securities and investment advisory activities of banks; by R. M Kurucza, R. G. Ballen, T. R. McTaggart.

Controls on technology transfer: an analysis of the Southern response to Northern technological protectionism. 13 *Md. J. Int'l L. & Trade* 301-29 Spr '89
Performance of electric utilities in developing countries: the Ghanaian and Nigerian experience. 11 *Loy. L.A. Int'l & Comp. L.J.* 515

Kurzban, Ira J.
Employer sanctions—two y
Ja '90

Kushner, James A.
An unfinished agenda: the
ment effort. 6 *Yale L. & Pol'y Rev.* 348-60 '88

Kushner, Joseph
Profit rates, risk, and size in Canadian banks and trust
34 *Antitrust Bull.* 683-93 Fall '89

Kutler, Stanley I.
A sword for a scabbard: reflections on the making of the Judiciary Act of 1789. 14 *Nova L. Rev.* 97-110 Fall '89

L

La Fleur, Catherine A.
Duty to defend: does a four corners approach cover all the bases? by D. H. Piper, C. A. La Fleur. 62 *Wis. Law.* 19-20+ Jl '89

La Fond, John Q.
Washington's diminished capacity defense under attack; by J. Q. La Fond, K. A. Gaddis. 13 *U. Puget Sound L. Rev.* 1-39 Fall '89

Laberge, Danielle
Femmes et criminalité: le contrôle social est-il sexué? Une analyse des données statistiques québécoises; by D. Laberge, S. Roy. 3 *Can. J. Women & L.* 457-64 '89/'90

LaBerge, Robert A.
Some of the more exotic risks associated with drug and alcohol testing; by L. P. DiLorenzo, R. A. LaBerge, W. M. Burke. 42 *N.Y.U. Conf. Lab.* 6.1-.38 '89

Labor, Migrant *See* Migrant labor

Labor arbitration *See* Industrial arbitration

Labor boycotts
See also
Picketing
Handbilling and the first amendment: a symbiotic relationship? The impact of DeBartolo v. Florida Building Trades Council [108 S. Ct. 1392]. J. P. Tielborg. 41 *Lab. L.J.* 235-48 Ap '90
Industrial protection: a new advance—the use of "employer injunctions" by trade unions. M. L. Worsnop. 63 *Law Inst. J.* 1046-8 N '89
Secondary boycotts after DeBartolo [Edward J. DeBartolo Corp. v. Florida Gulf Coast Building & Construction Trades Council, 108 S. Ct. 1392]: has the Supreme Court handed unions a powerful new weapon? 75 *Iowa L. Rev.* 217-34 O '89

Labor disputes
See also
Collective bargaining
Industrial arbitration
Labor boycotts
Unfair labor practices

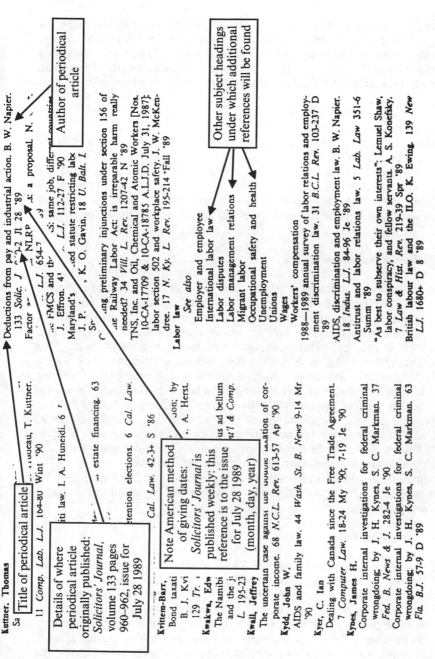

Figure 3.27 Extract from subject and author index of *Index to Legal Periodicals* 1989/90.

compiled from over 1,500 periodicals. Details of articles, with abstracts, are arranged under over 30 broad subject headings, one of which: social control, includes references to articles on the sociology of law, police, penology and correctional problems. Each entry not only includes details of where an article was originally published but also a brief summary of its contents.

3.8B7   Social Service Abstracts

Commenced in 1977, *Social Service Abstracts* summarises each month selected documents added to the stock of the Departments of Health and Social Security Library in London. Whilst the publication indexes publications dealing with social policy and social work, it is a useful source for references to articles on the law, its operation and reform, written from the point of view of social workers or social services personnel, rather than that of lawyers.

3.8B8   British Humanities Index

Whilst all the above indexing or abstracting services are related to a specific subject area, BHI might be termed an 'umbrella' service, for it covers the whole field of the humanities including the arts, economics, history, philosophy, politics and society, as well as non-specialist articles in science and technology. It indexes major newspaper articles as well as journals. This width of subject coverage is valuable when researching the impact of law on society; for example, articles in non-legal journals on housing law or reform of the law on homelessness will feature in BHI. Over 200 journals are indexed. BHI is published quarterly with a cumulated, annual bound volume published at the year end. The layout and presentation of index entries is good; 'see' and 'see also' references are amply provided and a recent innovation is the provision of brief, descriptive notes of the content of articles where the title of the original article is not very informative.

Because of its wide subject coverage BHI is one of the few indexing services mentioned in this section of the book which will be found in most academic *and* public libraries.

3.8B9   The Times Index

The Times Index is compiled from *The Times,* the *Sunday Times* and the various *Times* literary and educational supplements. It is an exhaustive monthly index (cumulated each year) to the entire contents of these publications. The individual index entries are so detailed as to include the date, page and column reference (lettered a to h from the left of the page) to where original articles will be found! The major problem with *The Times Index* is that it takes time to compile and publish, so the most recent issue is always at least three months behind the latest issue of the newspaper itself. (But see *The Times Newspapers* in 3.8C5). Virtually every academic and major public library will take *The Times Index.*

3.8B10   Clover Newspaper Index

This indexes all the quality newspapers (in alphabetical order: *Daily Telegraph, Financial Times, Guardian, Independent, Observer, Sunday Times* and *The Times*) and their 'colour supplements'. It first appeared in 1986 and is published weekly. It is available within two or three *weeks* of the issues of the newspapers indexed. Consequently, the subject indexing is more basic and the only information given about each article is its title (in its original, attenuated journalese). The index is, nonetheless, very useful because of its good currency.

3.8C   ELECTRONIC SOURCES

For background information on the use of electronic databases, see appendix 4.

3.8C1   Legal Journals Index

The electronic equivalent of the publication described in 3.8B1 is available updated every two weeks. The data are held on a disc which can be searched using a personal computer. For security and other reasons the disc may not be on public display in academic libraries, so ask library staff if the service is provided.

3.8C2   Index to Legal Periodicals

Approximately the last 10 years' indexing included in the printed database described in 3.8B3 is mounted on computers in the United States and can be searched by subscribers worldwide to a number of on–line host organisations. The *Index* is available on LEXIS, in the US law library: LAWREV. Your library will have details. In addition, the same 10-year database is available on CD-ROM; again, ask if your library has this service.

3.8C3   Sociological Abstracts

This on-line database corresponds to the printed equivalent described in 3.8B6 but only for the period from 1963 to the present. It may be searched through a number of on-line hosts – your library will have details. The database is also available on CD-ROM under the name *Sociofile/SOPODA* but includes the contents of *Sociological Abstracts* from 1974 onwards, only.

3.8C4   DHSS-DATA

The Departments of Health and Social Security Library Catalogues from which *Social Services Abstracts* (3.8B7) is compiled, are available on the Data-Star on-line host. Ask your library for details.

3.8C5   BHI PLUS

This is the CD-ROM equivalent to *British Humanities Index* (3.8B8) covering over 100,000 indexed articles from over 320 key humanities journals and daily newspapers from 1985 to the present. The discs are updated with the same frequency as the paper version.

3.8C6   *The Times Newspapers*

The full text, not just the index, of *The Times* and the *Sunday Times* newspapers, excluding advertisements etc., is mounted on the computers of three on-line organisations, the longest backfile of information being on FT PRO-FILE Information. FT PROFILE also contains the full text of the *Daily Telegraph, Sunday Telegraph, Independent* and *Independent on Sunday*, and the *Guardian*, which can all be searched at the same time. Further, the database is updated daily with the latest issues of these newspapers. Ask your library staff for further information.

A number of newspapers are now available on CD-ROM. The list includes *The Times, Sunday Times, Guardian, Independent* and the *Financial Times*. Each individual disc contains the full text of one of the newspapers, but generally only for 1990 onwards. New developments occur quickly in the CD-ROM field, and your library will be able to advise on current availability and coverage.

3.8C7   *British Newspaper Index*

This compact disc contains the indexes to nine quality newspapers including *The Times* and its literary and education supplements, *Sunday Times, Financial Times, Independent* and *Independent on Sunday*. The disc is up-dated cumulatively every three months and begins with 1990. Eventually up to five years indexing will be included on each disc.

3.8C8   *Legal Resource Index*

Although the vast majority of the 850 English-language periodicals indexed in this remote on-line database are American publications, some English titles are included. The database is updated monthly and may be searched by subscribers to any one of the several on-line hosts – ask library staff for further details.

3.8C9   *LEXIS*

LEXIS contains the full text of only a handful of English law periodicals. Issues of two are included from 1986 onwards, the remainder from more recent dates. To search the periodicals select the ENGGEN library and the UK journal file, entitled UKJNL, and then select whether you wish to search all the files in that library (i.e., all the periodical titles) or just an individual title. Your search request could be either for a subject, or an author, or mention of an Act or case by name, which you should type in the form you believe it would be mentioned in the text of the periodical, remembering to use 'connectors' where necessary. See appendix 6 for an explanation of how to search LEXIS.

3.8D   RESEARCH STRATEGIES

The sources you should use and exploit will depend on the type of information you require and how current the topic. If the subject is of very recent origin then you may find that only the most rapidly compiled periodical indexes (such as *Legal Journals Index*) or the remote on-line electronic sources (not the CD-ROM versions), will have indexed any articles which have been written on the topic. To help you match appropriate paper and/or electronic sources to the subject you want to research, a few general suggestions of titles to search are listed below; it will be profitable if, before you start your research, you talk over your precise information needs with library staff, who will be best able to advise on the most relevant sources and, more importantly, those readily available.

For English law use one or more of: *Legal Journals Index* (3.8B1, 3.8C1), *Current Law* (3.8B2), *Halsbury's Laws* (3.8B4).

For English law compared with other common law jurisdictions use one or more of: *Legal Journals Index* (3.8B1, 3.8C1), *Index to Legal Periodicals* (3.8B3, 3.8C2), *Legal Resource Index* (3.8C8).

For information on the profession of law and topics related to law use: *Legal Journals Index* (3.8B1, 3.8C1).

For information on related topics select from: *Criminology & Penology Abstracts* (3.8B5), Sociological Abstracts (3.8B6, 3.8C3), *Social Services Abstracts* (3.8B7), *British Humanities Index* (3.8B8, 3.8C5), *DHSS-DATA* (3.8C4), *Legal Resource Index* (3.8C8).

For information which might have appeared in newspapers select from: *The Times Newspapers* (3.8C6), *British Newspaper Index* (3.8C7), *The Times Index* (3.8B9), *Clover Newspaper Index* (3.8B10).

3.9   RESEARCH LITERATURE

3.9A   DESCRIPTION

Particularly when you are undertaking a final-year project, dissertation or longer piece of investigative writing, you may wish to check whether anyone else has completed, or is currently undertaking, postgraduate (e.g., masters or doctorate) or other advanced research into the precise topic or a related area in which you are interested. A number of lists or indexes of research are published and will be collected by academic libraries; you are unlikely to find public libraries keeping them. Usually under six copies of higher degree dissertations or theses are produced by the author, and one will be deposited in the library of the university or polytechnic at which the degree was awarded. It is necessary, therefore, to use the lists or indexes as a means of identifying relevant work and then ask your own library to obtain a copy of the thesis or dissertation via the inter-library loan service (see appendix 2 on how to use this service). The written product of research undertaken other than for a higher degree, for example, by a group of staff in a university, polytechnic or other institution, may be even more difficult to trace. It could be a research paper or memorandum published by the teaching department, or one or a series of periodical articles. One of the lists of ongoing research, *Current Research in Britain*, is valuable because it gives the names of the researchers and their departmental address, so you will be able to write to them seeking information about their research project and any published results.

However, before you decide to write, ensure you have checked sources of information about books (3.6) and periodical articles (3.8), so you are already aware of any material published by the researcher/s and can decide whether your enquiry with them is going to be a worthwhile use of both your, and their, time and effort.

3.9B   EXPLOITATION

3.9B1   Legal Research in the United Kingdom 1905–1984

Information for this list of completed research was collected by a survey, conducted by one of the leading academic legal research organisations, the Institute of Advanced Legal Studies (IALS), London, of over 40 universities and colleges throughout the UK. The list is arranged in alphabetical order by subject and within each subject chronologically. The only information given about the content and subject-matter of each thesis is its title. Author and geographical indexes (i.e., by jurisdiction) are also provided.

3.9B2   List of Current Legal Research Topics

Unfortunately, this publication prepared by IALS ceased with number 36, October 1988. Issued approximately annually this listed topics currently under investigation in universities and polytechnics and employed a similar layout and presentation to the list of completed research noted above,

3.9B3   Index to Theses

Index to Theses is the only comprehensive listing of British theses (regardless of subject). It commenced in 1950. From 1986 onwards the *Index* has appeared in four parts each year, listing over 9,000 theses annually, each entry including a substantial abstract or summary of the contents of the thesis. This publication is useful because it includes theses in subjects related to law as well as law itself.

3.9B4   Current Research in Britain

This is a national register of current research being carried out in universities, polytechnics, colleges and other institutions (e.g., government departments) within the UK. It is published in four sections, the volume for social sciences, revised annually, being most relevant to law. Each entry in the list includes details of the name of the principal investigator, and a brief description of the research topic and any publications. The entries are arranged by institution and department where the research is being undertaken, but helpfully constructed subject and keyword indexes at the back of the volume, allow information to be found by other routes. A CD-ROM version of this source is currently being planned.

3.9B5 Dissertation Abstracts International

First published in 1938, this is now a monthly compilation of abstracts of doctoral dissertations submitted to over 400 educational institutions in the United States and Canada. Dis. Abs., as it is commonly known, is divided into two sections, law dissertations featuring in section A, which covers the humanities and social sciences. The considerable interest in English law shown by overseas researchers is apparent, even from the most cursory glance over the subject indexes.

3.9C ELECTRONIC SOURCES

For background information on the use of electronic databases, see appendix 4.

3.9C1 Index to Theses on CD-ROM

During 1991 a CD-ROM version of the published index (3.9B3) for the years 1970–90 became available. The 1992 edition will cover the full period over which *Index to Theses* has been available: 1950–91. These discs correspond with the printed product.

3.9C2 Dissertation Abstracts Online

Dissertation Abstracts International (3.9B5) and two related databases are mounted on computers in the United States which can be searched worldwide by subscribers to a number of on-line hosts organisations. Your library will have details. Dis. Abs. is also available on CD-ROM (*Dissertation Abstracts Ondisc*) which can be mounted on a personal computer. Some libraries may have the service available – ask staff for information.

3.9D RESEARCH STRATEGIES

Are you searching for the products of research, i.e., theses and research publications? If so, use: *Legal Research in the United Kingdom 1905–1984* (3.9B1), *Index to Theses* (3.9B3, 3.9C1), *Dissertation Abstracts* (3.9B5, 3.9C2).

Are you searching for the names of people currently engaged in research? If so use: *List of Current Legal Research Topics* (3.9B2), but bear in mind the information it contains is becoming increasingly out of date; *Current Research in Britain* (3.9B4).

3.10   REFERENCE WORKS

3.10A   DESCRIPTION

The catch-all term 'reference works' embraces three distinct types of publication: dictionaries: which usually explain the meaning of legal terms and phrases; directories: which provide names and addresses of individuals and organisations; compendia: which provide a concise introduction to law.

The range of individual titles available is enormous and what follows is but a brief guide to the wide selection you will find in most law libraries.

3.10A1   Dictionaries

These fall into four groups:

(a)   Conventional dictionaries, which provide an explanation of a word or phrase to varying degrees of detail.

(b)   Judicial dictionaries of words and phrases, which provide details of and quotations from statutes and cases where the courts have considered the meaning of each word or phrase.

(c)   Indexes, or lists of legal abbreviations and citations, with explanations of their meaning.

(d)   Biographical dictionaries – 'who was who' in the legal profession.

3.10A1.1   Conventional dictionaries

A recent study of reported judgments (Clinch 1989, p. 481) found that the *Shorter Oxford English Dictionary* was the most frequently cited of all types of dictionary, with the *Oxford English Dictionary* placed second. These two accounted for over half the citations to all dictionaries.

Mozley and Whiteley's Law Dictionary (10th ed., 1988) provides definitions of legal terms across the whole field of law, including legal history. *A Concise Dictionary of Law* (2nd ed., 1990), on the other hand, is primarily intended for those without a qualification in law but who, like surveyors, accountants, civil servants, local government officers, social workers, probation officers, business people and legal secretaries, require some knowledge of the precise meaning and spelling of legal terms in their work. The entries therefore contain quite lengthy explanations but are chosen with modern-day practice in mind. *Osborn's Concise Law Dictionary* (8th ed., 1990) is intended for use by lawyers, and has the added bonuses of a list of law reports, with their abbreviations, and a table of the regnal years of English sovereigns (see 3.2.2 for the purpose and value of this). A number of dictionaries have been compiled which restrict entries to words found in a specialised area of law: *Dictionary of Employment Law* (1985), *Dictionary of Shipping Law* (1984), *Dictionary of Commercial Law* (1983), *Dictionary of Company Law* (2nd ed., 1985). So far all the dictionaries mentioned have been compact, single volume works, the sort of publication you might buy for yourself! *Jowitt's Dictionary of English Law* (2nd ed., 1977) is in two large volumes and is kept up to date by the publication of supplements every few years. It aims to be comprehensive, giving a definition and explanation of every legal term old and new.

3.10A1.2 Judicial dictionaries

Stroud's Judicial Dictionary of Words and Phrases (5th ed., 1986) published in six volumes and kept up to date by occasional supplements, provides details of the interpretations by judges of words and phrases, as well as references to definitions included in statutes. Two innovations in this edition are tables of cases and statutes in the sixth volume which enable you to look up the interpretation of a word or phrase from the case name or statute title. *Words and Phrases Legally Defined* (3rd ed., 1988–9), in four volumes with annual Cumulative Supplements, is similar but provides verbatim extracts from speeches and judgments, as well as a selection of statutory definitions.

Definitions of words and phrases can also be found by using the index to *Halsbury's Laws of England*, which will guide you to the appropriate Main Volume of the encyclopaedia. Recent interpretations by the courts are listed in the Noter-Up binder. *Current Law Monthly Digest* and *Current Law Yearbooks* provide similar listings, but lack the consolidated index which makes *Halsbury's* so much easier to use.

3.10A1.3 Indexes or lists of legal citations and abbreviations

A glance at the 'citation' sections of the discussions on law reports and law periodicals earlier in this book (sections 3.4 and 3.8, respectively) will reveal how little standardisation there is in the abbreviations used by authors to identify the material they cite. Many publications are commonly referred to by several abbreviations and many abbreviations have more than one meaning. The most comprehensive index available is Donald Raistrick's *Index to Legal Citations and Abbreviations* (1981) which includes not only abbreviations used in the United Kingdom, but also the Commonwealth, USA and Common Market. A word of warning, though; some students are baffled when, on checking an abbreviation for a law report or periodical title cited in their reading, they learn that it is a rather obscure overseas publication. The chances are that the citation abbreviation is a new concoction of the author, and really relates to a more well known publication in the English jurisdiction. So, a little guesswork, as well as delving into *Raistrick*, is required.

Much smaller lists of abbreviations will be found in *Sweet and Maxwell's Guide to Law Reports and Statutes* (3rd ed., 1959) and the University of London, Institute of Advanced Legal Studies, *Manual of Legal Citations*, part 1, The British Isles (1959). Lists will also be found in *Current Law Monthly Digest* and *Current Law Yearbooks, Index to Legal Periodicals*, the first volume of *The Digest* and the first volume of *Halsbury's Laws*. Each issue of *Legal Journals Index* carries a list of abbreviations to the 160 or more titles it indexes – this is particularly useful because of LJI's comprehensive coverage of the periodical literature.

3.10A1.4   Biographical dictionaries

Occasionally you may want to go behind the law itself and learn something of notable people in the legal profession. For those still alive the best source is *Who's Who* (annual).

For details of names from the past, the *Biographical Dictionary of the Common Law* (1984) edited by A.W.B. Simpson will prove invaluable. The more famous lawyers noted in Professor Simpson's work will also have entries in *Who Was Who* (published each decade) and the *Dictionary of National Biography* (originally published between 1885 and 1901 and updated every 10 years, and more recently by a new volume every five years).

3.10A2   Directories

These may be divided into two groups:

(a)   those specific to law and the law profession, and
(b)   titles of general coverage.

3.10A2.1   Directories for law

There are many; here is a selective list.

One of the most authoritative listings of solicitors and barristers is the *Solicitors' and Barristers' Directory*, published annually. It includes a list of solicitors and, in addition, official lists of barristers, Fellows of the Institute of Legal Executives and licensed conveyancers. The list of solicitors' firms and individuals is arranged geographically with details of the work they will undertake – very useful when you are seeking a placement or articles! Chambers and Partners' directory, *The Legal Profession*, is an annual guide to the top 1,000 law firms and all barristers' chambers, with useful specialist lists indicating which firms and chambers are best known for particular areas of expertise, and also includes regional listings. Indexes at the back of the volume enable you to identify those firms or sets of chambers handling particular types of business. *Havers' Companion to the Bar*, a new title to the bookshelves, is different yet again; as well as a conventional listing of barristers and their chambers it provides biographies of 4,000 individual lawyers, including details of leading cases in which they have appeared.

The Solicitors' and Barristers' Diary, a companion volume to the *Directory*, lists the courts and tribunals of England and Wales, their addresses and telephone numbers, and the names of judges, recorders and clerks. In addition it provides names and addresses for the members of the government legal service. *Shaw's Directory of Courts in the United Kingdom* (annual) provides similar information but includes Scotland and Northern Ireland.

Finally, a volume you will find useful when wishing to study in vacations, or when you wish to find a law library with a more comprehensive collection than is available locally. *The Directory of Law Libraries in the British Isles* (3rd ed., 1988) provides details of the names, addresses and telephone numbers, and in most instances a named contact, with brief details of collections and services for hundreds of law libraries in all types of organisation. Many are private, so if you are contemplating using them, it is essential to contact the librarian beforehand to discover whether you can gain admission and on what conditions. Discuss your need to use other libraries with your 'local' law librarian, who may be able to assist and advise on the best approach.

3.10A2.2   General directories

Again, there is a vast number, but here is a selection you should find invaluable, particularly when researching your final-year project or dissertation.

Civil Service Yearbook (annual) is a comprehensive listing of government departments and organisations, with brief details of the responsibilities of each right down to quite specific operational levels, names of key civil servants and enquiry point telephone numbers. *Municipal Yearbook* is in two volumes: the first, reviewing one by one the functions of local government, the second, comprising entries for every local authority in the United Kingdom including the names, addresses and telephone numbers of individual offices and departments. *Councils, Committees and Boards* (7th ed., 1989) is a directory of advisory, consultative and executive organisations working at national or regional level – very useful for tracing the names and addresses of obscure government advisory committees or public authorities. A companion volume, *Directory of British Associations* (10th ed., 1990), is even more valuable, for you can trace the existence of pressure groups, professional and trade associations, societies and similar organisations with voluntary membership. Details of their names, addresses, contact person, sphere of interest etc. are provided.

3.10A2.3   Compendia

I mention two, quite different in their aims and content. The *Oxford Companion to Law* (1980) contains thousands of dictionary-like entries on the principal legal institutions, courts, judges, jurists, systems of law, branches of law, legal ideas, concepts, doctrines and principles of law. References at the end of some articles and in one of the appendices provide leads to major sources of information. In complete contrast, *The Penguin Guide to the Law* (2nd ed., 1986) is a highly readable, lay person's guide to the law and the legal system in England and Wales. However, in using this particular publication you should remember it is a highly condensed view of the law, and the law changes fast, so parts of the book will be out of date. Little skill is needed to open and read a text such as the *Penguin Guide* – but, as a law student, you should be honing your research skills on some of the sources noted much earlier in this chapter!

3.11   OFFICIAL PUBLICATIONS

3.11A   DESCRIPTION

3.11A1   Definition

There is no agreed definition of what constitutes an 'official publication'. Her Majesty's Stationery Office (HMSO) is the publisher for Parliament, government departments and other organisations funded or controlled by government. All the publications required by Parliament to carry out its business (Parliamentary publications) are published by HMSO and comprise about half the 8,000 to 9,000 titles issued by HMSO each year. The other half are termed non-Parliamentary, and are published by HMSO on behalf of government departments and other 'official' organisations. However, in addition, as many titles again as are published by HMSO in total are issued direct to the public by government departments and other organisations, and not through HMSO at all.

Included in this huge output is a wealth of material relevant to the study of law. It is essential that you gain a basic grasp of the sources devised to help you find your way around this publishing maze and develop skills in using them.

What follows is a sketch of the main types of HMSO and non-HMSO official publication you are likely to come across in law or legal studies. They fall into three groups: Parliamentary publications; HMSO non-Parliamentary publications, and, finally, non-HMSO official publications.

3.11A1.1   Parliamentary publications

3.11A1.1.1   Parliamentary proceedings and debates

Both Houses of Parliament produce records of what was done rather than what was said; they are, respectively, the *House of Commons Votes and Proceedings* and *House of Lords Minutes of Proceedings*. They are of limited legal research value, save that the *House of Commons Votes and Proceedings* records amendments to Bills at committee stage submitted *before* the committee has met.

Of considerably greater research value are the *Official Reports of Parliamentary Debates*, which since 1943 have been officially known as *Hansard*, after the person most closely linked with the reports when they were published privately in the early 19th century. There are two series, one for Commons and one for Lords, and they report verbatim what was said in Parliament (see 3.2.1B3 for further details). Part of the process of scrutiny of Public Bills in the Commons requires that they be considered by a Standing Committee of between 16 and 50 members. A separate publication from Hansard, *Official Report of Standing Committee Debates*, reports verbatim the deliberations of the Committees. These reports are of considerable research value because of the detailed scrutiny of the meaning, and effect, of the provisions of a Bill (see 3.2.1B3 for further detail).

There appear to be several different ways of citing a reference in the *Official Reports of Parliamentary Debates*, but the method recommended here is adapted from the one used in Erskine May's *Parliamentary Practice*, the authoritative guide to Parliamentary procedure:

House Deb (Parliamentary session) volume number abbreviation col. followed by column number.

The following are examples of a reference to a House of Commons debate, a House of Commons written answer to a question and a House of Lords debate:

HC Deb (1990–91) 195 col. 311
HC Deb (1990–91) 195, written answers col. 41
HL Deb (1990–91) 529 col. 111

Official Reports of Parliamentary Debates in Standing Committees are published in a separate series. Each Standing Committee may scrutinise several different pieces of legislation each session, and the column numbering of the reports begins afresh with each new legislative title. It is essential, therefore, not only to cite the House, the Standing Committee identifying letter, Parliamentary session dates, and column number, but also the title of the legislation under discussion. The manner of citing from debates in Standing Committees is rather different from debates on the floor of the House, as the example shows:

Stg Co Deb (1980-81) Co E Finance Bill col. 46

title of series (Parliamentary Session) Committee letter Bill title abbreviation col., followed by column number.

Most academic and many of the major public libraries will subscribe to *Official Reports of Parliamentary Debates* for the House of Commons, fewer will subscribe to those of the House of Lords, and fewer still to the *Official Reports of Standing Committee Debates*.

The work of a quite different type of committee, the Select Committee, can provide unique background material when looking at the administrative and social context of government policy and legislation. Select Committees, as their title suggests, are composed of members selected by the House who are best qualified for the specialised, essentially investigative work of the Committee. Their main purpose is to review the work of government, especially in the financial field, and examine aspects of public life. A Select Committee is given a specific remit by the House and usually empowered to summon people (witnesses), and require papers and records to be presented to it. These witnesses are not only Ministers and officials of government departments, but also representatives of private organisations and pressure groups. Following its investigations and deliberations the Select Committee will issue a report, with appendices containing the verbal and written evidence given to it. The report and appendices are published as part of a much more extensive series of Parliamentary publications known as House of Commons Papers, or, for the Lords, House of Lords Papers. If the matter investigated touches on the actions of a government department it is usual for the department to respond to the committee's recommendations and observations. The response is frequently in the form of a Command Paper (see 3.11A1.1.3).

The House of Lords, with two exceptions, has a system of *ad hoc* Select
Committees which are convened as the need arises. The House of Commons
Select Committees number 25 at present, and 14 directly relate to the areas
of responsibility of the principal departments of government. These are of
the greatest interest to law students, and of the 14 the Home Affairs Select
Committee is probably the most relevant. The reports of this Committee
have influenced the nature of subsequent legislation, notably its criticism in
1980 of the use of the Vagrancy Act 1824 to arrest a person suspected of loi-
tering with criminal intent – the 'sus' law – and its effect on race relations. In
the following Parliamentary session the government introduced the Criminal Attempts Bill which repealed the 'sus' law.

A House of Commons Paper is identified by a serial number printed without brackets at the bottom left of the title page. Since a new sequence of
numbers begins each session, it is essential to include details of the session.
Variations can be found in the order in which the elements in the citation
are given but the citation must include an abbreviation for the House, dates
of the session of Parliament and the paper number as in the following
example:

HC (1990–91) 7

House of Lords Papers were, up to the Parliamentary session 1988/89,
issued in a numerical sequence which included House of Lords Bills as well.
Since then they have been separated. The serial number of each item is
printed in round brackets at the foot of the front cover. Again, variation
can be found in the order with which the elements in the citation are given
but the reference must include an abbreviation for the House, dates of the
session and the paper number, in round brackets, as in the following
example:

HL (1984–85) (244)

Very occasionally Joint Committees of the House of Lords and the House of
Commons issue reports. Citations to a Paper of *both* Houses are usually
given in the form:

HL paper number, HC paper number (session)

as in the following example:

HL 40, HC 15-viii (1981-82)

House of Commons Papers are likely to be held by most academic libraries
and the larger public libaries, but House of Lords Papers are not widely collected.

3.11A1.1.2   Primary legislation

Bills and Acts of Parliament are fully described in 3.2.1 and 3.2.2.

3.11A.1.1.3   Command Papers

These are documents which originate outside Parliament and are presented to Parliament 'by command of Her Majesty' usually by the Minister responsible. The Sovereign, in fact, is never personally involved, for the procedure is merely a technical device used by Ministers to place documents before Parliament which have not been created through the business of Parliament. About 300 to 400 are presented each year and, for lawyers, are one of the most frequently sought Parliamentary publications. There are several different types (the Cm and Cmnd references at the end of the examples below, are explained on p. 162):

(a)   Statements of government policy on a topic, which may indicate the broad lines of future legislation – these are often referred to as 'White Papers', a historical term for a Parliamentary Paper not thick enough to require a protective cover. A recent example is *Legal Services: a Framework for the Future* (Cm 740, 1989).

(b)   Reports of Royal Commissions: prestigious, investigative bodies set up under Royal Warrant to examine a topic of public concern where legislation seems desirable. The use of this type of investigation has diminished considerably during the last decade; an example of one of the most recent reports published is the Report of the *Royal Commission on Criminal Procedure* (Cmnd 8092, 1981).

(c)   Reports of Departmental Committees, set up by a Minister to carry out investigations into a matter of public concern, such as the *Departmental Committee on Section 2 of the Official Secrets Act 1911* (Cmnd 5104, 1972).

(d)   Reports of tribunals or commissions of inquiry set up to inquire into a matter of urgent, public importance such as *The Brixton Disorders 10–12 April 1981. Report of an Inquiry by the Rt Hon the Lord Scarman OBE* (Cmnd 8427, 1981).

(e)   Reports of a number of permanent investigatory bodies such as the Monopolies and Mergers Commission and the Law Commission. In the case of the Law Commission its reports may be published either as Command Papers or House of Commons Papers. In addition to bearing a Command Paper number or a House of Commons Paper number, the reports of the Law Commission are individually numbered in a single sequence. The citation is officially abbreviated, as in this example: Law Com. No. 196. If, as sometimes happens, this is all the information you have about the report, check the most recent annual report of the Law Commission which contains in an appendix a list of all those published. Helpfully, this list also provides details of any legislation enacted subsequently to the publication of a particular report. Many law libraries have a set of Law Commission reports bound in sequence number order, as well as copies of individual reports which will appear on the library catalogue. The Commission's working papers are published as non-Parliamentary papers (see 3.11A1.2.1).

(f)   Treaties and agreements with other countries and with international organisations – these form the largest single group of Command Papers.

(g)   Annual accounts and statistics, such as the annual report of the Commissioner of Metropolitan Police, or the Home Office compilation published each year, *Criminal Statistics, England and Wales*.

So far, this categorisation of Command Papers appears logical and reasonably clear cut, but in 1967 a new type of publication began to appear: the 'Green Paper'. In a House of Commons debate (HC Deb (1966–67) 747 col. 651), the Minister credited with having coined the term defined a Green Paper as 'a statement by the government not of policy determined but of propositions put before the whole nation for discussion'. Individual Green Papers are sometimes subtitled: 'a consultative document'. The choice of the collective title 'Green Paper' is the result of the colour chosen for the cover of the first one. At first these documents were published either by HMSO as non-Parliamentary papers or by government departments themselves. However, an increasing number are now published as Command Papers, yet according to the original, and frequently repeated intention behind their production, they are *not* statements of government policy but are published to stimulate discussion and enable the government to obtain the views of interested parties before making a policy statement (a White Paper).

Individual Command Papers are numbered sequentially in long series regardless of Parliamentary session. The running number, with a prefix, is printed at the bottom left-hand corner of the cover and title page. The prefix is very important, for it indicates which of the six series (the first began in 1833) the running number refers to. It is an abbreviation of the word 'Command'. The six series are as follows:

1st series	4th series
[1] – [4222] 1833–69	[Cmd 1] – Cmd 9889 1919–56
2nd series	5th series
[C 1] – [C 9550] 1870–99	Cmnd 1 – Cmnd 9927 1956–86
3rd series	6th series
[Cd 1] – [Cd 9239] 1900–18	Cm 1 - 1986 –

Examples of the use of the citation are given on p. 161.

Most academic and large public libraries will have collections of Command Papers usually running back, complete, over several series. Smaller libraries may have collections either much more restricted in the time period covered or composed of selected titles only. In some academic libraries you may find they subscribe to every Command Paper published, and so build up a 'reference only' set, and additionally purchase selected titles of particular relevance to the course taught. These selected copies may be available for you to borrow. Some of the less well-researched reading lists and books you read may refer to a Command Paper merely by its running number and prefix, with no indication of the title, Minister or government department responsible – some of the publications noted in 3.11B1 will provide assistance in tracing the publication from such a poor reference. In addition you may find that in some libraries, particularly those with a computer catalogue, it is possible to search for and locate a Command Paper solely from the prefix and running number. Ask the library staff if this is possible, and if it is, ask them to show you how it can be achieved.

3.11A1.2   HMSO non-Parliamentary publications

As their name suggests these are publications other than those required for the conduct of the business of Parliament. The range is huge but three broad categories have been identified (see Ollé 1973, p. 50): (a) statutory instruments (considered in detail in section 3.3.1 of this book); (b) reports; and (c) information publications.

3.11A1.2.1   Reports

Two types may be noted: annual reports of government institutions, and the reports of some permanent, and many *ad hoc* investigating committees and working parties. The Law Commission is a permanent body and its working papers, which have recently been renamed consultative documents, have green covers, and fall into this category. They are very valuable sources of information because they provide an account of the criticisms and supposed defects of the law, with a statement of the options for change, and the Commission's view of the preferred option. Because Law Commission working papers are an authoritative distillation and analysis of the law on a topic, they can be a very useful starting-point when researching why the law has developed in a particular way, and the alternatives for change. Following this consultation the Law Commission will issue a report which sometimes includes a draft Bill of Parliament (see 3.11A1.1.3 and also in 3.2.1A2). Law Commission working papers are numbered sequentially and over 130 have been issued since the Law Commission was set up in 1965. They are sometimes referred to solely by their number, without the title of the individual paper, as in Law Comm. WP115. To discover the title consult the latest annual report of the Law Commission which, in an appendix, contains a complete list of all those published. This list also very helpfully gives details of any Law Commission reports which resulted from working papers. Many law libraries have a set of Law Commission working papers bound in sequence number order, as well as copies of individual titles which will appear on the library catalogue.

3.11A1.2.2   Information publications

A wide variety of books, pamphlets, leaflets and periodicals fall into this category. They provide the public with information and advice, most of which is derived from experts in government departments and institutions. They range from codes of practice, such as those issued by the Home Secretary under the Police and Criminal Evidence Act 1984 and approved by Parliament (see 3.3.2), to guides on the practical application of particular legislation: for example, *A Guide to the HSW Act* prepared by the Health and Safety Executive (HSW stands for Health and Safety at Work).

Non-Parliamentary publications have no overall numbering sequence or system of citation. The publishing output is very large and although some academic and large public libraries will attempt to purchase all non-Parliamentary publications most libraries may be more selective in what they stock. You will probably find that although academic law libraries will take, for example, all the Law Commission working papers, public libraries may not, but instead, collect non-Parliamentary publications of wider public interest.

3.11A1.3   Non-HMSO official publications

This category embraces those documents published by government departments direct to the public, not through HMSO, and the publications of over 500 organisations controlled or funded by the government. Of these 500 or so organisations the most important in legal research are the *qu*asi-*a*utonomous *n*on-governmental *o*rganisation*s* (quangos), for example, the Equal Opportunities Commission, the Health and Safety Commission etc. One difficulty which has faced researchers in the past has been that few government departments and quangos have issued catalogues of their publications, so it has been very difficult trace what has been published and by whom. It is worth emphasising that a publication prepared by a government department or quango could be published by HMSO, or it could be published by the organisation itself – and this has had considerable implications when trying to trace information about it in indexes, explained in 3.11B and 3.11C.

3.11B   EXPLOITATION

3.11B1   HMSO catalogues

3.11B1.1   Daily List

Each afternoon, Monday to Friday, HMSO issues a list of the publications made available that day. The *Daily List* usually extends to three or four pages of entries, with publications grouped under four headings: Parliamentary publications, non-Parliamentary publications, agency publications (items sold through HMSO for British, European and international organisations), and statutory instruments. The purpose of the *Daily List* is to alert booksellers and the public to the very latest material. No subject or title indexes to the *Daily List* are produced, so it is an inappropriate source to search for more than recent publications. For research covering longer periods of time you should use the *Monthly Catalogue* and/or *Annual Catalogue*.

3.11B1.2   Monthly Catalogue

This contains entries for publications noted in the *Daily List* except for statutory instruments. It is published about four to six weeks after the end of the month to which it relates. Since 1976 it has been divided into four parts: Parliamentary publications; a classified section, including all non-Parliamentary publications and Parliamentary publications (excluding Bills, Acts, debates and Measures) listed under the responsible department or body; Northern Ireland publications; and, lastly, agency publications. In addition there is an alphabetical index with entries for subjects, authors, chairmen and editors all in a single sequence. Prior to 1976 there were just two sections, Parliamentary publications; non-Parliamentary and agency publications. The alphabetical index cumulates through the year so it is best to start your search with that in the latest monthly issue. A note at the beginning of the alphabetical index tells you to which monthly issue the page numbers refer.

3.11B1.3 Annual Catalogue

As you might expect this is an annual cumulation of the *Monthly Catalogue* but the contents are not quite identical. There are three parts: Parliamentary publications, a classified section and, finally, a list of Northern Ireland HMSO publications. Publications from British, European and international organisations for which HMSO is the UK agent appear in a separate, annual *HMSO Agency Catalogue*. Towards the back of the HMSO *Annual Catalogue* there is an alphabetical index including subjects, authors, chairmen and editors in a single sequence. Since the mid 1970s there have been marked improvements in the layout and helpfulness of the alphabetical index and it is now relatively easy to track down publications through it. However, should you need to consult *Annual Catalogues* from before that period, you will find the indexing rather rudimentary and you would be advised to ask for help from library staff.

At the back of recent issues of the *Annual Catalogue* there is a list of libraries which take a subscription to one copy of most HMSO publications, with the dates from when each library first took up this service. Before visiting one of these libraries you should telephone or write to find out whether the library does in fact keep the materials you want, since some libraries do not retain all the publications they receive from HMSO.

3.11B1.4 Sectional lists

The sectional lists are 20 or 30 individual booklets giving details of items in print, published by HMSO for certain departments or subjects. Parliamentary publications are normally excluded, as are non-HMSO and agency publications. For lawyers the most relevant sectional lists are those for the Home Office (list 26), employment, health and safety (list 21), Department of Health and Social Security (list 11) and Department of the Environment (list 5). Regrettably there is no sectional list for the Law Commission, nor are its publications listed in any other sectional list.

3.11B1.5 *Committee Reports Published by HMSO Indexed by Chairman*

Since 1983 HMSO has published each quarter, and as an annual cumulation, an index listing the chairmen of all committee reports it has published.

Entries are arranged alphabetically by the name of the chairman. This is a very useful index which, in extended historical research, can be used in conjunction with those noted in 3.11B2.3. Very often a major official report becomes known colloquially by the name of the chairman of the committee or investigator, for example, the Benson Committee, the Butler-Sloss Inquiry. This index will help in tracing the correct title, full name of the chairman and other publication details, so that you will have a better chance of tracing the material in a library catalogue.

3.11B1.6   Guide to Official Statistics

The government is the leading collector of statistics and publisher of the results of surveys. Some statistics are collected as a matter of routine and are published at regular intervals. Others are only collected as the result of a particular study of investigation. The most comprehensive guide to the government's published statistics, and to major non-official sources of statistics in the UK, is the *Guide to Official Statistics*. The latest revised edition of 1990 excludes most material published before 1985, but it is still a most valuable guidebook. The subject index at the back of the *Guide* will lead you to the appropriate section in the body of the work, where the content of each statistical publication is briefly summarised. For a law student, chapter 4 of the *Guide* describing social statistics will probably prove the most relevant, for it includes references to statistical publications on the operation of the civil and criminal justice systems, crime statistics, the police and treatment of offenders. The two major series of statistics you are likely to consult as a law student are *Judicial Statistics England and Wales*, and *Criminal Statistics England and Wales*, both published annually. There are also a number of occasional series of statistics relevant to your studies issued in the series, *Home Office Statistical Bulletins*, published by the Home Office itself.

As well as describing statistical sources the *Guide* contains, near the back, a list of government department contact points, giving the addresses and telephone numbers of sections within departments responsible for the collection of statistics. This is a valuable list to consult should you have any queries about the availability or content of statistics on a topic you are researching, which neither the *Guide* nor local library staff can resolve.

3.11B1.7   Government Statistics: a Brief Guide to Sources

This short guide is published annually and lists sources of relevance to law under the heading 'justice and law'. Although less comprehensive and descriptive than *Guide to Official Statistics*, the information given is more up to date.

3.11B2   Non-HMSO catalogues

3.11B2.1   Departmental catalogues

Some, but by no means all, government departments and agencies publish catalogues or lists of their publications. These are not fully comprehensive (for example, they frequently exclude such items as press releases). The *Cata-*

logue of British Official Publications Not Published by HMSO (3.11B2.2) is to be preferred.

3.11B2.2 Catalogue of British Official Publications Not Published by HMSO

First issued in 1980 by a private publisher Chadwyck-Healey, and now published bimonthly with an annual bound volume, this catalogue gives details of the vast publishing output of over 500 official organisations including government departments, nationalised industries, research institutes, quangos and other official bodies. The catalogue is as comprehensive as the compilers can make it, covering periodicals, newspapers, serials, single-sheet publications, leaflets and publicity material of value, as well as more weighty policy documents. The alphabetical index includes subjects, authors, chairmen etc. in a single sequence. Each reference in the catalogue to a publication carries a code number which appears in italics at the end of the entry and an index to these codes provides the names and addresses of the sources from which the publications may be obtained. This catalogue is now available on CD-ROM (3.11C2).

3.11B2.3 British Government Publications: an Index to Chairmen of Committees and Commissions of Inquiry

Currently in four volumes covering the period 1800 to 1982, the index is arranged in alphabetical order by the surnames of the chairmen, with details of the reports for which they were responsible. More recent publications are indexed in the HMSO list (see 3.11B1.5).

3.11C ELECTRONIC SOURCES

For background information on the use of electronic databases, see appendix 4.

3.11C1 British Official Publications

This remote on-line database includes similar information on HMSO publications issued since 1976 to that found in the *Annual* and *Monthly Catalogues*. It is updated monthly.

3.11C2 United Kingdom Official Publications (UKOP)

This is the CD-ROM equivalent of the *Catalogue of British Official Publications Not Published by HMSO* (3.11B2.2) *and* the HMSO publications catalogue from 1980 (3.11B1.2 and 3.11B1.3). It is a very useful and valuable database because it combines references to HMSO and non-HMSO official publications. Further, it is possible to search by author, title or keyword, making it easier to find relevant material than using the paper indexes.

3.11D RESEARCH STRATEGIES

3.11D1 How to find details of official publications on a subject

See figure 3.28.

> HMSO *Daily List* (3.11B1.1)
>
> (search backwards in time to the latest issues of *Monthly Catalogue*).

> HMSO *Monthly Catalogue* (3.11B1.2)
>
> (search backwards in time to either (a) the latest issue of the *Annual Catalogue* (3.11B1.3) and (b) the latest issue of the *Catalogue of British Official Publications Not Published by HMSO* (3.11B2.2) or, better still, the date of the latest issue of *United Kingdom Official Publications* (UKOP) (3.11C2); but to extend your research to before 1980 you will need to use the *Annual Catalogue* (3.11B1.3) and *Departmental Catalogues* (3.11D2.1). You could use *British Official Publications* (3.11C1) as an alternative to the HMSO *Monthly* and HMSO *Annual Catalogues* and take your search back to 1976.

Figure 3.28   Finding details of official publications on a subject.

3.11D2   How to find details of Law Commission publications

To find details of Law Commission reports follow figure 3.29.

To find details of Law Commission working papers or consultative documents, follow the same sequence as for reports but search the *Daily List* in the non-Parliamentary publications section. Note that in the body of the *Monthly* and *Annual Catalogues*, working papers or consultative documents are listed only once, under the classified section, subheading 'Law Commission', because they are not published as Parliamentary Papers.

3.11D3   How to trace details of an official publication when all you know is the name of the chairman

If you have an idea of the date of the publication, and it is pre-1982, check the appropriate volume of *British Government Publications: an Index to Chairmen of Committees and Commissions of Inquiry* (3.11B2.3).

If you believe it is a post-1982 publication, check *Committee Reports Published by HMSO Indexed by Chairman* (3.11B1.5).

If either British Official Publications (3.11C1) or UKOP (3.11C2) is available, use that as an alternative.

3.11D4   How to trace if statistics are published on a topic

Use *Guide to Official Statistics* (3.11B1.6) – check the subject index at the back and read the commentary at the chapter and paragraph number in the body of the *Guide* to which you are referred. Note the titles of any statistical sources mentioned and check your library's catalogue to see if they are in stock.

Alternatively use *Government Statistics* (3.11B1.7), but this is a rather poor substitute.

Reports: for those published in the last few months: HMSO *Daily List* (3.11B1.1) – search the section on Parliamentary publications. Take your search back to the latest issue of HMSO *Monthly Catalogue* (3.11B1.2).

Monthly Catalogue (3.11B1.2) – search the alphabetical index at the back of the latest issue under the heading 'Law Commission', and follow up the page numbers given. In the body of the catalogue entries for Law Commission reports will appear twice – once in the section on Parliamentary publications (since they are published as House of Commons Papers) and once in the section headed 'classified list' under the subheading 'Law Commission'.

To take your search further back consult either

| The latest issue of the annual report of the Law Commission (itself published as a Law Commission report) – use the appendix at the back of the annual report, which lists all reports published. | The latest issue of *Annual Catalogue* (3.11B1.3) and then previous issues. Note that entries will be duplicated for the same reason as given under *Monthly Catalogue* above. | *British Official Publications* (3.11C1) and for pre-1976 publications, *Annual Catalogue* (3.11B1.3). | UKOP (3.11C2), and for pre-1980 publications, *Annual Catalogue:* (3.11B1.3). |

Figure 3.29   Finding details of Law Commission publications.

Chapter 4

Researching the law of the European Communities

4.1 INTRODUCTION

On 1 January 1973 the United Kingdom joined the European Communities (EC), and agreed to apply and be bound by the law of the Communities. The gradual movement towards the harmonisation of laws across all member States, significantly quickened by the ratification of the Single European Act in 1987, has meant that EC law can no longer be considered in isolation as a separate unit of legal study or research, but now permeates English law as a whole. It is important for you as a law student to understand and know how to use the legal sources and materials of EC law, which are quite different from those of domestic English law.

Before looking at the structure of EC legal materials it is necessary to give a thumbnail sketch of the EC and its institutions so you will have a better grasp of the sources.

You may have noticed that the term Communities rather than Community has been used – there are in fact three European Communities:

(a) European Coal and Steel Community (ECSC).
(b) European Atomic Energy Community (Euratom).
(c) European Economic Community (EEC).

The legislation which set up these Communities not only created a system of law independent of national law but also created a number of bodies, known as 'institutions':

(a)   Council of Ministers - to take decisions on legislative proposals.
(b)   Commission - to enforce the application of EC law and instigate new
legislative proposals.
(c)   European Parliament - to advise on legislation.
(d)   European Court of Justice - to interpret EC law.

In addition to these institutions, there are a number of other bodies
which, with the exception of the European Investment Bank and Euratom's
Supply Agency, act in an advisory capacity only. Those you may come
across in law studies are likely to be:

(a)   Court of Auditors - to examine the accounts of all revenue and expenditure of the Communities and keep a check on the EC budget.
(b)   Economic and Social Committee – a body representing economic
and social interests in the Communities, such as employers' organisations
and trade unions, which is consulted by the Council together with Parliament, before final decisions are taken.

EC legal information sources, like those for England and Wales, may be
divided into primary (i.e., original) and secondary (i.e., commentary and description) – see figure 4.1.

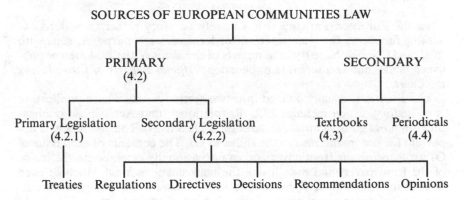

(The numbers in brackets indicate the section of this chapter where discussion of the
particular source will be found.)

Figure 4.1   The literature of European Communities law.

The primary sources (see 4.2) comprise:

(a)   Primary legislation - the founding treaties and later amending
treaties, concerned with the establishment of the Communities, treaties of accession as the membership of the Communities has been enlarged, and the

Single European Act, which aims to achieve a completely free market within the Communities (see 4.2.1).

(b)   Secondary legislation - laws setting out in detail how the objectives established by the treaties are to be met (see 4.2.2).

(c)   Case law - the decisions of the European Court of Justice (ECJ) (see 4.2.3).

The secondary sources comprise textbooks (see 4.3) and periodicals (see 4.4).

4.2   PRIMARY SOURCES

The authorised text of the treaties and secondary legislation of the EC is not made available in separate individual publications as the Acts and statutory instruments of England and Wales are, but are printed in the pages of the *Official Journal of the European Communities* (normally abbreviated to *Official Journal* or, simply, OJ). OJ is published almost daily and in several parts. The three parts in which you, as a law student, will be interested are:

(a)   The L series (Legislation), which gives the text of agreed legislation.

(b)   The C series (Communications and Information), which contains draft legislation, official announcements and information on EC activities.

(c)   The annexe, which contains the full text of debates of the European Parliament.

Since the European Parliament has merely advisory rather than decision-making functions, the main interest, for legal research purposes, rests with the L and C series. Note that the reports of decisions of the ECJ are *not* published in OJ, but as a separate publication, *Official Reports of Cases before the Court*.

The L series is usually divided into two sections: Acts whose publication is obligatory (which includes EEC Regulations), and Acts whose publication is not obligatory (which includes EEC Directives). The distinction is important for it is maintained in the Index to OJ. The contents of each issue of OJ are listed on the front cover and can occasionally extend onto the inside of the front cover, and even inside the back cover as well! Much of each issue contains legislative documents relating to agricultural policy or the customs union, which are often applicable for only a limited period of time. In the index these are listed in lighter type, whilst other measures are given in bold type with an asterisk.

Community publications are usually published in each of the languages of the member States. The covers of official EC publications are colour-coded according to the language of publication and English language publications have purple covers.

Since the publication of EC legislation and the reports of cases before ECJ is far more centralised than their counterparts in England and Wales, you might expect it to be relatively easy to master the necessary research skills. Regrettably this is not so, because of the sheer quantity of official publications and difficulties you will face in using the official indexes. Further, the reports of ECJ cases are delayed by as much as two years because of the importance attached to achieving a precise and accurate translation of the judgment and opinions into all EC languages.

Therefore, as you will see, whilst the authoritative text of legal documents is given in official publications, you will have to master the use of non-official indexes and publications to find your way through the vast quantity of EC publishing – the L and C series of OJ alone run to over 30,000 pages annually! Electronic sources of EC legal information exist and play a part in legal research, but again, considerable skill and experience is required, particularly with the remote on-line, as opposed to CD-ROM, databases, to extract information effectively.

Finally, where can you find EC official publications? Most law libraries are likely to subscribe to OJ. However, the EC have made efforts to ensure publications are accessible to encourage teaching and research as well as for consultation by the general public. Over 40 academic libraries (universities and polytechnics) in the UK have been designated European Documentation Centres (EDC) and receive a comprehensive range of EC material, although rationalisation in the late 1980s has meant some now only receive a selection. In addition 18 European Reference Centres (ERC) have been designated which receive a more limited range of publications. Finally, five EC Depository Libraries (DEP) with major collections intended for use by the general public have been designated in the UK. Staff at your law library will be able to provide addresses of all these special centres, or you can obtain a list by contacting the EC Information Office in either London, Cardiff, Edinburgh or Belfast – use a telephone book for the address and telephone number.

4.2.1 Community treaties

4.2.1A DESCRIPTION

See 4.2.

4.2.1B EXPLOITATION

The authoritative text, as we have seen, is given in various issues of OJ. However, for convenience the texts are brought together in a single title which has appeared in various consolidated editions, the latest (1987) in two volumes, published under the title: *Treaties Establishing the European Communities, Treaties Amending these Treaties, Single European Act and Documents Concerning the Accessions.*

When issued earlier as a single-volume edition, the publication was nicknamed (in its English-language version) the 'purple brick'!

A shortened version of the two-volume set: *Treaties Establishing the European Communities. Single European Act and Other Basic Instruments – Abridged Version,* excludes most of the associated annexes and protocols.

Unofficial versions of the treaties are given, with annotations, in the following:

(a) *Encyclopedia of European Community Law* – a loose-leaf publication in 13 volumes: the text of the treaties is given in volume B.

(b) H. Smit and P.E. Herzog, *The Law of the European Economic Community. A Commentary on the EEC Treaty* – a loose-leaf publication in six volumes.

(c) *Common Market Reporter* – a loose-leaf publication in four volumes.

(d) *Halsbury's Statutes of England*, 4th ed., vol. 50.

(e) *Sweet & Maxwell's European Community Treaties*, 4th ed. (1980) – a textbook edited by Sweet & Maxwell's legal editorial staff.

(f) Rudden, Bernard and Wyatt, Derrick (editors), *Basic Community Laws*, 2nd ed. (Oxford: Clarendon Press: 1986).

4.2.1C   ELECTRONIC SOURCES

For background information on the use of electronic databases, see appendix 4.

4.2.1C1   Celex

A computer in Luxembourg holds the text of the official legal database of the EC. The database is divided into a number of separate files which are further subdivided into sectors. The legislative file has four sectors. Sector 1 contains the full text of the treaties. Sector 2 contains the text of enactments passed in member States when each joined the EC, including the Act of Accession of the United Kingdom. Celex was originally designed for use by Commission staff and not by the public. There is a very large set of commands and the database is not easy to use. Celex staff expect users to attend a week-long training course to become proficient!

4.2.1C2   Justis-Celex

Justis-Celex is a bibliographic database – this means it does not contain the full text of documents but only details about them, such as the title, where they were published and cross-references to other documents which modify or have been modified by the original document. Justis-Celex uses a much simpler search language than Celex, and is useful for identifying publication details of a particular document before using an electronic 'gateway' to gain access to the Celex database to retrieve the full text.

4.2.1C3   Justis-Celex CD-ROM

This is the same database as Justis-Celex but available on a compact disc which is updated every three months.

4.2.1C4   POLIS

The *P*arliamentary *O*n-*L*ine *I*nformation *S*ystem was described in 3.2.1C1. As part of its coverage of UK Parliamentary information, it includes details, but not the text, of EC legislative proposals which have been considered by Parliamentary Select Committees since 1 January 1983, and also a selection of other EC documents published after 1 January 1984.

4.2.1C5   LEXIS

In its International Law Library (INTLAW), LEXIS includes a file (ECTY) which has the full text of the EC treaties. See appendix 6 at the back of this book for an introductory description of how to use and search LEXIS.

4.2.1D   RESEARCH STRATEGIES

The information given earlier should make clear how to find and use the EC treaties.

4.2.2   Secondary legislation

4.2.2A   DESCRIPTION

Whilst the treaties provide the overall objectives of the activities of the EC, secondary legislation sets out the fine detail of how these objectives are to be achieved. There are five different types of EC secondary legislation. Each has a different definition and purpose. Unfortunately, whilst the designated use in the EEC and Euratom treaties is the same, that in the ECSC treaty is different. Figure 4.2 provides definitions and illustrates the differences between the treaties.

ECSC Treaty Type of secondary legislation	Definition and purpose	EEC/Euratom Treaties Type of secondary legislation
Decisions (general)	Addressed to all member states — to be applied in full and directly applicable without the creation of national legislation.	Regulations
Recommendations	Addressed to all member States — lay down an objective to be achieved in a specific time but member States are left to legislate the details of implementation.	Directives
Decisions (individual)	May be addressed to member States, individuals, groups of individuals or companies — the means by which EC implements treaties or regulations.	Decisions
Opinions	Suggest a line of action or opinion and are not legally binding.	{ Recommendations { Opinions

Figure 4.2   Types of European Communities secondary legislation.

The two types of secondary legislation you are most likely to use during law studies are Regulations and Directives made under the EEC Treaty. They can be made by the European Commission or the Council of Ministers. A key point to remember is that whilst EEC Regulations do not require national legislation to bring them into force, EEC Directives can only be implemented through national legislation, which in the UK will be either an Act of Parliament or a statutory instrument. How the UK government selects which method to employ is discussed in an article by Bates (1989). It is very important when undertaking research on an EEC Directive to check whether it has been implemented within the jurisdiction with which you are concerned. You will *not* find this information in the Directive itself but will have to check the national sources.

So as to understand better the relationships between the various publications produced as part of the legislative process in the EC, it is necessary to sketch in the process itself. The following sequence is derived from a much fuller table printed in Thomson (1989).

(a)   Commission sends a proposal to the Council of Ministers – the text of the proposal and the explanatory memorandum are published as a COM document (the popular title for a range of working documents of the Commission), the text alone appears in the *Official Journal* C series.

(b)   Council consults the European Parliament and, in certain circumstances, the Economic and Social Committee. A committee of the European Parliament prepares a report on the proposal which is published in series A of the *European Parliament's Working Documents*.

(c)   The European Parliament in full session considers the report on first reading. The text of the debate is published in *Official Journal*, Annexe, while the text of the opinion they express is printed in *Official Journal* C series.

(d)   The European Social Committee gives an opinion – the text is printed in *Official Journal* C series.

(e)   The Commission considers amendments – the outcome is published in the same titles as was the proposal which began the legislative process – see (a) above.

(f)   The Council prepares a common position on the proposal accepting or rejecting amendments made by the European Parliament unless the Commission has made a modified proposal.

(g)   The European Parliament at second reading refers the common position to the European Parliament committee which made the first report.

(h)   The European Parliament committee makes recommendations (which may include rejection of the common position) to the full European Parliament – these are published in the same manner as in (b) above.

(i)   The European Parliament adopts a recommendation either to reject, accept with amendments, or accept without amendments the common position – this recommendation is published as for (c) above.

(j)   The Commission may re-examine the common position; it then forwards it to Council which may adopt it or amend it.

(k)   The proposal becomes law and is printed in *Official Journal* L series.

Thomson (1989) also provides an example highlighting the difficulties a researcher faces in discovering which stage any individual proposal has reached at any particular time.

During your law studies you will be mainly concerned with secondary legislation which has become law (i.e., printed in *Official Journal* L series), though occasionally you may need information on proposals (printed as COM documents with explanatory memorandum, or text only in *Official Journal* C series).

COM documents only become public after a considerable period of consultation with interested parties, and it is only the final version which is published. This fact is reflected in the way in which the documents are cited:

COM (year) running number, final

as in the following example:

Proposal for a Council Directive on safety glazing and glazing materials on motor vehicles and their trailers, COM (89) 653, final.

The text of this particular proposal was, as usual, published some time later in the *Official Journal* C series. References to the *Official Journal* take the following form:

OJ series issue number date of issue page number

as in the following example:

Proposal for a Council Directive on safety glazing and glazing materials on motor vehicles and their trailers (OJ No. C95, 12.4.1990, p. 1).

The L, C and S series of OJ are given a running number commencing at one in January each year, but the annexe series, covering European Parliament debates, is numbered quite differently.

A very small number of the most important proposals are given wider public notice by being published as supplements to the *Bulletin of the European Communities* (see 4.2.2B1.4). When referring to a particular piece of EC legislation printed in OJ the citation should include the following elements, though, with one important exception, there appears to be no standard order in which they should appear:

(a)   the institutional origin of the Act (Commission or Council)
(b)   the form of the Act (Regulation, Directive, Decision etc.)
(c)   a unique legislation number
(d)   the year of the enactment
(e)   the institutional treaty under which it is made (EEC, ECSC, Euratom)

(f)   the date the legislation was passed.

The important exception to note is that Regulations are normally cited with the name of the institutional treaty followed by the legislation number and then the year of enactment, whilst Directives and Decisions are cited by the year, legislation number and then the institutional treaty. It is very important to remember this system of citation when tracing references to legislation in indexes, otherwise it is easy to waste time finding the wrong document. Here are two examples of how the citations should be given; the first is an example of a Regulation, the second a Directive:

Council Regulation (EEC) No. 737/90 of March 1990 on the conditions governing imports of agricultural products originating in third countries following the accident of the Chernobyl nuclear power station.
Council Directive 87/102/EEC for the approximation of the laws, regulations and administrative provisions of the member States concerning consumer credit.

4.2.2B   EXPLOITATION

There are two ways of exploiting this vast output of EC secondary legislation: by using indexes, lists and directories compiled officially by the EC or by consulting the growing number of commercially produced publications. As you will see, whilst the EC publications are authoritative and the most up to date, the idiosyncratic subject indexing and the lack of cumulative indexes covering more than the legislation of a single year, have encouraged commercial publishers to try to overcome these deficiencies.

4.2.2B1   Official publications

4.2.2B1.1   Index to the *Official Journal of the European Communities*

The index to the *Official Journal* is published monthly with an annual cumulation. One of the drawbacks is that it does not cumulate over longer periods and so a search over several years can be time consuming. Additionally, and this is most regrettable, it indexes only the secondary legislation appearing in the 'L' series and excludes all references to draft legislation printed in the 'C' series.

The index is in two parts:

(a)   methodological tables
(b)   alphabetical index

The methodological tables divide legislation into the same two categories they were published under in the L series of OJ: Acts whose publication is obligatory and Acts whose publication is not obligatory. Within each category the different types of secondary legislation are listed in legislation number order. Each entry gives the title of the piece of legislation and the reference to where it was printed in OJ.

The alphabetical index – a sort of subject index – is potentially the more valuable part, but the terminology and phraseology of 'Euro-English' makes its use awkward. Matters have improved considerably with the preparation of EUROVOC, a thesaurus to 'a common documentary language' and a stage in the development of a 'harmonised vocabulary'. EUROVOC is now in its second edition and three of an anticipated five volumes have been published. This may sound a bit too much like the world of George Orwell's *Nineteen Eighty-Four*! Ask your library staff for help if you wish to trace legislation by subject using the indexes to *Official Journal*; fortunately, there are alternative ways of achieving the same result (see 4.2.2B2).

4.2.2B1.2   List of Pending Proposals

This is an irregular publication in the COM document series, which lists all Commission proposals under headings corresponding to the Directorate General (the equivalent of department) of the Commission sponsoring the proposal. There is no index.

4.2.2B1.3   General Report on the Activities of the European Communities

This is published annually, within a few months of the end of the calendar year to which it refers. The body of the report, which in recent years has run to over 400 pages, gives a synopsis of legal and other developments during the year with footnote references to secondary legislation appearing in the *Official Journal*, both as draft and enacted law. Annexes at the back of the volume give details of the progress during the year of a selection of directives. Researching the *General Reports* over a number of annual issues will provide you with a broad view of Community legislative activity on a topic, and valuable references to the *Official Journal* or other EC sources in which the original documents were published.

4.2.2B1.4   Bulletin of the European Communities

Published 10 times a year, this performs a similar function to the *General Report* except that the narrative synopsis of developments is replaced by brief notes on the progress and development of legislation, with full references to where the original materials were published. An annual index is published as part of an issue available early in the calendar year following. The value of the *Bulletin* is weakened by it appearing at least four months in arrears of the events it describes.

4.2.2B1.5   Directory of Community Legislation in Force

The *Directory* is published twice a year and contains information on legislation in force as at 1 June and 1 December. It is currently published in two volumes: Volume 1 contains the main body of the *Directory*, arranging references to legislation under 17 very broad subject headings and numerous more detailed subject headings. This arrangement means you will usually have to think of words of much wider meaning which include the topic in which you are interested and then narrow down once you have discovered the right major heading. For example, 'pollution' is not one of the 17 main subject headings but is a part of 'environment, consumers and health protection', which is! Volume 2 comprises chronological and alphabetical (i.e., 'sort of' subject) indexes, and the latter helps a little when using Volume 1 for a subject search.

4.2.2B2   Commercial publications

4.2.2B2.1   Encyclopedia of European Community Law

The whole of Volume C, which is currently published as nine loose-leaf binders (and expanding continually), comprises reprints of EC secondary legislation, with commentary and annotation (in a smaller type) provided by the editors. It does not include draft legislation. Each Volume is divided into a large number of parts, and the text of each part is divided into numbered paragraphs. There is a subject index to the whole of Volume C towards the back of the last binder, and a second, supplementary index right at the back, which covers the most recent additions to the encyclopaedia. The references given in the indexes refer to the volume letter, part and paragraph number (in arabic numerals) where information is to be found. Take care not to confuse this information with the roman numerals on the spines of the binders, which have no relevance to finding material in the publication. You can find your way around the binders by looking at the guide cards, which project from the edge of the pages, and mark the beginning of each part of the text. Each broad subject, such as company law, which comprises a whole part of the encyclopaedia, commences with a checklist of the secondary legislation, in EC reference number order, included in that part. If you know the reference number of the Regulation or Directive, these checklists, or the consolidated checklist to the whole of Volume C near the back of the final Volume, or the tables of Community secondary legislation at the front of binder CI, will enable you to find the part and paragraph number where the legislation is reprinted.

The more helpful subject indexing, coupled with the provision of annotations, make this encyclopaedia a better starting-point for searching for secondary legislation than OJ and its indexes. However, updating such a large work takes time and it is still necessary to check other, official sources for amendments.

4.2.2B2.2   Common Market Reporter

This four-volume loose-leaf work restricts itself to the secondary legislation of the European Economic Community, i.e., it excludes the laws of the ECSC and Euratom. It reprints secondary legislation, including some existing draft Regulations and Directives, in full, with editorial commentary. Draft Regulations and Directives are reproduced in the 'pending legislation' section, and cross-referenced to the main text of the *Reporter*. A cumulative index to new developments in Volume 4 links reports of new developments to the main work and should be checked to discover if any new proposals have been made whenever you use the main work. Volume 4 also contains a topical index (or subject index), preceded by a separate 'latest additions to topical index' which contains new or revised entries to the publication. From time to time these entries are incorporated in the main index to bring it completely up to date. The same Volume has 'finding lists' detailing different types of secondary legislation according to their official reference numbers.

Common Market Reporter also includes the texts of European Court of Justice rulings and quasi-judicial Commission Decisions, and is consequently a more comprehensive source for EEC law than the encyclopaedia noted in 4.2.2B2.1.

4.2.2B2.3 Law of the European Communities Service

This publication, which first appeared in 1990, is still in the course of being developed. In two loose-leaf volumes it currently contains the text of EC secondary legislation, arranged into 21 specific subject groups. Eventually it will include a commentary, Noter-Up of recent developments and lists of cases and new legislation. At the time of writing consolidated indexes have not been issued, so use of the work is hampered.

4.2.2B2.4 Halsbury's Laws of England, 4th ed., volumes 51 and 52

These bound volumes comprise an editorial commentary on EC law with copious footnotes giving references to where the original documents may be found. The volumes were published in 1986 and state the law correct to 30 November 1985. They have been kept up to date through entries in the Cumulative Supplement and service volumes to the whole *Halsbury's* service. Whilst the provision of a commentary is helpful, the lack of ready access, as part of the same publication, to the text of legislation prompted the publishers to develop the work in progress noted in 4.2.2B2.3.

4.2.2B2.5 European Communities Legislation: Current Status

Two hard-back volumes and a single, soft-cover volume (this reissued annually), all updated by a soft-cover Cumulative Supplement and alphabetical subject index published three times a year, list in official Community reference number order the secondary legislation of the EC. Each entry comprises the title of the EC legislation or a short summary, and details of whether the whole or any part of the legislation has been amended, repealed, deleted, added to or replaced and, if so, the Community reference number for the 'amending' legislation. The subject index appears to use similar index terms to those in the EC 'harmonised vocabulary' which means references may be hidden under terms you do not expect.

4.2.2B2.6 Guide to EEC Legislation

Three basic volumes, updated by Cumulative Supplements published annually, set out brief details of a large selection of EEC legislation, including draft legislation, with details of amendments. There are more up-to-date sources than this.

4.2.2B2.7   Completing the Internal Market of the European Communities 1992 Legislation

This joint publication of the Office for Official Publications of the European Communities and a private publisher, Graham and Trotman, merely arranges photocopies of legislation relating to the removal of trade barriers, taken from the pages of OJ under broad subject headings without commentary or indexes. It is loose leaf in six volumes with a bound handbook.

4.2.2B2.8   Weekly Information Bulletin of the House of Commons

This publication is also discussed in 3.2.1B1. Amongst its many listings it includes brief details of the latest COM documents containing draft legislation. Select Committees in both Houses of Parliament consider draft EC legislation and report their opinion whether the proposals raise questions of legal or political importance. Some proposals do, and of these a number are debated on the floor of the House of Commons. All the reports of the House of Lords Select Committee are debated. You will therefore find references to EC legislation in some of the other Parliamentary sources noted in 3.2.1B, especially *Hansard* (3.2.1B3).

4.2.2B2.9   Butterworths EC Brief

This four-page newsletter covering, in summary, all proposals for legislation, all enacted legislation of the EC and all UK legislation implementing it, is published weekly.

It is a current-awareness publication, designed to keep readers up to date with developments, but can be used for research. No indexes are published, so it is a matter of 'skim reading' through past issues to find the information you are looking for.

4.2.2B2.10   European Access

Published bimonthly, this publication is not confined to law but comprehensively lists, towards the back of each issue, new EC publications, and comment in newspapers, journals and books about the EC, including legislative developments.

4.2.2C   ELECTRONIC SOURCES

For background information on the use of electronic databases, see appendix 4.

4.2.2C1   Celex

A computer in Luxembourg holds Sectors 3 and 4 of the official legal database of the EC. These sectors contain the full text of secondary legislation as published in the L series of OJ. Sector 5 contains references to draft legislation in the form of COM documents. Development of Sector 7, which will give details of the national implementation of EC Directives is in progress.

Legislation on the database is updated weekly and the text is added usually about three to four weeks after its publication in OJ. As was noted in 4.2.1C1 above, Celex is not easy to use, and alternative electronic sources are noted below.

4.2.2C2 Justis-Celex

Justis-Celex is a bibliographic database – it does not contain the text of individual pieces of secondary legislation which have appeared in the L series of OJ, but only the full title, OJ reference, date of publication, date coming into force and details of other legislation it modifies or is modified by. Using Justis-Celex is a very helpful first step in searching the vast quantity of EC secondary legislation electronically for two reasons: first, the search language is easy to use and, secondly, once you have been able to identify a particular Regulation, Directive etc. and have written down details of its unique document number, you can transfer, through an electronic 'gateway' into the Celex database, and search for the full text using a far more concrete search query (the unique document number) than trying to negotiate EC subject indexing. The Justis-Celex database is updated weekly and is at least two or three weeks behind the publication of the original paper versions of the documents.

4.2.2C3 Justis-Celex CD-ROM

This version of the database featured in 4.2.2C2 includes the full text of secondary legislation which has appeared in the L series of OJ but also has the advantages of a helpful search language which will enable you to identify relevant documents. On the downside, however, is the poorer currency of the information it contains, for the discs are updated every three months; it is no use when you are searching for very recent secondary legislation. However, you can always undertake a search in two steps, using the CD-ROM version to search for older material by subject or whatever search query you wish to use, and then use the remote on-line version (4.2.2C2, above) to cover the most recent period.

4.2.2C4 LEXIS

In its International Law Library (INTLAW), LEXIS has included since January 1991, a file entitled ECLAW which contains the Celex database of secondary legislation. See appendix 6 for an introductory description of how to use and search LEXIS.

4.2.2C5 Spearhead

Produced by the UK Department of Trade and Industry, this database summarises all current and prospective EC measures in the single market programme and in other areas which have substantial implications for business. It is updated monthly and can provide a useful initial step to identify relevant EC legislation in summary form, before searching for the full text available on the appropriate sector of the Celex database.

4.2.2C6 Info 92

Info 92 is a bibliographic database with summaries of EC legislation, adopted and in preparation, on the progress towards the development of the single market. The database is in three parts: removal of physical barriers, removal of technical barriers and, finally, removal of fiscal barriers. Info 92 also includes details of the incorporation of EC legislation into the national law of member States. The database is updated daily.

4.2.2D RESEARCH STRATEGIES

4.2.2D1 Tracing the text of EC legislation on a subject

There are several ways of tackling this research.

Using electronic sources, LEXIS (4.2.2C4) or Justis-Celex (4.2.2C2) and Justis-Celex CD-ROM (4.2.2C3) would prove ideal. Only if the subject you are searching is related to the single market should you use Spearhead (4.2.2C5) or Info 92 (4.2.2C6). These two databases will only provide summaries with references to where in OJ the full text originally appeared, so you would eventually need to use paper sources.

Paper sources offer several different research paths. Three research strategies are given below; the first two are probably the better paths to follow.

(a) Either:

(i) go directly to the indexes of the *Encyclopedia of European Community Law* (4.2.2B2.1) or *Common Market Reporter* (4.2.2B2.2) or *European Communities Legislation: Current Status* (ECL: CS) (4.2.2B2.5). Then find the legislation in the body of the two first-named sources or, if you have used ECL: CS, go to OJ at the references provided. Or

(ii) go to *Official Journal Annexe to the Index: EUROVOC Alphabetical Thesaurus* to discover the words used in the compilation of *Official Journal: Alphabetical Index*. Then, if you know the year the legislation you require was published, check the appropriate annual volume of *Official Journal: Alphabetical Index*, and from the reference given, find the full text of the legislation in OJ. If you do *not* know the year the legislation you require was published, follow path (i), above, using the subject terms you have derived from the *EUROVOC Alphabetical Thesaurus*.

(b) See figure 4.3. Use of *Halsbury's Laws of England* is discussed fully in 3.4B4.1.

(c) See figure 4.4.

4.2.2D2 Tracing draft legislation

This is a difficult research task because the indexes to OJ do not cover the C series in which draft legislation is printed, and only the official electronic

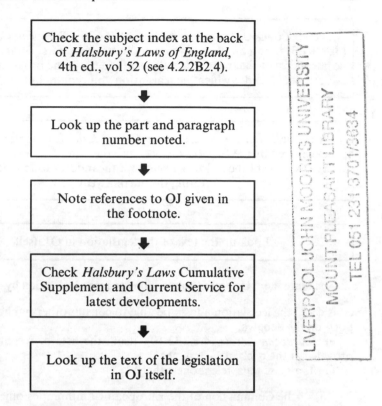

Figure 4.3 Using _Halsbury's Laws_ to trace EC legislation by subject.

database Celex, which is not easy to use, contains, in sector 5, references to draft legislation which appeared in the form of COM documents (see 4.2.2C1). Info 92 database (see 4.2.2C5) gives details of legislation in preparation but only that dealing with the single market.

Amongst paper sources the following alternatives are possible:

(a)   _List of Pending Proposals_ (4.2.2B1.2).

(b)   _Bulletin of the European Communities_ (4.2.2B1.4), in reverse chronological order until you overlap with information contained in the latest _General Report on the Activities of the European Communities_ (4.2.2B1.3).

(c)   _Common Market Reporter_ (4.2.2B2.2) using the cumulative index to new developments and the pending legislation sections.

(d)   _Weekly Information Bulletin of the House of Commons_ (4.2.2B2.8), working backwards in time and checking whether the draft legislation has been considered in Select Committee of either House of Parliament. A successful result of this research will provide you with the COM document number and even the reference to OJ C series in which the draft legislation was printed. You will also have the date when the UK Parliament

Check the *General Report on the Activities of the European Communities* (4.2.2B1.3) over a number of years and note any references to OJ. Use the contents list at the front of the *Report* to identify the broad subject area under which the legislation you require falls.

Check the *Bulletin of the European Communities* for the period to date not covered by the *General Report* – use the annual index published in an early issue of the following year and the indexes to individual issues during the current year.

Look up the text of the legislation in OJ itself.

Figure 4.4   Using EC publications to trace legislation by subject.

considered the legislation and so be able to consult other publications for reports on the debates.

(e)   *European Access* (4.2.2B2.10), using the lists of recent publications provided at the back of each issue.

(f)   If all else fails, telephone either:

(i)   the Commission of the European Communities offices in London or Cardiff or Edinburgh or Belfast, or

(ii)   the European Parliament Office in London, or

(iii)   the Centre for European Business Information, London or one of the 21 other European information centres in the UK.

4.2.2D3   Has this EC Directive become law?

To become law an EC Directive must be enacted by the UK Parliament. When development is complete, sector 7 of the Celex electronic database (see 4.2.2C1) will provide details of the national implementation of EC directives. Spearhead (4.2.2C5) and Info 92 (4.2.2C6) do already but only for Directives on the single market.

Amongst paper sources two may be consulted:

(a)   *Halsbury's Laws of England*, volumes 51 and 52 (4.2.2B2.4). Use either the tables at the front of volume 52 or the subject index at the back of volume 52 to trace commentary on the Directive. Details of implementation in the UK are given in the editorial footnotes in small type. Remember to check the Cumulative Supplement and Service volumes for the latest developments.

(b)   *Encyclopedia of European Community Law* (4.2.2B2.1). Use either the checklist or indexes towards the back of the final binder to volume C to find references to where the Directive is reprinted in the body of the encyclopaedia. Editorial footnotes in small type give details of implementation in the UK.

Note that *Common Market Reporter* (4.2.2B2.2) does *not* give details of the implementation of EC Directives in the UK.

4.2.2D4   Is this piece of EC legislation still in force?

Of all the electronic databases you can use to answer this research query, Justis-Celex (see 4.2.2C2) is probably the most helpful because it provides against each piece of legislation details of any later, modifying legislation.

Amongst paper sources the most authoritative but least easy to use is the *Directory of Community Legislation in Force* (see 4.2.2B1.5). The *Directory* is in two volumes, volume I being the main part of the work, and volume II comprising two indexes, one listing legislation in the order in which it was made (the Chronological Index), and the second by the subject-matter (the Alphabetical Index). If you know the EC reference number for the legislation check volume II, Chronological Index – the document numbering system by which this index is compiled is made up of the year and identifying number of each piece of legislation, with several other characters added to make the whole index appear initially rather confusing. But, if you read the 'information for readers' in volume I of the *Directory* the arrangement and structure of the Chronological Index will become more obvious. Having identified the legislation in volume II you can then turn to the appropriate page number in volume I where the legislation (if still in force) is noted with details of any amending legislation. If you do *not* know the EC reference number for the legislation but only its subject-matter, you will have to start with volume II, Alphabetical Index (of subjects). You may need to use the EUROVOC thesaurus (noted within 4.2.2B1.1) to help with the terminology for the topic to ensure you look under the most appropriate headings.

An alternative research path, not authoritative but easier to take, is to check: *European Communities Legislation: Current Status* (4.2.2B2.5).

If you know the EC reference number, look up the appropriate year and document number in the bound volume and soft-cover Cumulative Supplement.

If you know only the subject-matter, check the index volume and note the reference numbers given, then turn to the hardback volume and soft-cover supplement, which are arranged in year and running EC reference number order.

A further alternative is to check *Encyclopedia of European Community Law* (4.2.2B2.1) or *Common Market Reporter* (4.2.2B2.2) using either the subject indexes or checklist or finding lists to locate the legislation in the main part of the publication.

4.2.2D5 Has this EC legislation been considered in any cases before the European Court of Justice?

This research can be undertaken by using electronic or paper sources. Of the electronic, a search of LEXIS using the EURCOM library and CASES file of full text reports of ECJ cases, would probably be the easiest – see appendix 6 for an introduction to the use of LEXIS.

Amongst paper sources you should find the EC legislation in either the *Encyclopedia of European Community Law* (4.2.2B2.1) or *Common Market Reporter* (4.2.2B2.2) or *Halsbury's Laws* (4.2.2B2.4) and read the editorial footnotes. As an alternative to these encyclopaedic works use *Case Search Monthly*, an index to ECJ decisions, fully described in section 4.2.3B8.

4.2.3   Case law

4.2.3A   DESCRIPTION

The practice and procedure of the European Court of Justice, based in Luxembourg and founded in 1952, is quite different from that of the national courts of the UK. As a result, the reports of cases heard and judged by the court have a quite different structure. Individual case reports are in three parts:

(a)   Report for the hearing
(b)   Opinion of the Advocate-General
(c)   Judgment of the court.

The report for the hearing is a statement made to the court by a reporting judge outlining the facts of the case and giving a summary of the legal arguments. The opinion of the Advocate-General is an impartial review of the issues and prior decisions, with a discussion of the alternative choices available to the court and the Advocate-General's personal view of what in law should be done. The court usually follows the opinion of the Advocate-General in its judgment. Although the court is always composed of at least three judges, only a single judgment is given, and it is frequently short. Individual judges are not permitted separate or dissenting opinions.

In the *Official Reports of Cases before the Court*, more popularly known as *European Court Reports*, the report for the hearing is preceded by a summary of the judgment (comprising catchwords and headnote specially compiled for the publication), which has no binding force but, like its counterpart in domestic English law reports, is a useful indication of the subject-matter.

The court may deal with a case in any of the nine languages currently officially recognised by the EC. The only authentic version of a particular case is that printed in the procedural language employed. Each of the three parts of the case could have proceeded in a different language. *European Court Reports* contains only the English version, and a footnote to the first page of each part of the report of a case indicates in which language that part was originally heard. However, most law libraries in the UK are likely only to stock *European Court Reports*, and not sets of reports for each of the nine official languages.

The major drawback with *European Court Reports* is the time taken to publish case reports. Frequently 18 months to two years can elapse between the judgment being given and the report of the case being published. This is because considerable importance is attached to achieving a precise and accurate translation of the judgments and opinions into all EC languages.

However, copies of the judgments and opinions of Advocates-General are available from the court registry soon after they are delivered, but only in the language in which they were originally delivered. Some libraries do subscribe to this service.

The mode of citation recommended by the editors of the *European Courts Reports* is:

Case registration number. Names of parties [year] ECR Part number (only from 1990 onwards) page number.

Here are two recent examples:
Case C 3/87 *The Queen* v *Ministry of Agriculture, Fisheries and Food, ex parte Agegate Ltd* [1989] ECR 4459.
Case T-119/89 *Teissonnière* v *Commission* [1990] ECR II-7.

However, this method of citation is not suitable when ECJ cases are cited alongside English cases, which are not cited by registry numbers. Then it is better to put the case number after the names of the parties, thus:

The Queen v *Ministry of Agriculture, Fisheries and Food, ex parte Agegate Ltd* (case C-3/87) [1989] ECR 4459.
Teissonnière v *Commission* (case T-119/89) [1990] ECR II-7.

The case registration number is given at the head of each case report in ECR. Up to 1989 it comprised a running number which started at 1 at the beginning of each calendar year, followed by the year the application was filed with the court. In 1989 the new Court of First Instance was inaugurated and cases before this court have a registration number pre-fixed by the letter T whilst cases before ECJ are now prefixed C. It is important to remember that the case registration number merely refers to when the original application was filed with the court and *not* when the case was reported, which can be several years later.

The names of parties are frequently lengthy, and in common use are often abbreviated. The official index to ECR does not include these popular names, but some unofficial indexes helpfully do. Further, the official annual index to ECR is often several years late in appearing.

Reflecting the inauguration of the new court, beginning with Part 1 of 1990, ECR has been divided into two sections, each with a separate pagination. Section I contains reports of cases before the Court of Justice, Section II includes reports of cases before the new Court of First Instance.

4.2.3B   EXPLOITATION

The sources which will help you exploit EC case law fall into three categories:

(a)   Information about the progress of cases (4.2.3B1 to 4.2.3B3).
(b)   Alternative reports of cases to those published in ECR (4.2.3B4 and 4.2.3B5).
(c)   Guides, indexes and summaries of decisions (4.2.3B6 to 4.2.3B11).

4.2.3B1   Official Journal of the European Committees (OJ)

Probably the first indication that a case is being brought before ECJ is the appearance in OJ C series of a brief summary of the matter in dispute. If a case, once registered, is not pursued, the C series will again note its removal from the register. When a judgment is given by the court a brief summary – only a page or two long – will be printed in the C series. The reports of work of the ECJ are the *only* part of OJ C series to be indexed in the monthly and annual indexes. The structure and difficulties to be faced in using these indexes are described in 4.2.2B1.1.

4.2.3B2   Bulletin of the European Communities

This monthly publication provides brief summaries of new cases and the judgments of other cases, with references to where more details will be found in OJ C series. The summaries are usually printed within section 8 'Community Institutions' of the *Bulletin* under the sub-heading 'Community law courts', and individually grouped under subject headings. Unfortunately, the *Bulletin* is usually published at least four months after the events it documents.

4.2.3B3   Proceedings of the Court of Justice and the Court of First Instance of the European Communities

Each week the Information Service of the Court of Justice issues a typed bulletin giving brief details of the progress of cases during the week in question. The bulletin is in three sections: the first comprises summaries of recent judgments, the second indicates the subject of cases on which the opinion of the Advocate-General has been given (but without details of that opinion) and the third section lists cases at the oral procedure stage (an early stage in the court's consideration of the case). The summaries are not authoritative.

The bulletin is published about six to eight weeks after the events it describes and since ECR is so much delayed in publication, it is a valuable source of information on recent decisions. Unfortunately, use of the bulletin is not easy because indexes are published only annually.

4.2.3B4   Common Market Law Reports (CMLR)

CMLR, first published in 1962, is issued weekly. It does not report all EC cases, but only a selection. However, it does report EC cases more rapidly than ECR and, for this reason, you will find the series referred to frequently during your course. CMLR sets out reports of EC cases rather differently from ECR, adding after the headnote the names of those appearing in the action, with lists of cases referred to, perhaps in an attempt to make the reports look more like those from English courts. CMLR also carries reports of cases from national courts, of both member EC countries and non-members. Each weekly issue of CMLR carries an index inside the front and back covers. Each volume, there are usually three a year, carries a comprehensive range of indexes.

Since 1988 competition cases have appeared in a separate anti-trust supplement – *CMLR Antitrust Reports*. Subject collections of cases from CMLR have been published including *EEC Financial Services Cases 1964–1988*, *Industrial Property Law in the Common Market 1962–1988*, and *EEC Employment Cases*.

4.2.3B5 Common Market Reporter

Volume 4 of this loose-leaf encyclopaedia includes reports of ECJ cases relating to EEC law (cases relating to ECSC and Euratom law are *not* included). When volume 4 becomes full case reports are removed to a transfer binder and eventually replaced by a bound book. The case-reporting service is entitled *European Community Cases*, and this is the title you will find on the spine of annual bound volumes. The transfer binders of CMR carry reports of cases from 1961 onwards. However, whilst a slim paperback volume provides an alphabetical listing of the names of cases reported in the dozen or so transfer binders between 1961 and 1988, there are no other fully comprehensive indexes to the publication. There is a sort of subject index to the cases from 1974 onwards in volume 4 of the main service (it is titled 'cumulative index for transfer binders'), but for some types of research you will need to use the indexes in each individual transfer binder, which can be very tedious! However, the particular value of *Common Market Reporter* is that it links together the full text of both EC legislation and EC case law within a single publication.

4.2.3B6 Guide to EC Court Decisions

This publication gives brief details of cases, with a note of the judgment and EC legislation which was considered. Helpful annotations to journal articles and case notes (in which the decision has been analysed) are also provided. The whole publication is arranged in case registration number order. A bound volume published in 1982 is updated by another volume published annually, which in turn cumulates into a single supplement every three years. The work is useful for historical rather than current case research.

4.2.3B7 Gazetteer of European Law

This valuable work is marred by the fitful way in which it has been kept up to date, a disadvantage the publishers hope to amend in the near future. As originally published this was a two-volume guide to ECJ case law and much national and international case law on Community issues. It was based on a reworking of the indexes to *Common Market Law Reports* and the addition of material from *European Court Reports*.

It covered the period 1953 to 1983 and is both a *Citator* and comprehensive set of indexes to the whole body of law. There are five parts to the publication:

(a)   A master list arranged by court and within each court by official reference or docket number, giving details of the case name and where the text of the decision is reported – the master list is the heart of the publication since the other indexes generally give only the official court reference number for a decision.

(b)   An alphabetical index of cases, listing cases by title, with their official court reference number.

(c)   A chronological index, listing official court reference numbers by the date of the decision.

(d)   The case search, in which all cases referred to (cited) in later judgments are listed by their official court reference number, and beneath that number are given the reference numbers of the cases citing the decision. Three different grades of type face are used to indicate the extent to which the court has considered the earlier case.

(e)   A subject index.

In 1991 the publishers issued a third volume covering the same courts and publications, but only for the year 1989. It comprised the 12th and final cumulated issue of *Case Search Monthly* (see 4.2.3B8), and the first Annual Supplement to the *Gazetteer of European Law*. A single supplementary volume, covering the period 1984 to 1988, is in preparation. The indexes in the 1989 volume are not quite the same as in the 1953–1983 volume, comprising:

(a)   A master list.
(b)   An alphabetical index.
(c)   A chronological index.
(d)   A subject index.
(e)   A case tracker (formerly called case search).
(f)   A law tracker, lising all Community legislative provisions referred to in cases with the official court reference numbers of the citing cases.

4.2.3B8   *Case Search Monthly*

First published in 1989 and monthly since, this is an exhaustive index to ECJ judgments, EC Commission quasi-judicial decisions and judgments on EC law in national courts. Each issue cumulates previous issues for the calendar year and comprises six indexes; a master list, an alphabetical index, subject index, chronological index, case tracker and law tracker, fully described under the entry for *Gazetteer of European Law* (see 4.2.3B7).

4.2.3B9   Digest of Case Law Relating to the European Communities

This authoritative work is prepared by the Library, Research and Documentation Division of the Court of Justice. Unfortunately, this pedigree is no guide to practical usefulness. *The Digest* eventually will be in four series of loose-leaf volumes. To date only two series have been published and only series A, covering the case law of the Court of Justice, will be of interest to law students. It contains a subject–by-subject arrangement of quotations from *European Court Reports* based on the headings employed in the treaties establishing the Communities. The main drawbacks are that (a) it currently digests only cases published between 1977 and 1985 and (b) the latest issue of the digest containing this material was published five years later, in 1990! Lack of currency is a serious flaw in the research tool.

4.2.3B10   European Law Digest

Commencing in 1973 and published monthly, this publication arranges brief notes on recent legislation and cases under just three very broad subject headings. It covers not only EC law but also the European Free Trade Area (EFTA) and from early 1990 Eastern Europe also. It is modelled on the English law publication, *Current Law* (see chapter 3), so much so that from 1992 it has changed its name to *European Current Law* (see 4.2.2B11).

4.2.3B11   European Current Law

This new publication starting in January 1992 will contain, like *Current Law Monthly Digest*, summaries of recent legislation and cases, but drawn from all East and West European countries and the European Communities. It is due to appear monthly and at the year end will be consolidated into *European Current Law Yearbook*.

4.2.3B12   The Digest

Volume 21 of this publication, fully described in 3.5B2.3, contains summaries of major EC cases arranged by subject. The main drawback is that it can take up to 18 months from the date of the original report of the case for a summary to appear in the annual Cumulative Supplement to *The Digest*, so it is not useful for research on very recent cases. However, *The Digest* is a basic research source and is more widely available in law libraries than many of the sources noted elsewhere in this subsection.

4.2.3B13   Halsbury's Laws of England, 4th edition, volumes 51 and 52

These bound volumes comprise an editorial commentary on EC law with copious footnotes giving references to where the original documents may be found. The volumes were published in 1986 and state the law correct to 30 November 1985. They have been kept up to date through entries in the Cumulative Supplement and Service volumes to the whole *Halsbury's* service. See 3.4B4.1.

3.2.4C   ELECTRONIC SOURCES

For background information on the use of electronic databases, see appendix 4.

4.2.3C1   Celex

Sector 6 of this official legal database of the EC contains the full text of judgments and orders of the ECJ since it was established, and opinions of Advocates-General since 1965. Case law is updated monthly and summary information is available in the database about six to 10 weeks after the judgment has been delivered. The full text is not available until after the case has been published in ECR. As has been noted elsewhere, Celex is not easy to use – see 4.2.1C1.

4.2.3C2   Justis-Celex

Justis-Celex is a bibliographic database, i.e., it contains not the full text of ECJ cases but only abstracts with references to where the case has been fully reported in print or commented on. Having identified a case during a subject search of Justis-Celex and noted the case number and other details, you can pass through an electronic 'gateway' and retrieve the full text from sector 6 of the Celex database. Justis-Celex also includes the full English text of case reports which have appeared in *Common Market Law Reports*. This part of the database is useful because CMLR publishes reports of cases more rapidly than *European Court Reports*. The CMLR database file is updated weekly.

4.2.3C3   Justis-Celex CD-ROM

This is the same database featured in 4.2.3C2. The compact discs on which the database is stored are updated every three months so the currency of information is poorer. However, a search can always be undertaken in two steps, using the CD-ROM version to search for older material, and then the remote on-line version to cover the most recent period.

4.2.3C4   LEXIS

LEXIS contains the full text reports, in English, of *European Court Reports* (from 1954 onwards), *European Commercial Cases* (from 1978 onwards), *European Human Rights Reports* (from 1979 onwards), *Common Market Law Reports* (from 1959 onwards) as well as unreported ECJ cases from October 1980 onwards. All these reports are included in the EURCOM library, CASES file. The same materials may also be searched in the INTLAW library, ECCASE file. European Commission Decisions relating to competition will be found in both the EURCOM library, COMDEC file, and the INTLAW library, COMDEC file. For an introduction to the use of LEXIS see appendix 6.

4.2.3D RESEARCH STRATEGIES

4.2.3D1 Tracing a report of an EC case by name or by case reference number

This research query can be answered using either electronic or paper sources.

Any one of the electronic sources (4.2.3C) may be used. If you are using LEXIS, for example, select the EURCOM library and CASES file; if the case in which you are interested is *Vereniging Happy Family Rustenburgerstraat* v *Inspecteur der Omzetbelasting*, (case 289/86) you would type either:

Name (Happy Family)

or

Name (289/86)

and then press the TRANSMIT key.

If you were using paper sources, searching by the case name, check either:

(a) *Current Law Case Citators* (see 3.4B3.1) – the contents of both *European Court Reports* and *Common Market Law Reports* are indexed; or

(b) *Common Market Reporter* (4.2.3B5) – you will need to use not only the index to cases at the back of volume 4 but also the indexes to the annual volumes titled *European Community Cases* and the booklet, *Table of Cases Reported 1961–88*; or

(c) *Case Search Monthly* (4.2.3B8) and *Gazetteer of European Law* (4.2.3B9) – use the alphabetical index first, then having got the court official reference number use the master list to find the citation to *European Court Reports* – but note there is a gap in coverage 1984–88; or

(d) *Guide to EC Court Decisions* (4.2.3B6) – use the index of parties – but note the delay with which supplements are issued, so recent decisions will not be given; or

(e) the annual indexes to *European Court Reports* and *Common Market Law Reports* themselves, but only as a last resort, unless you know approximately when the decision has been reported!

Using paper sources with only the case reference number, check either:

(a) *Common Market Reporter* (4.2.3B5) – use the index to cases at the back of volume 4 and then methodically consult the table of cases by case number in each of the dozen or so transfer volumes; or

(b) *Case Search Monthly* (4.2.3B8) and *Gazetteer of European Law* (4.2.3B9) – use the master index, but note the gap in coverage 1984–88; or

(c) *Guide to EC Court Decisions* (4.2.3B6) – use the main body of the publication but remember recent decisions will not be noted; or

(d)   the annual indexes to *European Court Reports* and *Common Market Law Reports* themselves.

4.2.3D2   *Tracing EC cases by subject*

Either electronic or paper sources may be used for this research. LEXIS (4.2.3C4) or Justis-Celex (4.2.3C2) and Justis-Celex CD-ROM (4.2.3C3) would prove ideal.

With paper sources use either:

(a)   *Common Market Reporter* (4.2.3B5) – in volume 4 of the main services there is a sort of subject index to cases included in the transfer binders from 1974 onwards and in the new developments section – it is entitled 'cumulative index for transfer binders'; or

(b)   *Case Search Monthly* (4.2.3B8) and *Gazetteer of European Law* (4.2.3B9); or

(c)   *Guide to EC Court Decisions* (4.2.3B6); or

(d)   *The Digest* (4.2.3B12); or

(e)   *Halsbury's Laws of England*, 4th edition, volumes 51 and 52 (4.2.3B13).

4.2.3D3   *Has this ECJ case been referred to subsequently?*

Either electronic or paper sources may be used for this research. On LEXIS (4.2.3C4), for example, if you were tracing subsequent citations of the case of *Vereniging Happy Family Rustenburgerstraat* v *Inspecteur der Omzetbelasting*, (case 289/86) you would type:

happy w/8 inspecteur

and then press the TRANSMIT key.

If you are using paper sources check *Case Search Monthly* (4.2.3B8) using the case tracker index, and *Gazetteer of European Law* (4.2.3B7) using the case search index in the volumes for 1953 to 1983 and case tracker index for more recent volumes. Note that currently there is a gap in coverage 1984–88.

4.2.3D4   *Have there been any cases which have considered this EC Regulation or Directive?*

Electronic or paper sources can be used. On LEXIS (4.2.3C4), if you were tracing cases on Council Directive 77/388, you would type:

Council Directive 77/388

and then press the TRANSMIT key.

It is advisable not to use the reference numbers alone without stating the type of legislation, as with certain combinations of figures the computer will retrieve references to Regulations, Directives and any type of document referred to in the file of cases bearing the numbers you have requested.

Amongst the paper sources use either:

(a) *Case Search Monthly* (4.2.3B8) using the law tracker index, and *Gazetteer of European Law* (4.2.3B7) but only those volumes containing the law tracker index. Note that currently there is a gap in coverage 1984–88; or

(b) *Guide to EC Court Decisions* (4.2.3B6) – use the table of legal provisions but remember recent decisions will not be noted; or

(c) *Halsbury's Laws of England*, 4th edition, volumes 51 and 52 (4.2.3B13) – use the two tables of EEC etc. Decisions and Directives and EEC etc. Regulations given at the front of volume 52.

4.2.3D5 Tracing recent judgments

This is one type of research query where the paper sources may be a better place to start than the electronic. The reason is that the newspaper law reports, for example, will report a case with only a few days' or weeks' delay, whilst the electronic will wait on official references to the case to appear in the *Official Journal* or *European Court Reports*. If you wished to use electronic sources, LEXIS, for example, you would follow the steps outlined in 4.2.3D1.

Using paper sources conduct your research methodically backwards in time using:

(a) Newspaper law reports – *The Times* and other newspaper law reports are often the first to report a judgment, so check *Daily Law Reports Index* (see 3.4B2.1);

(b) Periodical notes of cases – the *Law Society's Gazette, New Law Journal* and *Solicitors' Journal* carry brief details of recent decisions which may be quickly followed by longer, explanatory articles; check *Law Journals Index* to trace references to them (see 3.4B2.1).

(c) *Bulletin of the European Communities* (4.2.3B2) – check recent monthly issues, which will provide references to summaries of decisions in the *Official Journal* C series.

(d) *Proceedings of the Court of Justice of the European Communities* (4.2.3B3) – check the contents pages of each issue.

Then, conduct your search following the steps outlined in 4.2.3D1.

4.3 SECONDARY SOURCES

4.3A DESCRIPTION

Both the EC itself and also many commercial publishers produce books, periodicals, booklets, pamphlets and reports on EC law. The closer integration of EC member countries means that many English law textbooks and periodicals carry valuable background information and comment on legislation and cases.

As was noted in chapter 3 on English law sources, the most efficient way to search for secondary sources such as textbooks and periodical articles is to use either indexing services, which arrange under subject headings brief details of original publications, when and where they were originally published; or abstracting services, which provide not only this so-called bibliographic information but also a short summary of the contents of each item listed.

4.3B   EXPLOITATION

4.3B1   SCAD Bulletin

SCAD (*S*ervice *C*entral *A*utomatisé de *D*ocumentation) is the Central Documentation Service of the European Commission. The *Bulletin*, published under this name since 1985, is a weekly publication listing a wide range of EC documents and also articles from non-EC periodicals. Over 1,200 different periodical titles are indexed, though only articles of substantial length are included. *SCAD Bulletin* includes references to about 15,000 new documents each year. The subject coverage is not restricted to law but covers the whole range of functions of the EC. Entries are arranged under about 30 broad subject headings. Whilst each issue includes a subject index and index to keywords (i.e., important words taken from the title of a document), the indexes are only published in French. Unfortunately there are no cumulative indexes, so to search the *Bulletin* for references to publications means searching the index of each issue. The *Bulletin* is therefore of most use for keeping up to date with recent developments by scanning each issue as it is published, rather than as a source for tracing references back over a long period of time. It is also available as an electronic database (see 4.3C1) and the computer version is more appropriate than the paper version for historical research.

4.3B2   European Access

See 4.2.2B2.10.

4.3B3   Legal Journals Index

See 3.8B1.

4.3B4   Current Law Monthly Digest

See 3.8B2.

4.3C   ELECTRONIC SOURCES

For background information on the use of electronic databases, see appendix 4.

4.3C1   SCAD

This is the remote on-line version of *SCAD Bulletin*. It contains items which appeared in the *Bulletin* and its predecessor from 1983 onwards. The database contains references to well over 100,000 publications. References to EC legislation and publications of the EC are noted in English but references to, and summaries of, periodical articles are given only in the original language and not translated. Since the database was originally designed for use only by officials of the EC it is not easy for an untrained person to use and the way information is presented on the screen is not easy to understand at first.

4.3C2 SCAD + CD

During 1991 the SCAD database became available on CD-ROM, using a search system devised not by the EC, but by a commercial company, Context Ltd, for its other products such as Justis-Celex. The CD-ROM version is probably the easiest method of searching SCAD, but the disc is updated only at six-monthly intervals so should not be used to search for very recent material.

4.3D RESEARCH STRATEGIES

If you are looking for some recent articles from periodicals on either a broad or narrow area of EC law, *Legal Journals Index* (4.3B3) is probably the easiest and quickest source to use. *Current Law Monthly Digest* (4.3B4) is also valuable but because of the less specific subject arrangement may prove tedious to use for detailed topics, and for research over more than a year or two. *European Access* (4.3B2) does not cover the range of law periodicals of either LJI or *Current Law Monthly Digest*.

SCAD, and particularly the SCAD + CD version (4.3C2), is probably the best service to use if you are researching a topic over many years and wish to draw material from the widest range of books, periodicals and other publications.

Chapter 5

Keeping up to date

The bulk of this book – chapters 3 and 4 – is about selecting and using legal publications which are appropriate to answering a particular information or research need. In contrast, this brief chapter is about the skill of keeping abreast with legal development and change. A vast quantity of new legal material is published each week and it is essential for you both as a student and, later, in your career to master the technique of keeping up to date. There are several ways this can be accomplished and it is wise to adopt one of them early in your studies so that you have developed a valuable research habit before you enter legal practice.

Weekly periodicals

Each of the three major weekly law periodicals designed for practising lawyers carries news sections and articles reviewing recent legal developments. The *Law Society's Gazette* (published each week except during August) contains a news section at the front of each issue with a legal update section of brief summaries of UK developments, and at approximately monthly intervals also includes a European update of recent EC cases and statutory publications. Sandwiched between the news and updates are brief 'feature' articles. *New Law Journal* also carries a news section at the front, but at the centre of each issue is a section entitled 'The Practitioner' which has fairly lengthy reports of one or two cases followed by NLJ digest of recent developments and a useful list of recently published statutory instruments. *Solicitors' Journal* also carries brief news reports followed by feature articles, and at the centre of each issue is 'Lawbrief', printed on coloured paper with pre-punched holes for the supplement to be removed and inserted in a separate binder, containing summaries of cases.

Some law students decide to take out personal subscriptions to one of these titles as a way of ensuring immediate access to news of latest developments.

Monthly reviews

Current Law Monthly Digest has been noted at several points in earlier chapters. It contains brief summaries of recent Acts, statutory instruments and case law (UK and EC), together with details of the authors and titles of new books and periodical articles, as well as major government publications. All this material is arranged under broad subject headings making it very easy to scan the sections of personal interest. Although *Current Law Monthly Digest* lacks the news and review content of the three law periodicals it is an excellent alerting service to a wide range of new publications.

Law Notes (published monthly) is specifically designed for articled clerks rather than undergraduates. It is edited by the Board of Management of the College of Law and has recently appeared in a much approved format. Brief notes of recent cases and statutory publications are included as well as one or two articles on legal practice topics. A glance at this publication during your final year at university, polytechnic or college will give you an idea of what study for Law Society examinations might entail!

One of the features of *Halsbury's Laws of England* is the Monthly Review, a booklet issued to subscribers to this encyclopaedic publication. The Monthly Review is filed in the Current Service binder. Each issue includes a few pages on recent developments whilst the bulk of the booklet comprises summaries of Acts, statutory instruments and cases, with references to articles which have appeared in a limited range of law periodicals. Information in the review is arranged under broad subject headings which match those used in the rest of the encyclopaedia.

Contents page services

Some law libraries and information units, especially those in large law firms and one or two in academic institutions, compile what are known as 'contents page services'. Quite simply, a photocopy is taken by library staff of the contents pages of law reports and periodicals received each day, along with copies of the covers or contents pages of other publications. At regular intervals, perhaps weekly or monthly, these photocopies are bound together and circulated amongst the staff of the law firm or the teaching staff of the university, polytechnic or college. Usually a copy of the 'contents page service' is available in the library for students to consult. Ask if your library provides such a service and, if it does, make a point of regularly setting aside a few minutes to glance over the pages and note details of new cases, periodical articles etc. – the time will have been profitably spent!

PART 3

AIDS TO IMPROVE THE QUALITY OF YOUR RESEARCH

Chapter 6

Recording and presenting research findings

6.1 RECORDING RESEARCH PROGRESS

When you undertake a piece of extended legal research over several months for, say, your final-year project or dissertation, you may consult quite a large number of the sources noted in chapters 3 and 4. Hopefully, you will come across references to a large number of original publications which you will need to either find in your library or ask the library staff to obtain for you via the inter-library loan service. You will appreciate that keeping a record of your research progress, a check on the sources you have already consulted, those you have yet to read, items you have asked the library to obtain for you – in short, being in control and organised about the progress of your research – will assume far greater importance than when, in the past, you were merely spending a few hours or days researching for an essay or assignment. If you are not methodical in the conduct of your research you may find you:

(a)   overlook a search of some vital sources of information;
(b)   cover the same or similar publications more than once, and so waste valuable time and effort by duplicating your references;
(c)   omit some vital element in a reference to a publication (such as the title or date of the periodical in which you found a valuable article) and have to retrace your steps to ensure you give a complete and accurate reference to it in your bibliography;
(d)   discover, when finally writing up your project or dissertation, that you should have checked indexes and catalogues under a subject term or

concept which you have only now realised is vitally connected with the topic of your research.

How do you avoid these common pitfalls?

(a)   Carefully consider the types of legal information you require to undertake your project – use the section headings in chapters 3 and 4 to help you decide which types of source are going to be relevant. For example, if you are researching the reform of a part of social security law, you will wish to consult a quite different range of sources as compared with research into equal opportunities in the legal profession.

(b)   Carefully consider the jurisdiction/s your research is going to cover: England and Wales, United Kingdom, European Communities, United States, or a comparison of practice and procedure between any number of jurisdictions.

(c)   Match your requirements in (a) and (b) above and read the relevant subsections of chapters 3 and 4, noting the appropriate sources for each relevant type of publication mentioned in each subsection B, on exploitation, and C, on electronic sources.

(d)   Develop a system of 'bibliographic check cards' which will indicate the sources you *should* check and the sources you *have* checked already (see Pemberton 1974, p. 48).

Buy a pack of 5in × 3in or 6in × 4in cards (or metric equivalent) and a flip-top box made to keep them in. Most stationers stock these. Write across the top of each card the title of a publication you have noted, from reading each subsection B, as being relevant to your search for information. In the body of the card note the years over which you consider it necessary to search issues of that publication. Figure 6.1 shows the layout of a bibliographic check card for *Index to Legal Periodicals*. As your search of the *Index* progresses you can cross off the issues you have consulted, and so always have an accurate record of the progress of your research.

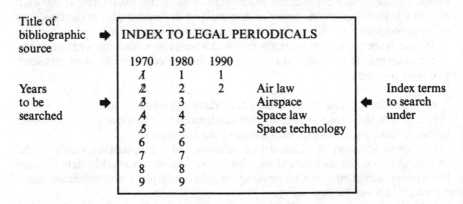

Figure 6.1   Example of a bibliographic check card.

Keep your bibliographic check cards in alphabetical order by the title of the publication, and occasionally review your total research progress by glancing over the whole set of cards.

This system of cards will:

(i) make you think about your research campaign and plan your progress;

(ii) help to ensure you check all your sources thoroughly, especially when you reach the shelves and find the next volume of a publication you wish to check is being used by someone else – on your check cards that volume will remain un-ticked and remind you to return to it later;

(e) Devise one or more cartwheels for your topic, as described in chapter 2, and run your list of subject terms against those used in each of the publications you have selected from the appropriate B subsections on exploitation. When you have discovered the subject headings used by the compilers of a particular publication under which you find relevant references, note the subject headings either in a space on the face of the relevant bibliographic check card (as in figure 6.1), or on the back, so that if you need to return to the publication at a later time you will immediately be able to consult the most appropriate subject headings. Rarely will you find two publications using exactly the same index terms under which to place information about a topic. Making a note of the terms used by a particular publication will speed your research.

(f) When you find a relevant reference in an index or catalogue, create a 'bibliography card' for it, which will provide you with details of information you have discovered (see Pemberton 1974, p. 48). Use similar cards to the bibliography check cards but keep your collections of bibliography cards and bibliography check cards separate.

Set out information on your bibliography cards to a standard pattern, and stick to that pattern – it will make the task of compiling the list of references, to be given at the end of your written work, much easier! Make up a specimen card for a book and a specimen card for a periodical reference and refer to them as you create new bibliography cards.

If the reference is to a book, complete the card as in the upper part of the illustration in figure 6.2; if it is to a periodical article, include the information given in the lower part.

You will notice that, near the bottom of each card, the source from which the reference was obtained is noted. This is useful information, because if you have made an error in copying the reference you can quickly look up the source index or catalogue again. Further, should you need to ask your library to obtain the item on inter-library loan, the request form you will need to complete will ask for your 'source of reference', so that if any errors in the transmission of your request between libraries occur, or the book or periodical article cannot be traced, library staff can verify that the reference is correct from the source information you have provided. You can also note near the bottom of the bibliography card whether you have had to ask

the library to obtain the item on inter-library loan, the date on which you
made the request, and whether your request has been satisfied. If you keep
these bibliography cards in alphabetical order by the name of the author,
you will be able to check, when you come across further references in a different index or catalogue, whether you have already discovered the material.
You will therefore ensure you do not note the same reference down twice
and duplicate the list of publications you need to consult.

BOOKS

BLOM — COOPER, LOUIS	← Author
Bankruptcy in private international law	← Title
London Butterworth 1954	← Place of publication
	Publisher
	Date
Univ of Cambridge Law Catalogue v 8 p470	← Where reference was found

PERIODICALS

SULLIVAN, G.R.	← Author
Intent, purpose and complicity	← Title
Criminal Law Review 1988 Oct p641–648	← Periodical title
	Year
	Month (or issue)
	Pages
ILL 4/4/89	
Index to Legal Periodicals Feb '89 p43 rec'd 18/4/89	

↑   ↑
Where reference was found   Details of request for this to be obtained on
                                       inter-library loan (ILL) and whether request
                                       satisfied.

Figure 6.2   Examples of bibliography cards.

You will discover that using bibliography cards, one card for each book
or article, is a very flexible way of holding information. When you come to
actually write your project or dissertation, you can plan the order in which
you quote or cite references merely by rearranging the order of your bibliography cards. Further, the group of cards containing references you cite in

a particular chapter can then be rearranged again into the order you require for the bibliography or list of references you will need to give either at the end of that chapter or, merged with cards used in other chapters, to form a grand, single bibliography at the end of the entire project or dissertation. Always use a flexible method of holding research information, such as cards – *never* note references to books or articles as you glean them from indexes or catalogues on to separate lines of a sheet of paper, cramming 30 or 40 references down the page. You will not be able to sort or reorder the references into alphabetical sequence, subject groups or the order of quotation. You will not be readily able to check whether you have already discovered the reference earlier in your research. In short, you will not have methodically organised the products of your research effort.

Some students may have access to personal computers and programs such as Cardbox-Plus which can simulate both the bibliographic check card and bibliography card systems outlined. Use them by all means, but do note that since most of the 'exploitation' sources you will be using will be reference-only items which you cannot borrow from the library and use at home, you will either need to use a laptop PC in the library or fall back on the 'old-fashioned' 5in × 3in cards described, and laboriously transcribe data from the cards compiled in the library to your computer file at home.

6.2 FOOTNOTING AND COMPILING BIBLIOGRAPHIES

Open almost any major law textbook and you will notice, at the bottom of some pages, numbered paragraphs in smaller type. These are footnotes; they have four main uses:

(a) to cite the authority for statements made in the text;
(b) to make cross-references to related information or publications;
(c) to make incidental comments on the text;
(d) to make acknowledgements.

Some lecturers encourage students to footnote their own essays and assignments, so it is worth remembering the precise purposes of footnotes. Overlong footnotes make the main thrust of the argument in the text less easy to follow and can be particularly off-putting if any one footnote extends over more than a page. If it really is necessary to provide that much incidental information, place it as an appendix at the end of the text.

However, lecturers are likely to be more concerned with your bibliography – the list of sources you have cited – than the construction of footnotes. The bibliography should be given at the end of your written work, and it serves two purposes: those marked (a) and (d), above.

You should get into the habit, if you have not already, of honestly acknowledging where your opinions and views came from. Lecturers are not expecting brilliant flashes of original thought from student essays, assignments, projects or dissertations – they may only come following long familiarity with a topic, and sometimes never at all! If you fail to give due acknowledgement to the authors of the textbooks or periodical articles you have used, and try to pass off their work as your own, lecturers will easily spot the change in style and use of language. Plagiarism will not be tolerated.

So that those who read your written work can find the books and articles you cite, can read and check the accuracy and appropriateness of your interpretation, you should use a system or standard form of citation by which the quotation or paraphrase in the body of your essay is linked to the full reference to the book or articles you provide in the bibliography at the end of your essay.

There are, in fact, at least three systems of citation in common use. Two, the numeric system and the name and date (or Harvard system) are widely used in all subjects from astronomy to zoology. The third, the Harvard Law Review Association's Uniform System of Citation, has been devised specially for use in legal publications, but its use is confined to the USA. Details of each are given in appendix 7.

Sometimes, especially when you are preparing for a longer piece of work such as a research project or dissertation in your final year, lecturers will specify which of the three systems you should use. For shorter pieces of work, such as essays and assignments, no such guidance will be given, so you will have to select one of the three systems and follow its requirements when preparing your work. Choose *one* of the three alternative systems for citing references and use it *consistently* through a single essay or assignment – do not mix use of the three systems in the same piece of work.

Appendix 1

Check your knowledge of how to use a law library

1. The stock of a law library is usually divided into books and periodicals. Is it here?

2. How is the stock arranged on the shelves?

    (a) by subject according to a classification scheme,
    (b) by jurisdiction,
    (c) by title,
    (d) by author,
    (e) by a combination of these.

3. Are there any separate sequences for particular types of stock, such as:

    (a) large books (folios, quartos or oversize),
    (b) thin books (pamphlets),
    (c) photocopies,
    (d) dictionaries,
    (e) general encyclopaedias,
    (f) directories,
    (g) bibliographies?

    If so, where are they located?

4. Over which periods of time can you borrow books, and where is the 'loan period' for a particular book marked on it?

5.   Are some books available for loan for very brief periods of time and, if so, where can you obtain them?

(a)   from the open shelves,
(b)   by asking at an issue desk or counter for staff to obtain them from a 'closed' collection.

6.   What type/s of catalogue system does the library have:

(a)   computerised,
(b)   microform,
(c)   card,
(d)   a combination of these.

7.   Which different ways can you search for books?

(a)   by author,
(b)   by title,
(c)   by subject,
(d)   by other routes, if so, what are they?

8.   Try the following searches to learn more about the information given in the catalogue:

(a)   An author search for ATIYAH, P.S. Are several different titles noted? Select one and discover from the entry the subject classification number (class mark) and details of where it is located in the library;
(b)   A title search for *Constitutional and Administrative Law*. Are several different editions noted? Select the most recent and discover from the entry the subject classification number (class mark) and details of where it is located in the library.
(c)   A subject search for books on 'contract'. If you are using a microform or card catalogue, what is the classification number or class mark? Use this mark to search the classified catalogue for authors and titles.
If you are using a computerised catalogue, select one of the entries in the list of authors and/or titles and identify its classification number (class mark).

9.   If you are using a computerised catalogue, does it tell you whether a particular copy of a book is on loan and, if it is, when it is due to be returned?

10.   If you want a book that is on loan, how do you ask the library to recall it from the reader who presently has it?

11.   Which different ways can you search for periodicals?

(a)   by title,

    (b) by subject.

12.   Try the following searches to learn more about the information given in the periodicals catalogue.

    (a)   Does the library keep the following periodical titles:

        (i)   *Criminal Law Review,*
        (ii)   *All England Law Reports,*
        (iii)   *Modern Law Review,*
        (iv)   *New Law Journal*?

    (b)   If it does, which issues of each does it stock?
    (c)   What information is given about the location of these periodicals in the library?
    (d)   Can you find the titles the library stocks, on the shelves?

Appendix 2

The inter-library loan service

What is it?

When you discover there are books or periodical articles that you require but which are not stocked by your library, you can make a written request on forms available in the library for the materials to be borrowed from another library for you. All academic (i.e. university, polytechnic and college) libraries and all public libraries are members of the national inter-library loan service. A large number of privately funded libraries (such as those in firms of lawyers) are also part of the network. Most items requested are obtained from the British Library Document Supply Centre (BLDSC) at Boston Spa, West Yorkshire, but some may be obtained for you from other academic libraries. Some items may be obtained from libraries abroad.

How do I use the service?

Your library may have inter-library loan application forms on public display for you to fill in with details of the publications you require. Often there will be two different types of form available for you to use: one type should be used for books, theses and the like, the other for periodicals, conference papers, and law reports.

When you request items you have discovered from a search of bibliographies, indexes and abstracts make sure you give full and accurate details of the item you require. Lack of information could cause delays in supplying the item. There will be a place on the form for you to quote your source of reference: the author or title of the book or bibliography, with page references, in which you discovered the item. This is important as it enables libraries to recheck your source if problems arise – it can be helpful if you attach a photocopy of the reference to your request.

Some further points to remember when making an application:

(a)   *Books:* give full details including the name of the publisher, date of publication and edition (very important in law where books pass through editions quickly), and the international standard book number (ISBN) – a 10 digit number which uniquely identifies one title or edition of a title from a specific publisher.

(b)   *Periodicals:* give full details of each article you require, the full title of the periodical in which the article appeared, year, volume, part and page references, as well as the author and title of the article itself.

(c)   *Law reports:* give full details of the names of parties to the action and the *full* title (not the abbreviated citation) to the series of reports, with year, volume and page references.

(d)   *Theses:* give details of the degree/awarding institution, type of degree (PhD, MPhil, LLM etc.) as well as the year, author and title. For British PhD theses you will also need to complete and hand in with your request a thesis copyright declaration.

How long does it take to obtain an item on inter-library loan?

It is not possible to estimate how long it may take to obtain each item – it depends on how readily a library holding the item you require can be located and, if the item is part of the borrowable stock of the library, whether it is on their shelves and not on loan to one of their library users at the time you request it.

How long may you keep an item obtained on inter-library loan?

If the item has been obtained from BLDSC, Boston Spa, you will have the book for three weeks with an automatic extension for a further three weeks so long as it is not required elsewhere. It is not usually possible to renew BLDSC loans.

If the item has been obtained from another academic library the loan period will be determined by the library lending the publication and this can vary. It is possible, however, to renew these loans.

Some items are supplied as photocopies of original documents and these you may keep.

Please remember to take particular care of all inter-library loans and to return promptly items obtained for you.

Appendix 3

Comparative table of generally accepted terminology for the division of Bills, Acts and statutory instruments

(Based in part on information given in University of London, Institute of Advanced Legal Studies, *Manual of Legal Citations*, part 1, the British Isles (London: The University, 1959) and Erskine May, *Parliamentary Practice*, 20th ed. (London: Butterworths, 1983).

Column A = division
Column B = abbreviation
Column C = symbol, i.e., an example of how the division is distinguished in the publication.

Bill			Act			Statutory Instrument		
A	B	C	A	B	C	A	B	C
Part	Pt	VIII	Part	Pt	VIII	Part	Pt	VIII
Chapter	ch.	VI	Chapter	ch.	VI	Chapter	ch.	VI
Clause	cl. (plural = cll)	3	section	s. (plural = ss.)	3	*article	art or (plural = arts)	3
						*regulation	reg. or (plural = regs)	3
						*rule	r. (plural = rr.)	3
Subsection	subs.	(2)	subsection	subs.	(2)	paragraph	para.	(2)
paragraph	para.	(d)	paragraph	para.	(d)	subparagraph	sub-para.	(d)
subparagraph	sub-para.	(ii)	subparagraph	sub-para.	(ii)	sub-subparagraph	sub-sub-para.	(ii)
Schedule	Sch.	3	Schedule	Sch.	3	Schedule	Sch.	3
Part (of schedule)	Pt	2	Part (of schedule)	Pt	2	Part (of schedule)	Pt	II
paragraph (of schedule)	para.	1	paragraph (of schedule)	para.	1	paragraph (of schedule)	para.	1
subparagraph (of schedule)	sub-para.	(2)	subparagraph (of schedule)	sub-para.	(2)	subparagraph (of schedule)	sub-para.	(2)

*terminology of division determined by whether the publication is titled an Order (article) or Regultions (regulation) or Rules (rule).

Appendix 4

Background information on the use of electronic databases

Remote On-line

Large governmental or commercial organisations have developed since the mid 1960s, machine-readable databases containing references to the wide range of publications they need to be aware of to fulfil their legal and/or business objectives. Much of the development work has been, and continues to be, carried out in the United States. Improvements in the extent and reliability of communications networks for the interchange of computer messages has led to the explosive growth in the 1970s and 1980s of both the number of databases publicly available and interest in using them.

The early databases, and still the majority, are known as bibliographic databases, because they contain descriptions of documents (i.e., author, title, subject-matter, perhaps even a summary of the contents, known as an abstract) but not the text of the document itself. Some others contain the full text of the document. One of the earliest full-text services was LEXIS, which although publicly available in the UK since 1980, was first developed by the Ohio Bar Association in the late 1960s and early 1970s. Because law is, pre-eminently amongst all subjects, literature based, it is not surprising that producers of databases and users have preferred to search the text of legal documents themselves: legislation and cases, rather than an index of descriptions of those documents.

Another important development was the setting up of organisations providing the computing facilities on which to store these databases and to enable searchers to communicate directly with the databases 'on-line'. These organisations are known as 'on-line hosts' and to be able to search one of their databases, a library or information unit has to be a recognised user and normally pay a charge to that organisation as well as for the use of the particular database. The major users of the databases mentioned in this book are law firms, followed by academic institutions. Large public libraries provide access to many of the databases but are much less likely to subscribe to the lawyers' specialist service: LEXIS.

Library staff of the academic institution in which you are studying will be pleased to discuss the advantages, pitfalls and problems associated with on-line searching, and, where appropriate, undertake searches for you. Although an increasing number of databases are providing 'menu-driven' searching (i.e., where the computer presents the user with a number of options at each step in the search process and the user merely has to choose between those displayed), many require the user to have a working knowledge of the search language employed by the system. For this reason, and because every second of time you are on-line not only is the library being charged by the database provider (with a few exceptions) but also the telecommunications network provider (e.g., British Telecom, or equivalent), on-line searching is usually only permitted after you have received training and supervised practice.

The first step is to discuss your information need or query with library staff so they can gauge whether an on-line search is going to be appropriate. They may encourage you to undertake some research amongst the paper indexes and encyclopaedias held by the library to clarify (a) the precise nature of your query, (b) the subject terms or keywords which might be used to describe it and (c) uncover the authors and titles of one or two relevant documents. Armed with this information the staff can construct a more precise search request, with a better chance of success. They will be able to search not only by subject or keyword, but also discover what other work a particular author has written and, on some databases, discover whether his or her work or a legal document has been cited subsequently.

Once this valuable groundwork has been laid, the on-line search may commence. First, using a personal computer with a 'modem' (a MODulator DE-Modulator), which converts messages from the computer into a form which can be transmitted down a telephone line, or a specialised or 'dedicated' terminal like that used for LEXIS (see appendix 6), communication with the remote computer database has to be achieved. A password will need to be given by the user and recognised by the remote computer, and once successfully 'logged on' to the database the search query can be transmitted to the computer.

A search query is made up of search terms and logical operators or connectors. Search terms may be a word or phrase. Logical operators such as AND, OR or NOT are used to combine search terms in a logical fashion. The effect of these operators can be best understood by reference to figure App4.1, where two search terms, 'sun' and 'moon', are displayed in different combinations.

'Sun and moon' will search for and retrieve documents in which both are discovered; 'sun or moon' will retrieve all documents containing either or both search terms. 'Sun not moon' will select documents which contain the term 'sun' but exclude documents with the term 'moon'. Some database

The shaded areas indicate the instances when documents would be retrieved in response to the search statement given.

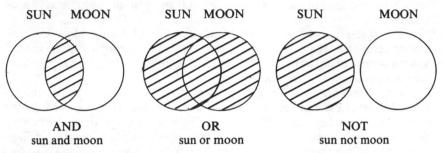

SUN MOON   SUN MOON   SUN   MOON

AND   OR   NOT

sun and moon   sun or moon   sun not moon

The following terms, used in different on-line retrieval systems, enable you to specify how close the two terms should appear within any document, for it to be retrieved.

W/   (meaning within)

near

phrase

Figure App4.1   The effect of the use of logical connectors in a search statement.

search programs will also allow you to state the maximum number of words which may separate the occurrence of the search terms in the document.

The search query should be worked out *before* going on-line because it will take time to develop it, and time is money when you are interrogating a remote computer database.

The actual search is performed by the computer looking for a match between your search query and the terms stored in the database – in a bibliographic database the search terms may be an author's name or a subject; in a full-text database single words or a phrase or the title of a document may be used. The essential point to remember is that the computer will search only on the specific request made to it; so, if the wrong terms are used or a spelling mistake is made, the result of the search may not be what was anticipated, and the request will have to be amended and repeated. 'Rubbish in, rubbish out'.

The result of the search will be displayed on the monitor screen and can be printed out if a printer is attached to the terminal. If the search result is a lengthy printout it is often more cost-effective for the result to be printed 'off-line' at the remote computer and posted to the user. Alternatively, the results can be down-loaded to a disc within the personal computer.

Menu-driven systems usually have a 'HELP' facility, so if, when you are on-line, something unexpected has occurred or you have forgotten what to do next, getting the HELP screens can sort out the difficulty. At the end of your search some systems will allow you to 'save' your search query for a limited period of time, so that you can return to it on your next search session.

The final step is to 'log-off' and break the communications link with the remote computer. It is at this point that on most computer databases and hosts a screen of information will appear telling you how long you have been on-line and, on some, the cost!

The result of your search may be a list of references to various documents or the full text of them, depending on the type of database searched. In the former case your next step will be to see if the library has these documents in stock. If it does not you may need to use the inter-library loan service (appendix 2) and ask the library to obtain them for you.

CD-ROM

A recent technological development has been the availability of an increasing number of remote on-line databases on CD-ROM. These 'portable' databases have been one of the growth areas of information search and retrieval in the late 1980s and look set to proliferate further in the 1990s.

During the 1980s most people became familiar with the use of compact discs and the development of compact disc read-only memory (CD-ROM) from their application in the audio world. In a short space of time CDs replaced vinyl long-playing records as the favoured medium for listening to music. Compact discs can store vast quantities of information which is read from the disc by a laser contained in a special CD player. For CD-ROM, a computer is also needed to control the searching and display of data stored on the compact disc.

Suitable products and equipment have only been widely available for a few years but libraries and information units have been quick to grasp the new technology. One of the main advantages of CD-ROM over remote on-line searching is that libraries or their users are not charged by the length or number of searches of the database made, so research can be more relaxed and not feel like a race against the 'taxi meter'. However, updated CD-ROM discs are expensive to produce and new issues are rarely distributed more frequently than three or four times a year. In contrast many remote on-line databases are updated weekly or even daily so reducing delay in the latest material appearing on the database. The two technologies complement one another – CD-ROM can be used initially to explore a database historically, to discover the subject index terms or keywords which retrieve the most relevant material, and then search the remote on-line database restricting a search to any material published since that included on the CD-ROM.

CD-ROM databases frequently offer a choice of search method. A menu-driven search is often referred to as 'novice' mode, whereas one where a search request using logical operators is required, may be called 'expert' mode.

Taken overall CD-ROM systems tend to be more 'user friendly' and in academic libraries are available for library users to search unsupervised, after the minimum of instruction. It is foreseeable that as more CD-ROM law or law-related databases become available, lawyers will be expected to possess not only research skills in the use of printed sources but also their electronic equivalents.

Appendix 5

An introduction to Lawtel

What is Lawtel?

Lawtel is a computer database of legal information which can be searched using the British Telecom Prestel videotex service. For a subscription, using a telephone line connected either to a videotex terminal or a personal computer with appropriate connecting hardware and software, you can gain access to the Prestel service, which includes separate databases of information on a wide range of subjects provided by hundreds of different organisations. Lawtel is just one of these databases. It has described itself as 'an on-line digest of current law' and contains brief summaries of, amongst others, Bills in progress, Acts, statutory instruments, cases and major government publications such as White and Green Papers. The Prestel service can be accessed by anyone with an appropriate terminal and a paid-up subscription to the service, but Lawtel is one of the databases in the Prestel service which is only available to registered users of (subscribers to) this particular database; it is therefore known as a 'closed user group' on Prestel. So, you need to be a subscriber to both Prestel and Lawtel.

How is Lawtel different from other electronic sources?

Lawtel is arranged rather like a huge encyclopaedia of law with thousands of numbered pages. As with a paper publication, in order to find the information you require you look in a series of indexes to find the appropriate page number. You are not required to devise a search request – a phrase describing the information you are seeking – but merely choose one of the alternative options Lawtel provides from the 'menu' on each of its index screens. Lawtel is a highly structured database, which means all the information in it has been organised by the database builder, and you have only to choose the appropriate path to the information you require.

Lawtel is updated daily – it aims to alert you to the latest developments as well as having very useful files of older material, some ranging back to the late 1970s. It is not designed, however, to contain a comprehensive collection of historic information.

Lawtel provides summaries of legal information, not the full text.

Lawtel is not just a legal database, but also includes a 'research bureau', which is designed to help users with research problems by directing them to the appropriate authorities. Unfortunately, the service is only available to standard-rate business subscribers, and many educational institutions take an alternative subscription which does not include access to this service! However, interesting research bureau questions and answers are also indexed by subject from the 'Subjects A-Z' menu and are identified by (RB).

How do I learn to use Lawtel?

Library or lecturing staff may give you instruction in using Lawtel; it is very simple to use and included within the database is a Lawtel tutorial to help you use the system. The Lawtel user guide, which should be found near the terminal, provides information, with illustrations, covering how to access Lawtel and the content of the database.

As with the use of any electronic source you *must* have a clear idea of what it is you are looking for *before* you connect your terminal to the database – the subject matter of the problem or the type of publication in which you are interested (a Bill, an Act etc.). Only then will you be able to choose correctly from the options presented you on each of the Lawtel screens. Particularly when you are to search for information on a subject you may find it helpful to follow some of the techniques suggested in chapter 2 of this book.

Appendix 6

An introduction to LEXIS

APP6.1   WHAT IS LEXIS?

LEXIS is an on-line computerised information retrieval service. Loaded in a computer in Dayton, Ohio, USA, is the full text of a very large body of law from a number of different jurisdictions including all Public General Acts and statutory instruments currently in force in England and Wales, virtually all cases reported since 1945 plus *Tax Cases* reports since 1875, and a large number of unreported cases of the Court of Appeal (Civil Division) and some of the High Court. It also contains a large body of European Communities law.

Unlike many computerised information retrieval systems, LEXIS is designed to be used by end-users (lawyers) themselves, rather than by intermediaries (librarians, information officers) carrying out the research on behalf of someone else. You will find the instructions given by the computer terminal are in plain English rather than computer jargon, and easy to follow.

APP6.2   HOW IS LEXIS DIFFERENT FROM PAPER SOURCES OF INFORMATION?

Paper sources, such as books and encyclopaedias, have pages of contents and indexes to help you identify the place in the text of the publication where the information you require is printed. The indexes are compiled of particular words or phrases selected by the indexer which describe facts or concepts. These facts or concepts may be expressed in the text of the publication in many different ways, but the art of the indexer is to construct the index so that all the references to a particular fact or concept, no matter how expressed, are brought together under a single index entry. By contrast, LEXIS is a full-text retrieval service. There is no index to LEXIS. You search the actual language used in the original legislation and judgments which form the database. Virtually every word is a potential index term! Consequently you need to take great care when using LEXIS, so that your search request specifies all the ways in which the fact or concept in which you are interested could be expressed in the documents you are asking the computer to search. Any documents which use a form of words different from the ones you specify will not be retrieved by the computer. Your search will be only partially successful.

As with any computer system the information can be retrieved only in response to requests structured in a way the computer can understand. You cannot browse through LEXIS as you would books at the shelves. You need to understand LEXIS search techniques.

The English courts have adopted a cautious attitude towards the citation of unreported cases retrieved from LEXIS (see *Roberts Petroleum Ltd* v *Bernard Kenny Ltd* [1983] 2 AC 192 and *Stanley* v *International Harvester Co. of Great Britain Ltd* (1983) *The Times*, 7 February 1983). A preference remains for the citation in court of decisions reported in the conventional manner; the House of Lords has prohibited the citation of unreported judgments of the Court of Appeal (Civil Division) before the House without special leave having been gained to do so.

LEXIS provides access to more primary sources of English law than might be found in many law libraries. It also includes a large body of European Community law and the law of a number of other jurisdictions. However, in both the English and EC jurisdictions, with a very minor exception, it does not provide access to the secondary sources of law (e.g., textbooks, periodical articles) and so it is not possible to obtain explanatory commentary on the law from this computer database.

In setting up and running a library, one of the greatest expenses is buying the stock and making it available on the shelves. Once purchased there is little difference in the overall cost to the library whether you use a book once or ten times. Contrast this with LEXIS, where there is a telecommunications charge (telephone bill) for a link to the London office of LEXIS, for as long as your terminal is connected to the computer in the USA, and also a charge levied by the company which provides LEXIS. Whilst you should not let these expenses worry you and upset your work at the terminal, it does mean you must prepare thoroughly before you use LEXIS so that the time spent on-line to the computer is productive to you and not unduly expensive to the library providing the service.

LEXIS is updated weekly. Although it takes a while for new Acts, statutory instruments and cases to be added to the database, LEXIS is more up to date than books.

APP6.3 HOW DO YOU LEARN TO USE THE SYSTEM?

Training in the use of LEXIS is given by teaching and/or library staff to students on most degree-level law courses in the UK. As part of the training session you will be given a password; you cannot gain access to the database without a password. If you are studying law independently and would like to be trained in the use of LEXIS, contact Butterworth Telepublishing Ltd, 6, Bell Yard, Temple Bar, London WC2A 2JR, telephone 071-404-4097 for details of their training programme – a charge will be made for attendance.

The checklists which follow will help remind you of the points made during your training programme. They cover only basic use of the system – LEXIS is a very sophisticated research tool but having mastered these basic steps you will be able to explore the full potential of the system using the LEXIS manual and training guides normally kept near the computer terminal.

APP6.4 BASIC SEARCHING USING LEXIS

App6.4.1 Before you go on-line . . . think!

Think about the legal problem you have to solve. What type of information are you searching for?

(a) Are you searching for the text of an Act or statutory instrument or a case by its title?

(b) Are you searching for instances when a particular Act, statutory instrument or case, the name of which you know, has been cited subsequently?

(c) Are you searching for references in Acts, statutory instruments or cases to a particular word or phrase?

If you wish to search for information under (a) or (b), check in paper sources *before* you go on-line that you have the correct spelling and dates for the titles you are going to search for on LEXIS, otherwise your computer search will be yet another example of 'rubbish in, rubbish out'.

Search (c) is the most difficult of the three to undertake, because 'words and phrases' are less concrete than searching for a particular document itself or references to it. Examples of how to search LEXIS for named documents or citations to them will be found in this book in the relevant 'research strategy' (subsection D) for the type of publication required. Therefore, the majority of the checklist which follows is concerned with preparing for a 'words and phrases' type of search.

Identify the key facts and legal concepts in your problem using the techniques described in chapter 2 of *Learning Legal Skills* (Lee and Fox 1991). Use law dictionaries, dictionaries of words and phrases and encyclopaedias to help you clarify the nature of the legal problem.

If you were going to rely on the paper sources of law in the library you would now go to the subject indexes of major works such as *Halsbury's*

Laws of England and try to match the words you have identified as describing the fact or concept (the keywords) against those selected by the indexer to the publication. But, as has been pointed out, LEXIS is not an index – it contains the full text of documents and the search is conducted on the full text. You need to think of synonyms, closely related terms, words of broader and narrower meaning, which might have been used in the text of legislation and judgments. So look back at chapter 2 of this book at the technique for effectively using indexes and draw up a 'cartwheel'.

App6.4.2   Now plan your search strategy

Consider how you need to link together the keywords you have identified.

Think about the relationships between the words.

Are there alternative words for the same fact or concept? For example: surveyor, valuer; negligence, negligently? *Widen* your search request to ensure the computer retrieves as much relevant material as possible by using the connector *OR*:

surveyor OR valuer;
negligence OR negligently.

Are there words which must occur together in the same document? For example surveyor and negligence. *Narrow* down your search by using *AND*:

surveyor AND negligence.

Within how many words of each other might you expect any two words to occur? The computer permits you to specify any distance between 1 and 255 words. The effect of this command is to narrow the search but if you choose too low a number, i.e., search for words close together, the computer may miss relevant documents. On the other hand, too high a number may result in irrelevant material being retrieved, particularly if one or both of the search words has several common meanings.

Surveyor w/15 negligence

This request means 'surveyor' and 'negligence' must both occur in the same document and within 15 words of one another.

Are there any words which have the same beginning (stem) but different endings, e.g., negligent, negligence, negligently etc? The computer will search for the occurrence of all these words if, instead of linking them by OR, you simply use the truncation mark!

Negligen!

Are there different spellings of the same word, e.g., Anderson, Andersen? An asterisk can be substituted either in the middle or end of a word to retrieve an alternative spelling:

Anders*n

But the asterisk requires LEXIS to search for all alternatives of the spelling of that single space which it occupies. So, for example M*cCleary will find MacCleary but not McCleary. M*cCleary tells LEXIS to search for a nine-letter word with any character between M and c; the eight-letter word 'McCleary' will not be found.

By this stage you may have at least one search request. That is fine, because if the first request you make to LEXIS does not retrieve relevant material, you can modify your search whilst on-line and use an alternative request. You may also find that your search request/s can each be divided into a number of discrete parts. You can transmit your search request to LEXIS all at once but unless it is extremely short you would be advised to break it up into parts or levels. Transmitting each separate concept or idea on a different level will enable you to track the progress of your search request and see which level is too restrictive or poorly constructed. For example, if LEXIS responds by declaring no documents found, it would not be possible to know which word in your search request has prevented LEXIS from finding something. It is advisable to start your search with a widely drawn request and use modifications to narrow it down, not only to help you to identify relevant material more quickly, but also to undertake your search in a cost effective way. The pricing structure for the use of LEXIS, both in academic institutions and in commercial practice, means making repeated new searches or changing an existing search request, is more expensive than using a single, wide search gradually and logically modified and refined down.

Now think about which parts of the database you wish to search. LEXIS contains the law of a number of different jurisdictions: England and Wales, European Communities, France, United States to name a few. Which do you want to search? The law of each jurisdiction is divided into 'libraries'. Each library contains the general law of a particular jurisdiction or the law relating to a specialist subject such as tax. Check the list of libraries normally kept in or near the LEXIS manual. Each library is divided into 'files', each file consisting of materials of a particular type, such as cases or statutes. Which do you want to search? Check the list of libraries and files.

Now you are ready to go to the LEXIS terminal!

App6.4.3   Becoming familiar with the layout of the keyboard of the LEXIS terminal

LEXIS can be searched using either dedicated equipment – that is, a terminal specially designed and only used for access to LEXIS – or a conventional personal computer running a special software program. The description which follows applies to the use of a dedicated terminal – different techniques not explained here are required for the use of other equipment.

Sit in front of the LEXIS terminal or study an illustration of it given in the red LEXIS manuals and guides. Spend a few minutes making sure you understand the layout of the keyboard – do not go on-line until you are familiar with the function and position of the major groups of keys.

The centre of the keyboard comprises grey keys, arranged like a type-writer or personal computer keyboard. These are the ones you will use to type your search request. Some have additional functions: two to note in particular are, first, H, which serves as a HELP key and when depressed will display a screen of help messages relevant to the stage your research has reached; secondly, M, which when depressed at certain stages in your search will allow you to change or modify your request.

To the right of the grey keys is a large green key labelled TRANSMIT. You press this to send the command or request you have typed, using the grey keys, to the LEXIS computer.

Above this key is an oblong red key marked STOP. You use this key when a bad telephone line interferes with the transmission of data. Sometimes, when the terminal fails to respond after pressing this key you will need to use the black RESET button above the keyboard. Full details of the se-quence to follow when you experience communications difficulties are given in App6.4.5.

To the left of the grey keys is a large blue key labelled SIGN OFF which you press when you have finished your search, and wish the LEXIS com-puter to take you through the steps to disconnect you from the database.

Both above and to the right of the grey keys are a number of groups of blue coloured 'function' keys. Moving from left to right they are:

(a)   A group of six keys; the three on the bottom row are the most use-ful:

CHG LIB allows you to change to a new library.

CHG FILE allows you to choose a new file within the same LEXIS li-brary – on pressing this key LEXIS will display the files in the library in question from which you can make your selection.

NEW SEARCH allows you to start a new search in the same library and file.

On the top row of this group the PRINT CASE key allows you to in-struct a high speed printer in the London offices of Butterworth Telepublish-ing to print the full text of the case or document which you are viewing on your screen. Additional charges are made for this service and lecturing and library staff at your library may advise you not to use this service.

(b)   A single, large key labelled MAIL IT can be used in conjunction with other keys to have printed in the London offices of Butterworth Telepublishing all the documents, either complete or just selected parts, re-trieved as a result of your last search. Again additional charges are made for this service and you may be advised not to use it.

(c)   A group of five keys: the display keys. Once LEXIS has retrieved some documents you will be asked to press one of these keys to determine how much information about each one is to be displayed on your screen.

FULL displays the full text of the documents.

CITE in the CASES file this will display case names and their citations, the most recent case listed first; in STAT, SI or STATIS files the sections of Acts or statutory instruments will be displayed commencing with the most recent.

SEGMTS enables you to display particular parts or segments of the documents.

KWIC displays a 25-word window of text each side of each occurrence of the words you specified in your search – it is useful for helping you quickly decide whether the context within which the words are used in a particular document is relevant to the problem you have to solve.

VAR KWIC performs the same function as KWIC except that you can specify the size of the window up to 50 words either side of your search terms. You do this by pressing your selection from the grey number keys before pressing VAR KWIC, e.g., 15 VAR KWIC.

(d) Five larger keys starting with NEXT PAGE – these allow you to browse amongst the pages of a document and are pressed after you have selected from the display keys (see (c) above). Their function is self-explanatory, except for ROLL UP and ROLL DOWN which allow you to roll up or roll down material one line at a time. To move quickly through a document and skip pages you can press grey number keys before pressing NEXT PAGE or PREV PAGE and the screen will jump intermediate pages – however, you need to remember that to move from page 1 to page 6 is a jump of 5 pages (not six) so your instruction would be to press the number key 5 and then NEXT PAGE.

(e) Four larger keys starting with NEXT CASE – these allow you to browse amongst a number of documents. Again, their function is self-explanatory and to skip over documents you would press the appropriate grey number key and then NEXT CASE or, to go to a particular document, type its number and press TRANSMIT.

(f) A group of nine keys – these allow to alter or edit your search request before sending it from your screen to the LEXIS computer. When LEXIS is ready to accept your search request a small white line will appear at the top left-hand corner of the screen. This is known as the cursor. The arrow keys allow you to move the cursor in the direction indicated and the HOME key takes the cursor back to the top left corner of the screen. INS CHAR inserts a gap immediately to the left of the cursor to divide a word or add a character. To substitute one character for another merely type over the old character. DEL CHAR deletes the character immediately above the cursor. To erase characters to the right of the cursor press the long grey space bar across the bottom of the keyboard and nearest you.

(g) A single, oblong key marked PRINT – pressing this enables you to print the screenful of text you are viewing on the high-speed printer attached to your terminal. Since there is no extra charge for making prints by this means it is the method lecturers and library staff will recommend.

Two buttons to note are, first, the black button with a red neon light marked POWER located above the keyboard to the right, which switches the terminal on and, secondly, the button marked ALARM, which when depressed will cause the terminal to make a brief, high pitched 'peep' after LEXIS completes each of your commands – some people find this helpful as it indicates positively when LEXIS is ready for your next instruction, other people find it irritating and press the button so it returns to the raised position and the 'peep' is switched off.

Are you sitting comfortably? Then let us begin to use LEXIS!

App6.4.4   Going on-line

If you need assistance at any point in your search follow the instructions in App6.4.5.

These step-by-step instructions assume the terminal is completely switched off before you begin. If, in fact, you are taking over from someone who has used the terminal before you, you may only need to press CHG LIB to have the full list of LEXIS libraries displayed, and start your search from that point (step 10, below).

1.   Press the POWER button so that it glows red.

2.   Some terminals require the use of a telephone, some do not. If yours does, the telephone should be near your terminal. It may have a telephone lock fitted to the side of the base. If so, unlock the telephone using a key available from staff responsible for the LEXIS terminal.

3.   Pick up the telephone handset and dial the London telephone number given in the instructions near your terminal: 071-242 9722. Wait while the ringing tone is heard.

4.   When the ringing tone is replaced by a high-pitched whine, press the DATA button on top of the telephone and if your telephone is fitted with a red indicator light near the dial face, it should glow.

5.   Replace the handset (in effect, hang up!).

6.   Wait until a message 'Welcome to LEXIS' appears on the screen – if nothing appears within a minute or so, begin again at step 3.

7.   Type your LEXIS identification number and then press TRANSMIT. You will have been given a number during your training session.

8.   Does the computer recognise your identification number? If no, then try again, checking you have entered the numbers and letters correctly. If yes:

9.   A screen will appear with numbers and dots at the top left-hand corner. Lawyers in practice may type here a client's number or file reference so that when the bill for the cost of the LEXIS search arrives it can be debited to that client's account. Unless instructed otherwise by your trainer you should not type anything but simply press the TRANSMIT key.

10.   A list of libraries will appear. The English law libraries are given in the first column on the left side of the screen. Select the library you require and type in the abbreviated code name and then press the TRANSMIT key.

11.   A list of files contained in the library you have selected will appear. Choose a file, type in the code name and then press the TRANSMIT key.

12. A screen appears on which LEXIS asks you to type in your search request – do so, ending your instruction by pressing the TRANSMIT key.

13. LEXIS may respond in one of several ways:

(a) That it is working on your request – it may take what seems a very long time to you but is normally under 60 seconds, be patient! Go to step 14.

(b) That it has found over 500 cases in response to your search request – LEXIS will interrupt the search and give you an opportunity to amend your request or continue with the search and view the materials discovered.

(c) That there is an ambiguity in the way you have constructed your search request, particularly in the use of logical connectors (OR, AND, w/). Depending on the error LEXIS may either assume you meant a particular relationship between the words and continue the search on that basis, or stop the search and ask you to clarify your search request.

14. When LEXIS has completed the search it will display a screen telling you how many documents it has found which match your request. If it has found none it could be because:

(a) you have misspelt your search request – check it carefully; or
(b) you have made the request unduly restrictive by using too low a number following w/.

If LEXIS has found no documents then the cursor will go to the top of the screen ready for you to amend your search request (use the editing keys: see App6.4.3(f)). Alternatively you can type in an entirely new search. If LEXIS has found some documents choose the format in which you wish the computer to display the results (use the display keys: see App6.4.3(c)). CITE is probably the best format to choose at this stage, as it will list on a single screen citations to about seven or eight documents (depending on the length of the document name and citation). If you have done some research in paper sources before using LEXIS you may recognise some of the citations, which will help to confirm your search has been on the right lines.

15. If you pressed CITE and the screen of citations has been displayed you may wish to make a print of this list on the high-speed printer attached to the terminal. Press PRINT.

The PRINT command can be used only once the cursor has completed its course across the whole screen, do not press the key before then . . . be patient! If there is more than one screen of information to display, press NEXT PAGE, wait for the complete screen of new information to be displayed and then press PRINT again.

16. To read the first case in the list on the screen press FULL, located directly above the CITE key. Move around within that document using the PAGE keys (see App6.4.3(d)). To find where in that document the words you searched on occur, press KWIC, located above the CITE key.

17. To move from one document to the next use the CASE keys (see App6.4.3(e)).

18. At any stage you can obtain a print of the page on the terminal screen by pressing PRINT.

19. If you wish to refine your search further you can request LEXIS to search on the cases already discovered for the occurrence of more specific terms. You do this by using the following sequence:

(a) press the M (MODIFY) key;
(b) press the TRANSMIT key;
(c) type in your connector: AND, w/, or OR to connect the additional search request to the previous request;
(d) type in the additional words or phrases;
(e) press the TRANSMIT key.

20. When you have completed your search and wish to leave the terminal, press SIGN OFF and follow the instructions on the screen. LEXIS gives you the option of storing your search request until 7.00 a.m. the next morning so you can return to it later – helpful for practitioners, but students usually wish to complete the search at one sitting. So, in response to this screen press N and then the TRANSMIT key.

21. LEXIS then tells you how long you have been on-line and automatically disconnects your terminal from the computer. Do not forget to switch off the terminal itself by pressing the black POWER button.

App6.4.5 Getting help

Do you need help with the logic of your search problem and how to respond to the questions LEXIS puts to you? If yes, go to 1 below. If no, do you need help because of a telecommunications problem? If yes, go to 2, below.

1. Help messages can be displayed relevant to the stage your search has reached by pressing the H key and then the TRANSMIT key. If, after reading these messages, you are still unsure, remain on-line and seek help from lecturing or library staff but *only* if they are nearby. If help is not to hand write down the stages of the search you have completed, the difficulty you have encountered and press the R key and then the TRANSMIT key which will display your search request. Once that search request is on the monitor screen press PRINT to obtain a copy from the high speed printer on your terminal. This will be a helpful record for future investigation. Finally, press SIGN OFF (steps 20 and 21, in App6.4.5). If library or lecturing staff are unable to assist with your problem, LEXIS customer service is available by telephoning 071-405 1311.

2. If there is a telecommunications failure, for example, in response to a command the cursor merely moves down an otherwise blank screen, follow these steps:

(a) press the red STOP key once only;
(b) wait 40 seconds;

(c)   when the terminal responds follow the instructions on the screen;

(d)   if the terminal does not respond: press the RESET button once (situated near the POWER button); wait a few seconds and then press the RED stop key again, once only;

(e)   wait 40 seconds;

(f)   when the terminal responds follow the instructions on the screen.

If the terminal does not respond leave the terminal power on and using *another* telephone call LEXIS customer service on 071-405 1311. You will be asked to quote your LEXIS identification number, so make sure you have it with you.

Inform lecturing or library staff responsible for the LEXIS terminal of the problem, the steps you have taken and whether it has been resolved or not.

Appendix 7

Systems for citing documents in written work

Standards for systems of citation are set out in a British Standard BS 5605: 1978 which incorporates systems recognised in a more complex standard BS 1629: 1989.

Two systems of citation are generally recognised: the numeric and the name and date or Harvard system. In addition, lawyers writing in law reviews in the USA employ a hybrid system devised by the Harvard Law Review Association.

NUMERIC SYSTEM

In this system cited documents are numbered in the order in which they are first referred to in the text. At every point in the text at which reference to a particular document is made, its number is inserted in brackets or parentheses or as a superscript (little number).
Examples:

'In a recent study (26) it is shown . . .' or
'In a recent study [26] it is shown . . .' or
'In a recent study [26] it is shown . . .'

When different parts of a document are cited at different points in the text add the page numbers with the reference number in the text.
Example: 'In a recent study (26, p. 629) it is shown . . .'.

References describing the documents cited are given in a list at the end of the text arranged in numerical order. The sequence of elements in the reference is normally as follows:

(a) *For a book*: name of author; title of book; name of editor, compiler or translator (if any); name of series in which the book appears (if any); number or name of edition, if other than the first; place of publication; name of publisher; date of publication.
Example:

26. Devlin P., *The Judge* (Oxford: Oxford University Press, 1979).

(b) *For an article in a periodical*: name of author; title of article; date of volume; volume number; abbreviated titles of periodical; page number.
Example:

27. Tang, Chin-Shih, 'The law of citation and citation of law' (1986) 10 Dalhousie LJ 124.

A major drawback of the numeric system is if, in the final stages of preparing a document you wish to add an extra reference or remove an existing one, all references following the change will need renumbering. Modern word processing systems can, however, reduce the work involved.

NAME AND DATE OR HARVARD SYSTEM

In the Harvard system, at every point in the text at which reference to a particular document is made, its author's surname and the year of its publication are given.
Example:

'Laster (1988) describes . . .'
'In recent study (Brenner 1990), it is described as . . .'
'Scharf (1989a) discussed this briefly . . .'

If the author's name occurs naturally in the sentence give the year of publication in brackets; if not, then give both name and year. When the same author has published more than one cited document in the same year, distinguish between the documents by adding a lower-case letter (a, b, c etc.) after the year inside the brackets.
Bibliographic references describing the documents cited are arranged in alphabetical order of author's names and then by year and letter.
Examples:

Brenner, Susan W. (1990) 'Of publication and precedent: an inquiry into the ethnomethodology of case reporting in the American legal system' 39 De Paul L Rev 461.
Scharf, Harry M. (1989a) 'The court reporter' 10 J Legal Hist 191.

Detailed recommendations for compiling references by the numeric and Harvard systems are contained in section 6 of BS 5605.

Another method of referencing is described by Turabian (1973), who recommends that the first time a work is mentioned in a footnote, the entry should be in complete form unless a full bibliography is added at the end of the essay or paper. Once a work has been cited in full, subsequent references to it should be in abbreviated form.

HARVARD LAW REVIEW ASSOCIATION

This system of citation is quite complex and employs slightly different rules for the system depending on the type of document in which the citations are made. The details and examples given below are based on the requirements for law review footnotes. For further details consult: Harvard Law Review Association, *A Uniform System of Citation*, 14th ed. (Cambridge Mass: Harvard Law Review Association, 1986).

In the text, references are set out as for the numeric system (e.g., 'in an authoritative study (26) . . .') whilst the sequence of elements in the footnotes or bibliography is as follows:

(a) *For a book*: name of author – with initials placed before surname; title of book; page number(s); and then in parentheses: edition number and date. For example:

26. W. HOLDSWORTH, A HISTORY OF ENGLISH LAW 278 (6th ed. 1938).

(b) *For a periodical article*: name of author – without initials unless there is a citation elsewhere in the work to another author of the same surname; title of article; volume number; title of periodical; page number(s); and then in parentheses, date. For example:

27. Hutcheson, *A Case for Three Judges*, 48 HARV L REV 795 (1934).

References

Anon. (1983) 'Commencement – the latest' 4 *Statute Law Review* 42.

Bates, Jane (1989) 'The conversion of EEC legislation into UK legislation' 10 *Statute Law Review* 110.

Bates, T.StJ.N. (1986) 'Parliament, policy and delegated power' 7 *Statute Law Review* 114.

Bennett, Andrew F. (1990) 'Uses and abuses of delegated power' 11 *Statute Law Review* 23.

Brown, Paul (1989) 'Law reporting: the inside story' 20 *The Law Librarian* 15.

Clinch, Peter (1989) *Systems of Reporting Judicial Decision Making*. Unpublished PhD thesis. University of Sheffield.

Clinch, Peter (1990) 'On making law reports easier to use' 21 *The Law Librarian* 62.

Cole, Stuart (1988) 'Transcripts of unreported cases' 19 *The Law Librarian* 89.

Cross, Charles and Bailey, Stephen (1986) *Cross on Local Government Law*, 7th ed. (London: Sweet & Maxwell).

Drewry, Gavin (1989) 'Public Bills in the Westminster 1987–88 Parliamentary session' 10 *Statute Law Review* 200.

Durnford, Charles and East, Edward (1786) *Reports of Cases Argued and Determined in the Court of King's Bench* (London: Whieldon).

Ferguson, R.N. (1988) 'The legal status of non-statutory codes of practice' [1988] *Journal of Business Law* 12.

Harrison, Nicholas (1984) 'Unreported cases: myth and reality' 81 *Law Society Gazette* 257.

Holland, James A. and Webb, Julian S. (1991) *Learning Legal Rules* (London: Blackstone Press).

Lee, Simon and Fox, Marie (1991) *Learning Legal Skills* (London: Blackstone Press).

Lord Chancellor's Department (1940) *Report of the Law Reporting Committee* (London: HMSO).

Moran, C.G. (1948) *Heralds of the Law* (London: Stevens).

Morris, R.J.B. (1990) 'Finding and using local statutory instruments' 11 *Statute Law Review* 28.

Noel-Tod, Alex (1989) 'What's in a name? The statute book and popular titles' 20 *The Law Librarian* 29.

O'Keefe, J.A. (1991) *The Law Relating to Trade Descriptions*, issue 47 (London: Butterworths) loose-leaf.

Ollé, James (1973) *An Introduction to British Government Publications*, 2nd ed. (London: Association of Assistant Librarians).

Pearson, R.P. (1986) 'Open justice' 130 *Solicitors' Journal* 969.

Pemberton, J.E. (1974) *Undertaking Enquiries*, part 2, Literature search and compiling a bibliography (Open University. Social Sciences. A Third-Level Course. Public Administration. Course D331. Block III, Part 2) (Milton Keynes: Open University Press).

Pollock, Sir Frederick (1896) *A First Book of Jurisprudence* (London: Macmillan).

Statsky, William P. (1982) *Legal Research, Writing and Analysis*, 2nd ed. (St Paul, Minn: West Publishing Co.).

Thomson, Ian (1989) *The Documentation of the European Communities. A Guide* (London: Mansell).

Turabian, Kate L. (1973) *A Manual for Writers of Term Papers, Theses and Dissertations*, 4th ed. (Chicago: Chicago University Press).

Winfield, Percy (1925) *The Chief Sources of English Legal History* (Cambridge Mass: Harvard University Press).

Index